The Future of Children

PRINCETON - BROOKINGS

VOLUME 17   NUMBER 1   SPRING 2007

Excellence in the Classroom

Introducing the Issue

Susanna Loeb, Cecilia Rouse, and Anthony Shorris

A high-quality education is critical to the future well-being of a child—and thus also to the nation as a whole. By one estimate, a high school dropout in the United States will earn nearly a quarter of a million dollars less over his lifetime than a high school graduate who completes no further education. He will also contribute $60,000 less in tax revenues. Aggregated over a cohort of eighteen-year-olds who never complete high school, these losses add up to $200 billion.[1] Moreover, gaps in the educational achievement of children by race and social class are large and persistent. For example, among eighth graders in 1988, 95 percent from the most advantaged families had received a high school diploma within six years, compared with only 66 percent from the least advantaged families.[2] According to the National Assessment of Educational Progress, 9 percent of black and 13 percent of Hispanic eighth graders perform at or above the proficient level in mathematics, compared with 39 percent of whites.

Concern about the overall quality of U.S. education, and in particular about the troublesome gaps in achievement, has led many policymakers and parents to demand reform of the educational system. But for reform—whether increased education revenues, smaller class sizes, or greater accountability—to make a difference, it must penetrate the classroom and affect the quality of teaching. Indeed teachers are so important that, according to one estimate, a child in poverty who has a good teacher for five years in a row would have learning gains large enough, on average, to close completely the achievement gap with higher-income students.[3] Improving the quality of teachers is thus crucial to efforts to raise student achievement and narrow achievement gaps. But schools with high concentrations of black students, Hispanic students, and students in poverty have serious problems in recruiting and retaining effective teachers. According to one study, three times as many black students as white students in New York State had teachers who failed their general knowledge certification exam on their first attempt (21 versus 7 percent).[4]

But although almost everyone recognizes the importance of effective teachers, it is much less clear how to improve the teaching workforce. One difficulty is the sheer size of that workforce. Teachers make up about 10 per-

www.futureofchildren.org

Susanna Loeb is associate professor of education and director of the Institute for Research on Education Policy and Practice at Stanford University. Cecilia Rouse is the Theodore A. Wells '29 Professor of Economics and Public Affairs, director of the Education Research Section at Princeton University, and a senior editor of *The Future of Children*. Anthony Shorris is Executive Director of the Port Authority of New York and New Jersey and former director of the Policy Research Institute for the Region at Princeton University.

cent of all college-educated workers. With
more than 40 percent of schools' operating
expenditures going to instructional salaries,
even small changes in compensation or in the
number of students per teacher can have
huge revenue implications. Total spending on
teacher salaries in U.S. public schools is more

> *With more than 40 percent
> of schools' operating expen-
> ditures going to instructional
> salaries, even small changes
> in compensation or in the
> number of students per
> teacher can have huge
> revenue implications.*

than $160 billion a year.[5] Thus, a 5 percent
salary increase—$2,338 for an average
teacher—would cost taxpayers more than $8
billion a year.[6]

A second difficulty for schools and districts is
how to identify effective teachers. On one
level, most people know a good teacher when
they see one. As Lee Shulman, president of
The Carnegie Foundation for the Advancement of Teaching, notes (see box 1), good
teachers engage the class and motivate student participation. They inspire students to
challenge themselves and help them develop
values, commitments, and identities. But how
districts are to pick out such people before
they enter a classroom, or educational institutions are to guide them to reach this ideal, is
much less clear. Equally problematic is precisely which qualities of the ideal teacher
should form the basis of policy reform.

Nevertheless, researchers have established
that carefully designed public policies can
strengthen teacher quality. The articles in
this volume explore key tools available to policymakers to do just that—from changes in
the way teachers are certified, to investments
in professional development, to wage policies, to financial and other incentives, to policies that affect unions and collective bargaining. The volume also examines the special
challenges facing rural and urban districts
and synthesizes relevant experiences from
other developed and developing nations.

What Have We Learned?
Before reviewing the main findings of the articles in this volume, we must stress how hard
it is to know whether a particular policy
makes a difference. Although most observers
would agree that good teachers do more than
simply raise the test scores of their students,
measuring other outcomes is problematic. In
addition, when student learning improves, it
is difficult to be certain whether the gain is in
fact attributable to a particular policy intervention, such as a new professional development program. Perhaps the gain would have
happened even in the absence of the intervention.

The challenge is to determine what social scientists call the counterfactual—what learning
gains students would have made had their
teacher not, for example, received professional development. To construct the counterfactual, researchers might look at similar
students, similar classrooms, and similar
teachers who have not participated in the reform, or they might look at the same student
during two different periods. By making such
comparisons, researchers hope to tease out
the causal effect of the policy on students.
But because researchers can rarely be completely confident of the accuracy of the coun-

terfactual—are the students, classrooms, and teachers they are comparing similar in all respects or just in the few characteristics observed?—the research base on many policies is surprisingly thin, a fact that is reflected in the articles in this volume.

A Framework

The first step in recognizing potential weaknesses in the nation's system of public education, and in seeing how to address those weaknesses, is to understand the institutional framework within which teachers and their employers work. In the leadoff article in this volume, Richard Murnane and Jennifer Steele provide just such a framework. They describe how wages and working conditions both in teaching and in competing occupations influence the number and skills of people drawn to teaching. Growing job opportunities for women during the 1970s and 1980s, for example, dramatically affected the supply of teachers, pulling away many women with the strongest academic backgrounds. Because wages and working conditions vary from school to school, the supply of teachers varies as well. Similarly, because alternative job opportunities are greater for some teachers than for others, the supply of teachers also varies by teacher characteristics. For example, greater opportunities for people with strong science backgrounds decrease the supply of science teachers relative to teachers in fields such as history and English.

The demand for teachers—the number of teachers that schools and school districts need to hire—also varies over time and across locations, driven by factors such as the number of students, the desire for particular class sizes, and retirement trends among teachers. Declining student-teacher ratios over the second half of the twentieth century, for example—from roughly 27:1 in 1955 to 16:1 by 2001—increased the demand for teachers by 41 percent.

When considering a job, a prospective teacher looks at both wages and working conditions. Salary schedules almost always reflect years of teaching experience and educational attainment, though there is some leeway to provide added pay for added responsibilities (such as coaching) or, in rare instances, for performance as a teacher. Within districts, salary schedules are usually the same for all schools and for all teachers, regardless of field. This salary structure creates difficulties for schools with less desirable working conditions and for fields in which opportunities outside teaching are better or the work in the classroom is more difficult. The wide disparity among schools in the characteristics of their teachers is one manifestation of this structure. To address these problems, policymakers have proposed a variety of reforms, including across-the-board pay increases for teachers, more flexible pay structures, and reduced requirements for certification. Murnane and Steele address these approaches briefly and lay the framework for the remaining papers, which address these and other policies in more detail.

The Benefits—and Costs—of Certification

Every state has its own procedures for certifying teachers, and every public school is expected to hire teachers certified by the state. All states require a bachelor's degree, and all but two require applicants to pass at least one certification exam that covers general knowledge and subject-area knowledge, as well as pedagogy. Some states require high school teachers to have a major in the subject area that they teach, and most require teachers to complete coursework in education. Further, most teacher candidates must spend time as a

Box 1. Good Teaching

By Lee S. Shulman

"What does good teaching look like?" It's a question I get often, more frequently from my colleagues in the academy than from my neighbors down the street. My colleagues are almost always referring to teachers in general, much less often to the teachers in their children's schools. They are almost never talking about themselves.

For an economist doing research, good teaching can be simplified into an estimate of the regressed gain scores of pupils who have studied with a teacher during some specified time period. That estimate of impact is often further corrected by estimating the cost of the teaching during that period. But I have yet to read of an economist who defined good teaching that way for her own kids or for a university professor of economics.

Nevertheless, the attributes of good teaching can indeed be specified, and I'd wager they are not all that different for a third-grade math teacher, a high school history teacher, and a college economics teacher. A good teacher operates on at least four dimensions concurrently—intellectual, practical, emotional, and moral. For research purposes we typically simplify teaching and concentrate on only a particular feature of a single dimension, but we delude ourselves if we fail to realize how profoundly our simplifications have distorted the phenomenon we are studying. Thus the Nobel laureate Carl Weiman has studied college physics teaching and documented how students can make positive (albeit modest) gains in understanding the elements of physics while taking on a negative attitude toward science and misconstruing utterly the nature of scientific inquiry. A researcher studying gains in knowledge of physics concepts and facts—which is the norm—would deem the course a great success.

---

student teacher before becoming fully eligible to teach in a public school system.[7]

Donald Boyd, Daniel Goldhaber, Hamilton Lankford, and James Wyckoff raise a salient policy issue regarding these certification processes. In theory, certification can improve the quality of teachers in the classroom by establishing a floor on quality. To the extent that certification can distinguish bad teachers from better teachers, it can keep the worst teachers from entering the classroom. However, certification can fail to meet its goal in two ways. First, it can fail to distinguish good teachers from bad. Second, it may drive away potentially good teachers. If the certification process itself is so onerous that it keeps good teachers from pursuing a teaching career, then it may in fact lower the overall quality of teachers, even if it does screen out the worst teachers. Assessing the value of certification systems therefore requires evaluating both their ability to screen out the worst candidates and the extent to which they discourage potentially good candidates.

There is surprisingly little research that sheds light on how any element of certification affects classroom teaching. This does not mean that certification has no effect, just that there is no convincing evidence one way or the other. What little research there is suggests that teachers who score higher on exams tend to add more to the achievement gains of their students than do their lower-scoring peers, though these effects are not large. The au-

So what does good teaching look like? In the classroom of a good teacher, students are visible, engaged, attentive, and participating. They aren't looking off into space, surfing the net, or dozing. They are engaged in public performances of their understanding and misunderstanding. In good teaching, students are not silent partners. As the educator Deborah Meier observed, "teaching is mostly listening, learning is mostly telling." In good teaching, students are responsible for their learning; they are accountable for their understanding. Accountability is not determined by midterms and finals alone, but by the continuity of their participation, engagement, and interaction with the teacher and one another. Good teaching is passionate, and it induces an emotional response in students. Students may even feel a tad anxious because something they care about is at stake. That doesn't mean that good teaching is intimidating; mental paralysis can be induced by teachers who are gratuitous pedagogical terrorists. Good teaching starts with inducing habits of mind, but doesn't stop there. Good teaching engages practical thinking and problem-solving skills that can be applied in a variety of settings. And good teaching affects students' values, commitments, and identities. A good teacher of writing does not stop at teaching students to write a five-paragraph essay. He teaches students to think of themselves as readers and writers, who are competent, comfortable, and committed to their literacies.

Yes, good teaching is not a simple independent variable. It is rich, nuanced, complicated, internally and longitudinally inconsistent and produces different impacts on different students and in different contexts. Like all good scientists, we simplify any phenomenon in order to study and understand it. Teaching is no different. The danger arises when we forget how much of value we chose to ignore in order to explain a phenomenon like teaching and we treat our scientific conclusions as if we never compromised at all.

Lee S. Shulman is president of The Carnegie Foundation for the Advancement of Teaching and Charles E. Ducommun Professor of Education Emeritus and professor of psychology emeritus (by courtesy) at Stanford University.

thors were not able to identify any high-quality studies of how coursework or field experiences influence teacher effectiveness. The best evidence for the effect of field experience, and particularly student teaching, comes from the tendency of teachers to improve over their first few years. Students of first-year teachers, on average, learn less than students of more experienced teachers—a finding that suggests that classroom experience helps make teachers more effective.

Many states have introduced new routes to teaching that lessen coursework requirements. These new routes vary in their characteristics and content. Several studies of the most highly selective of these alternative routes, Teach for America, find that TFA teachers appear to perform at least as well in math as do the other teachers in their school, though (depending on the analysis) not quite as well in reading. But TFA is not representative of all alternative routes because it is highly selective, national, and aimed only toward recent college graduates. Given the enormous investment in teacher preparation and certification and the potentially negative consequences of certification for teacher supply, the lack of evidence is disturbing.

Professional Development: Unrealized Promise

Although some policies focus on improving new teachers, the fact that 82 percent of teachers have at least four years of teaching experience highlights the importance of policies aimed at veteran teachers as well.[8] On-the-job training—professional development—is important for several reasons. First, the alternative routes into teaching, with their reduced coursework and field experience requirements, mean that new teachers often arrive with less preparation than before. Second, it is not easy for schools and districts to know how effective teachers will be before they begin teaching. Third, many schools find

Teachers can make better use of the material provided by their schools and districts if their professional development is tied closely to it—a practice that is surprisingly uncommon today.

it almost impossible to fire poorly performing teachers because of tenure and due process rights at the state level, together with teacher contract provisions at the distict level. In all these cases, professional development can, in theory, help teachers develop the knowledge and skills that they lack. Finally, as states and districts aim to implement new standards and new curriculums, teachers may need help incorporating the new material into their practices.

Heather Hill describes some common professional development activities and reviews the research on their effectiveness. The average professional development program is of little benefit; however, a few programs have demonstrably improved teaching and student learning. Hill identifies three important characteristics of these high-quality programs.

First, they involve a substantial time commitment, such as a two- to four-week summer program. One-day programs, in most cases, are not worthwhile. Second, the program content is targeted—for example, on specific content knowledge, subject-matter-specific instruction, or student learning. Broad programs do not appear to be effective. Third, professional development is linked to the instructional goals and curriculum materials of the district or school. Teachers can make better use of the material provided by their schools and districts if their professional development is tied closely to it—a practice that is surprisingly uncommon today.

Wages, Working Conditions, and Teacher Labor Markets

Teaching is influenced not only by programs and policies that affect the current workforce, but also by those that influence who goes into teaching, who stays in teaching, and in which schools teachers choose to work. Both wages and working conditions affect the appeal of a teaching job. In their article in this volume, Eric Hanushek and Steven Rivkin address salaries and working conditions broadly. They find that the wages of teachers relative to those of other college graduates have fallen over time. In addition, salaries vary substantially from one region to another, with the highest wages found in the Northeast and the lowest in rural areas. There is little difference, on average, however, between wages in urban and suburban districts. In some metropolitan areas urban districts pay more, whereas in others, suburban districts pay more. But working conditions do differ substantially between urban and suburban districts, with urban teachers reporting less support from administrators and parents, poorer materials, and greater student problems. These difficult working conditions appear to drive much of the turnover of teachers and the transfer of teachers across schools.

Although the authors note that both wages and working conditions affect teachers' choices and result in a sorting of teachers across schools, they find less evidence on whether this sorting of teachers is actually detrimental to students. For example, teachers with higher test scores may be more likely to leave the lowest-performing schools, but these teachers might not be the most effective teachers. Although research in this area is sparse, existing studies indicate that the teachers who leave are not better at producing student learning gains than those who stay.

Teacher preferences, as affected by salaries and working conditions, are central to understanding the distribution of teachers across schools. But they are not the only factors. The preferences of hiring authorities, the effectiveness of district personnel decisions, and the institutional constraints within which they operate are also important, driving both who gets hired out of the pool of available teachers and the setting of wages and working conditions that then determine the pool of interested teachers. Teachers unions operate in all fifty states, and all fifty states have tenure laws. Thirty-five states and the District of Columbia have laws guaranteeing collective bargaining rights for teachers. These state policies and resulting teacher contracts often limit the ability of districts to hire, transfer, and fire teachers as they would like. They also set the current salary schedules, which, as Hanushek and Rivkin note, often do not reward teachers for student learning.

The Challenge of Building Incentives into Pay Structures

Teachers may have many incentives to work hard. The satisfaction of seeing their students learn, appreciation from students' parents, and recognition from their colleagues and principal may all motivate teachers. But only a few school districts, both in the United States and abroad, base teacher salaries on performance in the classroom. One such district is Denver, where in November of 2005 voters approved a $25 million tax increase to fund "merit pay" rewarding elementary and secondary school teachers for a variety of accomplishments, including their own demonstrated knowledge and skills and their students' academic growth. Victor Lavy synthesizes the research on pay for performance.

He notes that performance-based pay can take innumerable forms. It can reward individual teachers, groups of teachers, or schools; it can be based on student test performance or principal or peer evaluation; it can be large or small; it can include sticks as well as carrots. Each of these elements can substantially shape the incentives created for teacher performance. Clearly the benefit of performance-based pay is that it increases teachers' incentives to improve their students' learning. But as Lavy points out, it may also create perverse incentives—discouraging teachers from helping their peers or encouraging them to cheat or to restructure their class time in ways that improve students' test performance but not their long-term learning. The empirical research on the programs implemented to date has not found consistently positive effects from these reforms.

Lavy examines several practical challenges in implementing performance-based pay and concludes that the most daunting is to devise a way to measure performance. Such a measure must reflect the student outcomes of interest, minimize error, and discourage cheating and other unintended consequences. Implementing a system of performance-based pay that works is not a one-time task. Even with the best preparation, initial implementation is likely to be problematic. But if commitment to reform is ongoing, it may be possible to make progress gradually in addressing each of the challenges. As evidence, Lavy cites two carefully designed incentive programs in Israel that generated significant student gains.

How Unions Affect Teacher Labor Markets and Teaching

Some challenges in implementing any new policy, such as performance-based pay, are technical; others are political. Unions have played and continue to play a considerable role in schools, affecting not only teacher labor markets but also standards, curriculum, and other aspects of schooling. They have not always supported reforms favored by school administrators. In his article, Randall Eberts synthesizes the research on teacher unions and collective bargaining, focusing on how both affect compensation, student outcomes, and education policy.

Teachers unions, like unions in other occupations, increase worker pay and benefits. Teachers who are union members and teachers in highly unionized states receive higher salaries. Moreover, the higher the share of unionized teachers, the larger the gap in wages between new and experienced teachers. On average, collective bargaining increases education spending by roughly 15 percent. How unions affect student outcomes is much less clear. Although some studies find that unions improve student learning, others suggest that union efforts to increase salaries force a trade-off with other productive inputs and thus decrease achievement and increase dropout rates. An alternative explanation, says Eberts, is that unions force a standardization inside classrooms and schools

that increases the achievement of students who perform close to the average but decreases outcomes for lower- and higher-achieving students.

Unions are central to contemporary education policy. If districts and states are to enact successful reform, they must work collaboratively with them. Eberts notes that the traditional stance of unions against policies that enhance local discretion may be susceptible to change in light of other policy reforms, such as accountability, that shift the focus from schools' resources (class sizes and teacher salaries, for example) to student outcomes and expect local actors to respond to their inherent incentives.

The Unique Challenges of Urban and Rural Settings

Urban and rural schools each face particular challenges in attracting, retaining, and making the most of their teacher workforce. Brian Jacob identifies the challenges and potential policy solutions for urban schools; David Monk, those for rural schools.

Most of the lowest-performing schools and students in the United States are in urban districts, where poverty is highly concentrated and large shares of students have limited English proficiency and perform poorly on achievement tests. These districts often face unusually high costs. Higher wages in other occupations make it more costly for schools and districts to hire workers; space is often expensive; and high crime rates increase facilities requirements and tend to make upkeep more expensive. Urban districts are often far larger than other districts. Although increased size may offer some advantages in terms of reduced rates from suppliers, it also presents problems. As Jacob points out, to manage their many schools, large urban districts often institute unwieldy bureaucratic systems that slow the pace of operations. They also tend to face powerful teachers unions that hamper their actions even further. Urban districts thus face challenges both in attracting teachers to their schools and in optimizing their hiring, transfer, and retention policies so that they are able to bring the best available teachers into their classrooms and retain them.

In examining the recruitment and retention of teachers in rural areas, David Monk begins by noting the unique characteristics of rural communities—small size, sparse settlement, distance from population concentrations, and an economic reliance on agricultural industries that are increasingly using seasonal and immigrant workers to minimize labor costs. Many, though not all, rural areas, are seriously impoverished. Classes in rural schools tend to be small, and teachers often report good working conditions and relatively few discipline problems. But compensation tends to be low, perhaps because of a lower fiscal capacity in rural areas. Moreover, rural areas often have a smaller pool of college-educated workers from which to recruit teachers. Teacher turnover is often high, and the share of highly trained teachers is low. Relatively large shares of students with special needs and of highly mobile children of low-income migrant farm workers can also complicate recruiting and retaining teachers. Thus, while much of the policy focus has been on urban schools, the small size, remote location, and often poor and mobile student populations of rural schools create other obstacles to improving the teacher workforce.

Lessons from Other Countries

Helen Ladd puts U.S. educational policies and practices into international perspective by focusing on educational policies and practices in industrialized countries. She documents that students in countries with high teacher salaries do not, in general, perform better on international tests than do students in countries with lower teacher salaries, but notes that many factors, such as cost, could obscure an underlying relationship between teacher

The lesson, says Ladd, is that effective policy must simultaneously address a variety of issues, such as teacher preparation and certification, working conditions, the challenges facing new teachers, and the distribution of teachers across geographic areas.

wages and student outcomes. She also points out that in countries with low teacher salaries, teachers tend to have weaker qualifications. In high-salary countries like Germany, Japan, and Korea, for example, only 4 percent of teachers are underqualified, as against more than 10 percent in the United States, where teacher salaries are relatively low.

Throughout the developed world, policies that make salaries uniform across academic subject areas and across geographic regions hamper schools' efforts to recruit qualified teachers in math and science and in large cities. Among the strategies used to combat resulting teacher shortages are paying teachers different salaries according to their subject area and offering financial incentives, including bonuses and loans, for teachers in specific subjects or geographic areas. Other developed countries are also creating alternative routes into teaching to attract qualified teachers. To retain effective teachers and reduce attrition, they are providing more support staff for teachers, recognizing and celebrating effective teachers, improving school leadership, and reducing teacher burnout through part-time work, sabbaticals, and extended leaves. The lesson, says Ladd, is that effective policy must simultaneously address a variety of issues, such as teacher preparation and certification, working conditions, the challenges facing new teachers, and the distribution of teachers across geographic areas.

Finally, Emiliana Vegas reports on how the world's developing countries fill their classrooms with qualified teachers. Although schools in the world's poorest countries may seem unusual models to inform U.S. educational policy, in fact, those schools often resemble difficult-to-staff urban U.S. schools. Severe budget constraints and a lack of teacher training capacity have pushed developing nations to try a wide variety of reforms, including part-time or assistant teachers, pay incentives, and school-based management. Hiring teachers with less than full credentials has had mixed results at best. A more promising approach has been to increase pay to improve teacher quality, although the specific policy of providing incentive pay has had mixed results. Finally, school-based management reforms that devolve decisionmaking authority to the schools have improved both teacher performance and student learning. In Central America, for example, such reforms have lowered rates of teacher absenteeism, increased teacher work hours, increased homework assignments, and improved parent-teacher relationships. These changes are especially promising in schools where educational quality is low.

Implications

Although almost everyone agrees that school reforms are unlikely to improve student performance if they do not directly affect what happens in the classroom, to date there is strikingly little evidence to indicate exactly which policies are most likely to enhance teaching, and thus student learning. But research does point toward some approaches as more effective than others, and recent changes in local and federal policy will make it possible to learn more about teacher policy more quickly than has yet been possible.

First, research has made clear the shortcomings in teacher pay structures. Although some districts offer higher compensation for particular fields of specialization, especially special education, math, and science, that practice is not the norm. In most districts, all teachers in all schools are generally subject to the same salary schedule, leaving some fields and regions with teacher shortages, others with surpluses. A good short-term solution to these staffing problems may be to target large pay incentives for highly effective teachers in hard-to-staff subject areas or less desirable schools. But in the long run, it may be more productive—though expensive—to address working conditions directly by reducing class sizes, increasing release time for planning, providing instructional supports such as coaches, and ameliorating adverse conditions such as crime and dilapidated buildings.[9] Incorporating elements of pay for performance into salary structures is another reform with much theoretical appeal. Although experience with such policies has generated mixed results on student outcomes, much could be learned from carefully designed and implemented pilot programs.

Teacher preparation and certification is a second policy area that warrants further consideration and potential reform. The paucity of evidence on the effects of different elements of states' certification requirements is no reason to eliminate those requirements. Not knowing what effect they have is not the same as knowing that they have no, or even a negative, effect. In the absence of solid evidence, policy must be based on common sense and professional consensus. One thing that researchers have definitively established is that entry requirements strongly affect the pool of people interested in teaching. Policies that have loosened entry requirements have not only dramatically increased the number of people interested in teaching but also raised their average academic performance. It is thus crucial to evaluate entry requirements closely, especially in communities that have had trouble attracting qualified teachers.

Reform in ongoing teacher education is a third area worth pursuing. Although professional development can, in theory, benefit schools and districts, so far the nation has little to show for its substantial investment in this area. As Heather Hill points out, hours spent in general and unspecified professional development do not improve instruction. Instead, the work must be linked to the curriculum, have substantive content, and be sustained over time. Coaching and release time for directed collaboration among teachers are both promising forms of professional development.

Research has also uncovered some structural impediments to improving the teacher workforce. In particular, given how hard it is to identify good teachers, the constraints that keep schools from removing poorly performing teachers likely hurt students. Easing these restrictions may have large payoffs when an ample supply of potential replacements is available, especially if schools and districts can also offer teachers incentives to improve

student learning. In addition, cumbersome bureaucracies keep many large urban districts from adjusting to changing needs or even making predictable hires in a timely manner. As an example, streamlining the process so that these districts could hire teachers earlier in the year could help increase supply.

Finally, the papers in this volume demonstrate that strengthening the teacher workforce is not a one-time policy initiative. The effort must be ongoing—for schools, districts, states, and even the federal government. The introduction of assessment-based accountability systems over the past two decades has yielded a rich harvest of data that can help practitioners and policymakers assess the effectiveness of policy initiatives, especially those that are implemented with an eye toward careful evaluation. Education policy in individual districts, and in the nation as a whole, would be well served if reform initiatives were designed from the outset with credible evaluation elements, especially when it comes to collecting data about how the reform affects students facing various challenges. Without careful evaluation, the nation will continue to commit enormous public resources to one of society's most important investments without any real analytic support.

Researchers have begun to learn more about potentially effective interventions in teacher labor markets, many of which are described in the articles that follow. But much work remains. That research has not yet unlocked the "secret" of something as complicated as effective classroom teaching should be neither surprising nor discouraging. Our aim, in this volume, is to contribute to the continuing search for practical policy steps to improve teaching—the single most important element in student achievement—especially for children facing the greatest barriers.

Notes

1. Cecilia Elena Rouse, "Inadequate Education: Consequences for the Labor Market," mimeo (Princeton University, September 2005).

2. Lisa Barrow and Cecilia Elena Rouse, "U.S. Elementary and Secondary Schools: Equalizing Opportunity or Replicating the Status Quo?" *The Future of Children* 16 (2006): 99–117.

3. Eric A. Hanushek, Steven G. Rivkin, and John J. Kain, "Teachers, Schools and Academic Achievement," *Econometrica* 73, no. 2 (2005): 417–58. Here, a "good teacher" is defined as one with an average value added that is one standard deviation greater than the average. This does not include knowledge depreciation.

4. Hamilton Lankford, Susanna Loeb, and James Wyckoff, "Teacher Sorting and the Plight of Urban Schools: A Descriptive Analysis," *Education Evaluation and Policy Analysis* 24, no. 1 (2002): 37–62.

5. This estimate comes from multiplying the average teacher salary from 2003–04 ($46,752 at www.nea.org/edstats/images/05rankings.pdf) by the number of teachers given above.

6. Thomas D. Snyder, Alexandra G. Tan, and Charlene M. Hoffman, *Digest of Education Statistics 2005* (U.S. Department of Education, National Center for Education Statistics, July 2006), table 28, downloaded from http://nces.ed.gov/programs/digest/d05/tables/dt05_028.asp?referer=list (October 26, 2006).

7. Susanna Loeb and Luke Miller, "State Teacher Policies: What Are They, What Are Their Effects, and What Are Their Implications for School Finance," Getting Down to Facts Report, unpublished (Stanford University, December 2006).

8. G. A. Strizek and others, *Characteristics of Schools, Districts, Teachers, Principals, and School Libraries in the United States: 2003–04 Schools and Staffing Survey* (U.S. Department of Education, National Center for Education Statistics, 2006), http://nces.ed.gov/pubs2006/2006313.pdf.

9. Bringing in effective administrators is likely to be even more helpful, but unfortunately this is a substantially more difficult undertaking, since administrator labor markets are no less complicated than teacher labor markets.

What Is the Problem? The Challenge of Providing Effective Teachers for All Children

Richard J. Murnane and Jennifer L. Steele

Summary

Richard Murnane and Jennifer Steele argue that if the United States is to equip its young people with the skills essential in the new economy, high-quality teachers are more important than ever. In recent years, the demand for effective teachers has increased as enrollments have risen, class sizes have fallen, and a large share of the teacher workforce has begun to retire. Women and minorities have more career options than ever before, making it increasingly difficult to attract and retain the many effective teachers who are needed. Moreover, schools are limited in their ability to identify and reward the most effective teachers.

Perhaps the most urgent problem facing American education, say Murnane and Steele, is the unequal distribution of high-quality teachers. Poor children and children of color are disproportionately assigned to teachers with the least preparation and the weakest academic backgrounds. Teacher turnover is high in schools that serve large shares of poor or nonwhite students because the work is difficult, and the teachers who undertake it are often the least equipped to succeed.

Murnane and Steele point out that in response to these challenges, policymakers have proposed a variety of policy instruments to increase the supply of effective teachers and distribute those teachers more equitably across schools. Such proposals include across-the-board pay increases, more flexible pay structures such as pay-for-performance, and reduced restrictions on who is allowed to teach. Several of these proposals are already being implemented, but their effectiveness remains largely unknown. To measure how well these policies attract effective teachers to the profession and to the schools that need them most, rigorous evaluations are essential.

Murnane and Steele also note that policymakers may benefit from looking beyond U.S. borders to understand how teacher labor markets work in other countries. Although policies rooted in one nation's culture cannot be easily and quickly transplanted into another, it is important to understand what challenges other countries face, what policies they are using, and how well those policies are working to enhance teacher quality and improve student achievement.

www.futureofchildren.org

Richard J. Murnane is the Thompson Professor of Education and Society at the Harvard Graduate School of Education. Jennifer L. Steele is an advanced doctoral student in administration, planning, and social policy at the Harvard Graduate School of Education.

P ublic education in the United States has long been viewed as a means of expanding economic opportunity, enhancing social mobility, developing a skilled workforce, and preparing young people to participate in a democratic society.[1] High-quality public education is especially crucial today, as advances in the U.S. economy have made cognitive skills more important than ever in determining labor market success. But today's public schools are not equipping all students with the skills needed to thrive in a rapidly changing economy, and the economic consequences are becoming more serious for students who leave school without critical skills.

Cognitive skills are strong predictors of educational attainment. Students with weak skills are the most likely to drop out of school before earning a high school diploma, whereas those with strong skills are the most likely to enroll in college and to graduate with a four-year degree.[2] Wage trends of workers with differing levels of formal education illustrate the growing importance of cognitive skills in the American labor market. As shown in figure 1, real hourly earnings (net of inflation) for American workers who graduated from high school but did not go to college were no

higher in 2003, on average, than they were thirty years earlier. High school dropouts fared even less well: their real wages fell 14 percent over the same period. But the real wages of four-year college graduates grew during this period, and the wages of those with advanced degrees grew even more. These are remarkable trends, especially because a simultaneous increase in the share of the labor force with four-year college degrees created downward pressure on the relative wages of college graduates.

The problem facing American education is not that schools are less effective than they were thirty years ago. As figure 2 illustrates, the math and reading test scores of black and Latino students are significantly higher today than they were in the early 1970s, when the National Assessment of Educational Progress (NAEP) first began measuring the math and reading skills of American students. The NAEP scores of white students have also risen.[3] The problem is that technological advances have routinized manufacturing and clerical jobs and facilitated international competition, thereby increasing the demand for cognitive skills, especially problem-solving and communication skills. The nation's educational problem, in other words, is that an education that was good enough to

Figure 1. Real Hourly Wage for U.S. Workers by Education, 1973–2003

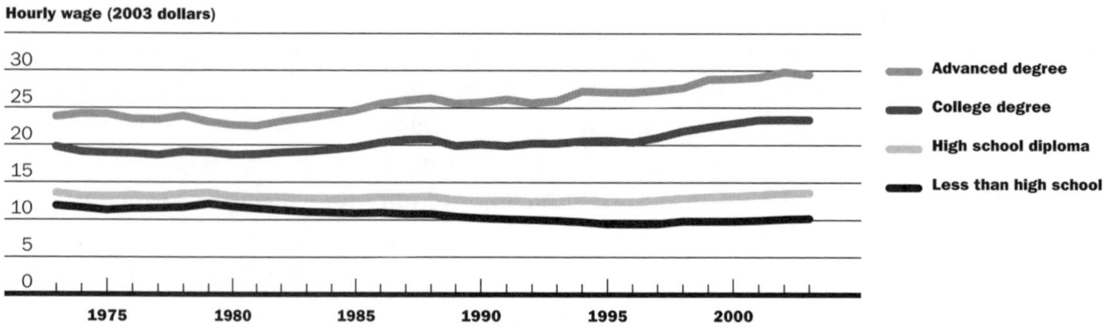

Source: Based on data from the Economic Policy Institute Data Zone, available at www.epinet.org/datazone/05/wagebyed_a.xls.

Figure 2. Trends in NAEP Scores in Math and Reading: Eighth-Grade National Averages

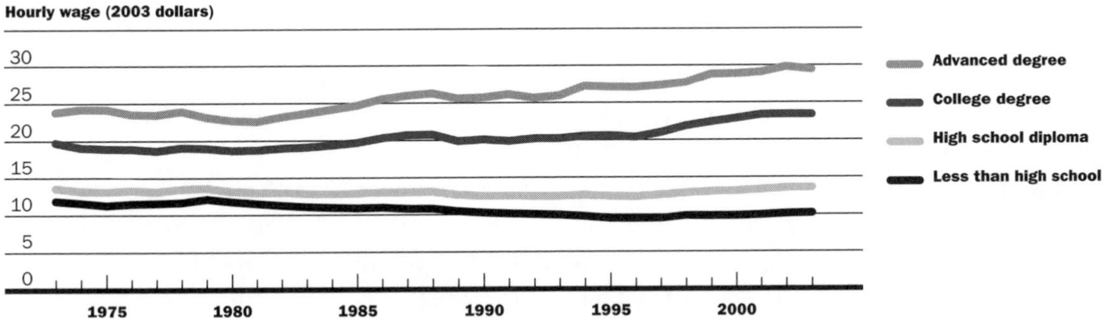

Hourly wage (2003 dollars)

Source: Based on data for eighth graders (thirteen-year-olds) from the National Center for Education Statistics, available at nces.ed.gov/nationsreportcard/ltt/results2004/age_13_math_avg_score.asp and nces.ed.gov/nationsreportcard/ltt/results2004/age_13_reading_perf.asp# score.

allow Americans to earn a decent living in the economy of 1973 is not good enough to enable them to earn a decent living today.[4] As a result, the gulf between those who thrive and those who struggle financially is increasingly driven by differences in skills. And these skill differences are influenced by variation in the quality of K–12 education—variation that depends heavily on the quality of teachers in the nation's classrooms.

In the next section, we describe how supply and demand work in the labor market for teachers in America, and we explain several economic concepts that recur in articles elsewhere in this volume. We describe forces affecting the demand for and supply of teachers and show how changes in these forces have contributed to the challenge of providing all students with skilled teachers. We conclude with a brief discussion of policy approaches to increasing the supply of effective teachers and improving their distribution.

Understanding Teacher Labor Markets

In this article, we focus on the labor market for *effective* teachers, defined as those who are skilled at raising the achievement levels

of their students. Today's policy challenge is not simply to place enough adults in front of classrooms, but to recruit and retain teachers who have a strong positive impact on students' learning. In this section, we assume that effective teachers are a single, homogeneous category, with no differences by subject specialty, years of experience, or educational credentials; and that all effective teachers are paid the same salary. We also assume that everyone agrees how to identify an effective teacher. These assumptions are clearly unrealistic (and we later take such complications into account), but they are helpful in explaining the concepts of demand and supply.

Supply and Demand in Teacher Labor Markets

The number of effective public school teachers that will be demanded by a particular school district depends on student enrollments, class size policies, curriculum requirements, the district's fiscal capacity, the priorities of district residents, and the wage level of effective teachers. School districts will want to hire more teachers if the level of teachers' wages is low than if it is high. For instance, if market conditions are such that effective teachers command a very high wage, districts may increase class sizes to accommodate that high cost.

Changes in labor market conditions other than wages shift the demand for effective teachers outward or pull it inward, meaning that more or (in the latter case) fewer teachers would be demanded *at any given wage*. For example, an increase in student enrollment would shift demand outward, which

---

School districts often respond to a shortage of effective teachers at the prevailing wage not by leaving teaching positions vacant, but by filling them with ineffective teachers.

---

means that a school district will want to hire more effective teachers at any prevailing wage level.

The supply of effective teachers who are willing to work in a particular school district depends on the wage they will be paid, the working conditions they will face, the wages and working conditions available to them in other occupations, and the cost of services such as child care that they need to purchase if they decide to work outside the home. A greater number of effective teachers are willing to provide their services to schools if the wage is high than if it is low.

As with the demand side of the market, a change in supply-side factors other than wages will shift the supply of effective teachers outward or pull it inward. An outward

shift in supply means that more teachers are willing to provide their services to schools at any given wage; an inward shift means that fewer teachers are willing to teach at any given wage. For example, an increase in the wages that effective teachers can command in other occupations would mean that at any given wage level, fewer effective teachers would be willing to provide their teaching services to schools.

The teacher labor market is in equilibrium when the number of effective teachers who are willing to teach is exactly equal to the number of effective teachers that the school district is willing to employ. The quantity supplied is equal to the quantity demanded at only a single wage, which economists call the market-clearing, or equilibrium, wage.

At any wage greater than the market-clearing wage, the quantity of effective teachers willing to provide their labor exceeds the quantity demanded by the school district. The result is a labor market surplus. At any wage below the equilibrium wage, the quantity of effective teachers demanded is greater than the quantity supplied, yielding a labor market shortage. School districts often respond to a shortage of effective teachers at the prevailing wage not by leaving teaching positions vacant, but by filling them with ineffective teachers.

The critical point to understand about labor markets is that a shortage can be ameliorated by raising the wage, just as a surplus can be ameliorated by lowering it. Given this adjustment mechanism, why do shortages of effective teachers sometimes persist for an extended time? The answer to this question has several parts. First, a variety of "shocks" affect the teacher labor market, changing either the demand for teachers or the supply of teachers and also changing the equilibrium wage. For example, increases in student enrollment shift the demand for teachers outward, thus increasing the equilibrium salary. The prevailing teacher wage therefore needs to increase if the district is to avoid a shortage of effective teachers.

Second, actual teacher salaries adjust only slowly to changes in the equilibrium wage. Teacher salaries are typically negotiated for extended periods, so it may take several years for wage levels to be reconsidered. Also, it often takes considerable time for school district leaders to convince school boards and taxpayers that they do indeed face a shortage of effective teachers at prevailing wages. School board members know that diligent human resource directors typically can find adults with college degrees to fill teaching vacancies. That many of these applicants lack the skills to teach successfully is typically not obvious. Indeed, as we explain later in the article, information available at the time of hiring does not distinguish effective teachers from ineffective ones very well. Consequently, it takes time even for skilled school district leaders to marshal evidence of a shortage of effective teachers at prevailing wage levels. In the interim, with demand expanding and the wage remaining unchanged, there is a shortage of effective teachers.

Third, it can take a year or more for college students and other adults who decide they want to teach to acquire the necessary credentials. The slow pace at which teacher wages increase means that individuals are slow to receive the signal that financial opportunities in teaching have improved. When they do receive the signal, those who lack the necessary credentials need time to earn them. Consequently, an increase in teacher wages will yield a smaller increase in the sup-

ply of effective teachers in the short run than in the long run.

Why Money Matters

Some effective teachers are willing to work at wages below the equilibrium wage. The problem is that there are not enough effective teachers to meet the quantity demanded at that wage. Of course, there also are effective teachers whose employment decisions are based on factors other than wage. It is not that financial incentives do not matter. Rather, they matter because they influence the occupational choice for people who would like to teach and are on the fence about whether it makes sense to do so. One such person could be an experienced teacher who takes a leave of absence to bear a child. After learning that high-quality child care is costly, she may find that her decision about whether to return to the classroom is very sensitive to the wage she can earn by teaching.

To appreciate how teaching salaries help determine the supply of effective teachers, it is also important to understand the concept of *opportunity cost*—that is, what must be given up as a result of a decision to teach. The opportunity cost for a college graduate trained in computer science who decides to become a teacher, for example, is the highest wage she could have earned elsewhere in the economy. The opportunity costs for teachers trained in different disciplines differ substantially. For instance, Dan Goldhaber and Daniel Player show that during the mid-to-late 1990s, starting salaries in engineering, mathematics, and computer science occupations were 14 percent to 30 percent higher than starting salaries in liberal arts occupations.[5] The opportunity cost of becoming a teacher is thus much greater for a college graduate trained in computer science than for one trained in history. Studies based on data from the United States, the United Kingdom, and Australia show that college graduates' decisions about whether to enter and remain in teaching depend not only on salaries in teaching, but also on opportunity costs.[6] Because almost all U.S. school districts pay computer science teachers and history teachers on the same scale, it is not surprising that many districts find they are not able to attract strong applicants to teach computer science, while they have an abundance of strong applicants to teach history.

Why Working Conditions Matter

People's decisions to enter teaching and to teach in a particular school depend not just on financial incentives but also on a wide range of nonpecuniary incentives, such as working conditions. Working conditions include easily measurable conditions such as class size and contract hours, as well as more difficult-to-measure conditions such as facilities quality, parent support, school leadership quality, collegiality within the school, and curricular autonomy.[7]

The experiences of two hypothetical neighboring school districts—Oceanside and Rivercity—make clear the importance of working conditions. Both districts have the same number of students and the same demand for effective teachers. But Oceanside has new facilities, nationally recognized school leaders, and strong parent support, whereas Rivercity's schools have dilapidated facilities, frequent turnover among struggling school leaders, and weak parental support. Under these circumstances, fewer effective teachers will want to work in Rivercity at any given wage level than will want to work in Oceanside. In other words, the supply of effective teachers to Oceanside will be greater than the supply of effective teachers to Rivercity. The equilibrium wage for Ocean-

side—the wage at which the demand for effective teachers is equal to the supply—would result in a shortage of effective teachers in Rivercity.

Even if Rivercity pays enough to avoid a technical shortage of effective teachers—that is, if it pays its market-clearing wage—it still will not have as many effective teachers as Oceanside. Given its inferior working conditions, Rivercity would need to pay a wage even higher than its own equilibrium wage to attract the same number of effective teachers as Oceanside. Economists use the term *compensating wage differential* to refer to the wage premium that Rivercity would need to pay over and above the equilibrium wage in Oceanside in order to attract the same number of effective teachers that Oceanside attracts.

The evidence is clear that urban school districts serving large concentrations of low-income students have trouble attracting and retaining effective teachers.[8] Some school districts have responded to this problem by offering higher salaries to teachers willing to work in hard-to-staff schools. To date, researchers have only limited evidence on the size of compensating wage differentials that schools with poor working conditions would need to pay to attract a full faculty of effective teachers. Old and dilapidated physical facilities can be part of the problem, but of greater importance may be the difficulty of serving large numbers of children with complex needs without adequate resources to do the job well.[9] Offering compensating wage differentials makes sense, but only if accompanied by the resources needed to educate well the children in these schools. Recently a number of urban districts have introduced initiatives to improve education in schools serving high concentrations of poor children

Figure 3. Public School Enrollment in Pre-K through Grade 12, 1965–2015

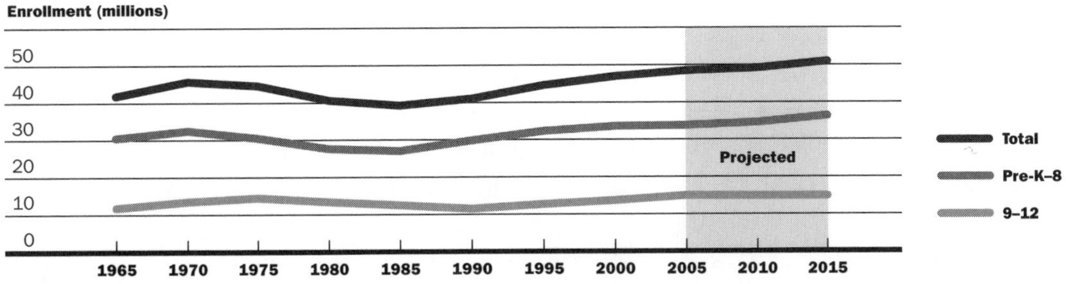

Enrollment (millions)

Source: Adapted from Patrick Rooney and others, *The Condition of Education 2006* (Washington: Institute of Education Sciences, National Center for Education Statistics, 2006). Data for 1965 through 2000 are in five-year intervals in the fall of given year; data for 2005 though 2015 are projected for the fall of given year.

by offering higher teacher salaries and providing additional resources such as a longer school day and longer school year, as well as more support services for students. The initial evidence on the consequences of these initiatives is positive, but much more needs to be learned.[10]

The Demand Side of the Teacher Labor Market

We next focus on the demand side of the teacher labor market. We begin with factors that influence the quantity of teachers demanded. We then consider factors that influence the demand for effective teachers, and we explain the difficulty of distinguishing effective teachers from ineffective ones.

The Quantity of Teachers Demanded: What Hasn't Changed

One striking feature of the quantitative demand for teachers is how little it has been affected by the technological changes that have been reshaping the larger economy. The technological advances that have dramatically raised output per worker in many fields and reduced the demand for labor have left education almost unchanged. Though some teachers use computer technology to enhance their teaching practices and prepare students for the knowledge-based economy,

computers have not sufficiently reconfigured the core tasks of teaching to produce notable efficiency gains or cost savings in public education.[11]

The Quantity of Teachers Demanded: What's New

Public school enrollments in the United States are on the increase, driven by immigration and a greater number of births.[12] Though the fertility rate (the number of live births per 1,000 women aged fifteen to forty-four) has fallen since 1970, when it stood at 87.9, it has risen modestly in recent years, from 64.6 in 1995 to 66.1 in 2003. Similarly, the number of live births rose from 3.9 million in 1995 to 4.1 million in 2003.[13]

Given that most students start school around age five, it takes roughly five years for elementary schools to feel the effects of changes in the number of births, and naturally it takes longer for these changes to be felt in secondary schools. This lag in enrollment trends between primary and secondary schools is visible in the pre-K–8 and high school enrollment lines in figure 3, where the peaks and valleys in the high school trajectory appear later than those in the pre-K–8 trajectory. As shown in figure 3, the National Center for Education Statistics (NCES) estimates that 48.7 million students were enrolled in public schools in the fall of 2005, an increase of more than 8 percent over 1995 enrollment levels. By 2013, U.S. public school enrollments are projected to reach 50 million students.[14]

Also on the rise are the shares of children of color and children living in poverty. Between 1970 and 2003, the share of impoverished children in the United States rose from 14.9 percent to 16.7 percent, and the share of students of color in public schools rose from 30.9 percent to 41.5 percent.[15] These trends create a demand for teachers who can meet the needs of students who historically have not been well served by America's public schools. Two recent, well-designed studies find that students benefit academically from having teachers whose race or ethnicity matches their own.[16] But the share of teachers of color in the workforce remains low, at 15 percent in 2005.[17] The changing demographics of American schoolchildren suggest an increasing demand for effective teachers of color in particular and, in general, for teachers who are effective at raising the achievement of students from disadvantaged or minority backgrounds.

Class sizes also affect the demand for teachers, and average class sizes have declined in recent decades. State policies such as the California Class Size Reduction Initiative of 1996, which paid schools to cap class sizes at twenty in grades K–3, have been one factor contributing to the increasing demand for teachers.[18]

The most commonly cited indicator of trends in class size, the average ratio of students to teachers, has fallen steadily in the United States since the 1950s. In 1955, the ratio was 26.9; by the fall of 1985, it was 17.9; and by 1995, it had fallen to 17.3. The NCES has es-

timated that the ratio was 15.5 in 2005 and that it will drop to 14.5 by 2014.[19]

Although the trend in the average student-teacher ratio is informative, it is important to realize that student-teacher ratios are typically smaller than average class sizes. One reason is that schools generally employ enough faculty members to grant each teacher a preparation period during the school day.[20] A second reason is that student-teacher ratios usually include all licensed educators working in a school, though many of these, including counselors, librarians, and resource teachers, are not teachers of record for a particular class.

One federal policy that has contributed to the decline of student-teacher ratios in the past three decades is the Individuals with Disabilities Education Act (IDEA). First implemented in 1975 and reauthorized most recently in 2005, IDEA requires schools to provide accommodations for students with learning disabilities.[21] Many schools have hired additional teachers to support students and to manage the act's extensive reporting requirements. In a review of the research on class size effects, Eric Hanushek found that IDEA implementation explained about a third of the decline in student-teacher ratios over the past fifty years.[22]

The Demand for Quality Teachers: What Hasn't Changed

The commonsense belief that teacher quality matters is supported by a great deal of evidence, much of which comes from studies showing that children in some classrooms learn a great deal more over a school year than do demographically similar children in other classrooms.[23] The evidence highlights the importance of improving the quality of the nation's teacher workforce. This challenge, however, is complicated by considerable disagreement among educators and policymakers about how to identify highly effective teachers.

Historically, the demand for teachers has been driven by local preferences, and hiring decisions have not always been based on estimates of teachers' instructional effectiveness. Some districts and schools have based hiring decisions largely on a prospective teacher's ability to coach athletics or connections within the community.[24]

Another reason schools have not always made instructional effectiveness a priority in their hiring decisions is the complexity of their scheduling needs, especially at the secondary level. For instance, if a school needs to staff three sections of biology and two sections of algebra, the principal may hire a certified biology teacher to cover both the biology and algebra sections because it would be more difficult either to find a person who is trained in both subjects or to hire two part-time teachers. When teachers are assigned to teach classes for which they lack academic preparation, they are said to be teaching "out of field." Using 1993–94 data from the NCES Schools and Staffing Survey, Richard Ingersoll found out-of-field-teaching to be widespread in grades seven through twelve, especially in schools serving a large share of low-income students. Overall, he found that 57 percent of physical science teachers, 53 percent of history teachers, and 33 percent of secondary math teachers lacked degrees in the subjects they were teaching, though the shares were closer to 20 percent for more broadly defined subjects like social studies and general science.[25]

Even if districts and schools make instructional effectiveness a top priority, they may still find it hard to select the most effective teachers because information available at the point of hiring does not predict well how effective a teacher will be in enhancing students' skills. For example, teachers with two years of experience appear to be more effective, on average, than teachers with no classroom experience. But most studies do not find that experience beyond the initial two or

---

Historically, the demand for teachers has been driven by local preferences, and hiring decisions have not always been based on estimates of teachers' instructional effectiveness.

---

three years results in improved student test scores. Similarly, most studies find that whether a teacher holds an advanced degree does not predict student achievement gains.[26]

One teacher characteristic that *is* somewhat helpful in predicting student outcomes is academic ability, as measured by verbal aptitude scores, ACT scores, or undergraduate college selectivity.[27] Academically talented teachers are better, on average, at raising student achievement than teachers with fewer academic skills. But the measures of teachers' academic ability that are available in personnel records and in quantitative research studies explain only a small part of the variation in teachers' effectiveness as measured by student test score gains.

Recent years have seen considerable debate about whether a teaching license is a useful indicator of a teacher's effectiveness. Teaching licenses, also known as certificates or credentials, function much like licenses in other trades and professions in that they signal to employers that a teacher has completed the level of training and preparation required to practice the occupation within that state. The requirements for licenses in most states include completion of a bache-

Another new feature of the demand for teacher quality is the growing interest among policymakers and school administrators in measuring a teacher's "value added"— that is, her effectiveness in raising students' test scores.

lor's degree and certain education course requirements, as well as student teaching. Teacher licensing regulations are designed to prevent districts and schools from hiring people whom the state does not deem acceptable—namely, those lacking a bachelor's degree or formal teacher preparation.[28] Some observers argue, however, that the costs associated with licensure requirements deter talented people who do not major in education from entering the profession.[29] In general, empirical studies find little or no difference in average effectiveness between those teachers who are traditionally licensed and those who enter the profession through alternative routes.[30]

Since 1987, the National Board of Professional Teaching Standards has provided a na-

tional voluntary teacher certification program for teachers who choose to submit detailed portfolios and pass a rigorous examination that evaluates their professional mastery. Unlike traditional licensure programs, national board certification appears to be a useful indicator of teacher effectiveness. Using data from North Carolina, Dan Goldhaber and Emily Anthony found that that national board certified teachers are more effective at raising test scores than both those who do not apply for board certification *and* those who apply but do not pass.[31] The evidence on national board certification is discussed in greater detail in subsequent articles in this volume.

The Demand for Quality Teachers: What's New

The No Child Left Behind Act of 2001 (NCLB) has established an unprecedented role for the federal government in regulating teacher quality. In particular, the law required that teachers be "highly qualified" by 2006 in schools that receive federal Title I funding, earmarked for poor children. As defined by NCLB, a highly qualified teacher has a bachelor's degree as well as a state teaching license and demonstrated competence in the academic subject(s) he or she teaches.[32] This definition addresses the problem of out-of-field teaching by ensuring that all students are taught by teachers who are knowledgeable in the subjects they teach. Among all the provisions of NCLB, however, the highly qualified teacher requirement has been the least thoroughly enforced.[33]

Another new feature of the demand for teacher quality is the growing interest among policymakers and school administrators in measuring a teacher's "value added"—that is, her effectiveness in raising students' test scores. Advances in data storage and data processing have enabled a growing number of states to create long-term databases linking students' and teachers' records, making it possible to estimate value-added contributions. Indeed, although NCLB has raised interest in these measures, some states have estimated value added for many years. For example, Tennessee has used value-added modeling (VAM) as one of several ways to estimate school effectiveness since 1992, and in 1996 it began using three years' worth of VAM estimates to assess the effects of individual teachers on student learning.[34] Although VAM estimates are not used in their formal evaluations, Tennessee teachers have the option of using their value-added results to demonstrate that they have met the state's definition of a highly qualified teacher under No Child Left Behind.[35]

Some researchers see VAM as a powerful tool in efforts to recruit and retain better teachers. For example, Thomas Kane and Douglas Staiger argue that because it is so hard to predict a teacher's effectiveness at the point of hiring, schools should use value-added measures to evaluate teachers carefully after their first or second year on the job. Typically in the United States, teachers are granted tenure in their third or fourth year of teaching. Although tenure does not offer unlimited job security, it does offer protection from termination without rigorously documented due cause.[36] Rather than granting teachers tenure and job security almost reflexively, Kane and Staiger recommend hiring teachers with probationary status for the first one to two years and terminating at the point of the tenure decision those who are least effective at raising student achievement.[37]

Other analysts, however, have found that some teachers respond in undesirable ways to high-stakes pressure to increase test scores. For instance, Brian Jacob and Steven Levitt discovered incidents of teachers' outright cheating in 4–5 percent of classrooms, with more cheating in classrooms that had fewer students who were exempt from score reporting.[38] Other researchers cite the empirical uncertainty of value-added models as a reason for caution about their policy applications (see box 1).

What's True Internationally

The United States is not the only industrialized nation experiencing growth in primary and secondary school enrollments. Internationally, enrollments increased 15 percent in North America and 10 percent in Europe between 1990 and 1997.[39] Nevertheless, the school-aged population is growing faster in the United States than in other industrialized nations. For instance, between 1993 and 2003 the number of youth aged five to nineteen grew 12 percent in the United States, but only 7 percent in Canada and 5 percent in the United Kingdom.

While a growing student population creates the challenge of finding enough skilled teachers, a declining student population introduces a different problem. For example, in Japan, where the population of five- to nineteen-year-olds fell 21 percent from 1993 to 2003, there are relatively few opportunities to invigorate the teaching profession with young, energetic teachers.[40]

Like the United States, several countries are experiencing mismatches between the ethnic composition of their teaching forces and their increasingly diverse student populations. For instance, in the Netherlands, ethnic minorities constitute 12 percent of primary school students but only 4 percent of teachers.[41] The situation is similar in Norway, where the mostly white, Norwegian-speaking teaching

Box 1. Measuring Teachers' Effectiveness through Value-Added Modeling

Under the No Child Left Behind Act of 2001, schools must make "adequate yearly progress" (AYP) by showing improvements in test scores from one year to the next. Critics of AYP often point out that the gains required by NCLB are not long-term measures of student growth. Rather, they are cohort-to-cohort, cross-sectional measures that compare last year's students to the current year's students in a given class or grade. For instance, instead of looking at how much Mrs. Smith's fifth graders improved since they were tested in fourth grade, the cross-sectional approach asks how well Mrs. Smith's fifth graders this year performed in comparison with the fifth graders she taught last year.

One criticism of the cross-sectional approach is that it assumes that this year's fifth graders are the same as last year's fifth graders in their baseline skills. A related criticism is that it does not encourage schools or teachers to focus on individual students' progress over time.

Given these limitations of cross-sectional school improvement measures, interest is growing in how to measure schools' and teachers' effectiveness by tracking the performance of individual students over time through value-added modeling (VAM). Value-added models estimate the academic progress that students make in a given teacher's class (or in a given school) from one year to the next, and they attempt to isolate the impact that a particular teacher or school has on student achievement.

A major advantage of value-added models lies in their attention to teachers' (or schools') contributions to the learning of individual students over time. But the tremendous potential of VAM to measure teachers' effectiveness is constrained by several statistical and measurement challenges.

First, isolating a teacher's effect on students' achievement requires estimating what would have happened to the students' achievement under an alternative scenario. (Economists call this estimating the counterfactual.) It is not always clear whether the counterfactual means being taught by the average teacher in the district or by the least effective teacher. Nor is it clear that the teacher's effect would be the same with entirely different students.[1]

A second challenge lies in specifying statistical models that take into account the correlations between an individual student's test scores from one year to the next. Such models require statistical assumptions about the persistence of teacher effects over time, and using different assumptions can generate different estimates of teachers' effectiveness.[2]

Third, value-added models must attempt to account for the relatively small numbers of students with whom most teachers work. The smaller a teacher's student load, the more weight any one student will exert on the estimate of a teacher's effectiveness, so estimates may be less reliable for teachers who have fewer students. The statistical procedures that minimize this problem have the disadvantage of also minimizing the impact of the very strongest and weakest teachers.[3]

A fourth challenge lies in the difficulty of disentangling contextual effects, such as school and classroom characteristics, from teacher effects. Because students are not randomly assigned to classrooms or schools, and because teacher effectiveness may be systematically related to student characteristics, it is difficult to distinguish statistically between effects that are due to teachers and effects that are due to other characteristics of the students' classroom, school, and district environments.

Missing student test scores or missing links between students and their teachers pose a fifth challenge to value-added modeling. In most district-level and state-level data on student achievement, it is not unusual to encounter missing or incomplete information. If students with missing data are systematically different from their peers (as may be true for students who change schools frequently or are absent on testing days), then value-added models may produce biased estimates of teachers' (or schools') effectiveness.

A sixth challenge concerns the suitability of the standardized tests used in the value-added models. Because VAM seeks to measure students' achievement gains from one test administration to the next, it is essential that the scores be measured on the same scale and that the tests measure comparable content. It is also essential that the tests measure content that the teachers have covered, which is more difficult to ascertain in higher grades, where there is greater curricular differentiation among classrooms.[4] In fact, VAM's potential for large-scale teacher evaluation is constrained by the fact that students are not tested in all grades and subjects under NCLB. In many states, data are inadequate for measuring the value added of high school teachers or teachers of subjects other than math and language arts.

Researchers have estimated that VAM can reliably identify the roughly one-fourth to one-third of teachers whose effectiveness is much greater or much less than that of the average teacher.[5] But more precise rankings are hard to obtain because of the small number of students taught by each teacher.[6] These challenges suggest the limitations of heavy reliance on VAM estimates in drawing high-stakes conclusions about teachers' skills. Nevertheless, VAM can provide useful insights about teachers' effectiveness that would be difficult to obtain in the absence of such methods.[7]

1. Daniel F. McCaffrey and others, *Evaluating Value-Added Models for Teacher Accountability* (Santa Monica, Calif.: RAND Corporation, 2003).

2. Ibid.

3. Ibid.

4. Daniel M. Koretz, "Limitations in the Use of Achievement Tests as Measures of Educators' Productivity" 37, no. 4 (2000): 752–77.

5. Daniel F. McCaffrey and others, "Models for Value-Added Modeling of Teacher Effects," *Journal of Educational and Behavioral Statistics* 29, no. 1 (2004): 67–101.

6. J. R. Lockwood, Thomas A. Louis, and Daniel F. McCaffrey, "Uncertainty in Rank Estimation: Implications for Value-Added Modeling Accountability Systems," *Journal of Educational and Behavioral Statistics* 27, no. 3 (2002): 255–70.

7. McCaffrey and others, *Evaluating Value-Added Models for Teacher Accountability* (see note 1).

force is increasingly called on to teach immigrant youth who arrive speaking only Urdu, Arabic, or Somali.[42]

Other countries also face challenges in identifying effective teachers. Like the United States, most industrialized nations use teacher salary scales that base compensation on years of teaching experience and educa-tional credentials. Most of these countries, like the United States, screen before the point of hiring and do little screening for effectiveness once they have placed teachers in schools. But in some countries it is much more difficult to enter the teaching profession than it is in the United States. For example, in countries like Korea, Hong Kong, and Singapore, entry into teacher education depends on a strong academic background in one's subject area. Other nations, including France, Germany, Greece, Italy, Japan, Korea, parts of Mexico, and Spain, require aspiring teachers to take competitive examinations to obtain teaching certificates or job placements.[43]

The Supply Side of the Teacher Labor Market

It is somewhat misleading to speak of a national teacher labor market in America. In reality, the U.S. market is localized in such a way that teachers in one geographic region typically do not compete for jobs in another region. Thus, teacher shortages are often specific to certain regions or even to specific districts or schools within a region.

Another feature of teacher supply is the relatively high attrition rate among new teachers. Indeed, some researchers argue that so-called shortages result not so much from a paucity of licensed teachers as from a revolving door into and out of the profession.[44] Using data from the nationally representative 1991–92 Teacher Follow-Up Survey (TFS), David Grissmer and Sheila Kirby found that the attrition rate for teachers with one to three years of experience is roughly 8 percent annually, compared with 4.5 percent for teachers with four to nine years of experience.[45] Using TFS data from 1989–90, 1991–92, and 1994–95, Ingersoll calculated that roughly one-third of new teachers leave the profession within three years of entry, and that almost half leave within five years.[46] Neither of these estimates, however, considers the number of teachers who leave the classroom and later return. In the past, this "reserve pool" of licensed teachers who are not currently teaching has been an important source of supply when demand for teachers has risen.[47]

Teacher Supply: What Hasn't Changed

The supply of teachers—the number of eligible (that is, traditionally, alternatively, or temporarily licensed) people willing to teach at a given wage—has always been a function of workforce demographics, salaries, opportunity costs, and working conditions.

Over the past forty years, the supply of teachers has varied by academic subject area.[48] Supply has been less adequate relative to demand for teachers who have high opportunity costs—those trained in fields such as mathematics, computer science, chemistry, or physics—than for those trained in fields that have lower opportunity costs, such as the humanities.

Special education is another area in which the supply of teachers has often been inadequate. One reason may be that special education teachers work with students who face greater academic, and in some cases behavioral, challenges than other students. Furthermore, special education teachers must complete, update, and implement Independent Educational Plans (IEPs) for their students in order to comply with the Individuals with Disabilities in Education Act (IDEA). Thus, special education positions often entail more administrative responsibilities and paperwork than do general education positions. A national sample of principals surveyed in 1999–2000 reported difficulty staffing 75 percent of their special education openings and 77 percent of their mathematics openings, as against only 30 percent of social studies openings.[49]

There is considerable evidence that the supply of effective teachers is not equitably distributed across U.S. schools. A 2002 study by Hamilton Lankford, Susanna Loeb, and James Wyckoff found that New York State schools serving high concentrations of poor, nonwhite, or low-achieving children were disproportionately staffed by teachers who were inexperienced, were uncertified in subjects they taught, had graduated from noncompetitive colleges, or had failed their licensing examination on the first attempt. For instance, in schools with more than 20 percent of students scoring at the lowest proficiency level in fourth-grade English language arts in 2000, 35 percent of teachers had failed their licensing examination on the first try and 26 percent had degrees from noncompetitive colleges, as against only 9 percent and 10 percent of teachers, respectively, in the highest-scoring schools. The authors also found that roughly a third of this sorting occurred within districts where compensation differences did not play a role.[50]

The distribution problem is not confined to New York. National board certified teachers in North Carolina, for example, disproportionately work in suburban schools serving economically advantaged students.[51] Also, throughout their schooling, African American students in North Carolina are especially likely to be taught by novice teachers.[52] Along similar lines, a national study of the Teach for America (TFA) program found that non-TFA teachers working in socioeconomically disadvantaged schools served by TFA were far less likely than the average U.S. teacher to have attended a selective college or to have completed student teaching before becoming a teacher.[53] Just as the problem is not confined to one geographical area, it is not new. Howard Becker described it in the Chicago public schools as early as the 1950s, and it remains one of the most pressing challenges facing public education today.[54]

The likely explanation for why well-educated, experienced teachers tend to avoid working in schools serving high concentrations of low-income children or children of color is that working conditions in these schools are especially difficult. Many books by journalists support this proposition.[55] But because few quantitative studies include direct measures of working conditions in schools serving different types of student populations, few data exist about which working conditions con-

Because few quantitative studies include direct measures of working conditions in schools serving different types of student populations, few data exist about which working conditions contribute to the distribution problem.

tribute to the distribution problem. One study based on the 1991–92 Teacher Follow-Up Survey does indicate that among teachers who transfer, those who transfer from urban high-poverty public schools are more likely than the broad population of such teachers to cite the following as reasons for their dissatisfaction: "student discipline problems" (29 versus 18 percent), "lack of faculty influence" (26 versus 13 percent), "lack of student motivation" (27 versus 10 percent), "interference in teaching" (12 versus 5 percent), and "lack of professional competence as colleagues" (23 versus 8 percent).[56]

Teachers' preferences for working in areas close to or similar to those where they grew up also contribute to the distribution problem. Using New York State data from 1999 to 2002, Donald Boyd and colleagues found, for instance, that 61 percent of new teachers took jobs within fifteen miles of where they went to high school and that 85 percent stayed within forty miles of home.[57] Because economically disadvantaged areas have fewer college graduates than more affluent areas do, they also have more trouble providing their own educators. Thus the lack of educational attainment in these areas becomes a self-sustaining cycle.

Late hiring in school districts serving many disadvantaged students also exacerbates the distribution problem. For example, a three-state survey of 374 new teachers showed that 28 percent of new teachers in low-income schools were hired after the start of the school year, compared with only 8 percent in high-income schools.[58] The problem of late hiring in urban districts is explored more fully by Brian Jacob in his article in this volume.

One component of teacher supply that has received little research attention is substitute teachers—a group that, from the beginning of kindergarten to the end of grade twelve, teaches the typical American public school child for about two-thirds of a school year.[59] Although the No Child Left Behind legislation required that all teachers become highly qualified by 2006, it explicitly excluded substitute teachers. In fact, nineteen states do not even require substitutes to hold a bachelor's degree.[60] Although some substitute teachers use these temporary jobs to gain entry into permanent positions, there is little research on the qualifications or skills of the substitute pool, whether these vary by type of school district, and what share of substitute teachers eventually moves into permanent teaching positions.[61]

Teacher Supply: What's New

We now turn to a discussion of changes in the supply of teachers over the past two decades. Because the supply of teachers is a function of population demographics, salaries, opportunity costs, and working conditions, we examine how trends in each of these factors have affected teacher supply.

Demographics. The teacher workforce in the United States has aged steadily since the mid-1970s and is on the verge of a large wave of retirements. In 2005, 42 percent of teachers were aged fifty or older, compared with 25 percent in 1996. The distribution of teacher experience shows the same trend. In 2001, 38 percent of U.S. teachers had more than twenty years of experience—up from 28 percent in 1986 and 18 percent in 1971.[62] The implication is that more teachers will be needed to replace the many who will retire soon.

In the past, two sources of supply have been important in responding to increased demand for teachers. One is the share of college students who train to become teachers, which has grown. The second is the reserve pool—licensed teachers who return to teaching after a period spent in another activity. Undoubtedly, both sources of supply will be important in responding to the increase in demand for teachers in the years ahead. But, as we show, several labor market developments have made it much harder for today's schools to attract talented college graduates.

Salaries and Opportunity Costs. The supply of teachers in the labor market has been adversely affected by increasing labor market opportunities for women and minorities. Before the civil rights and women's movements, opportunities for women and people of color

Figure 4. Distribution of New Female Teachers, by High School Ranking, Selected Years, 1964–2000

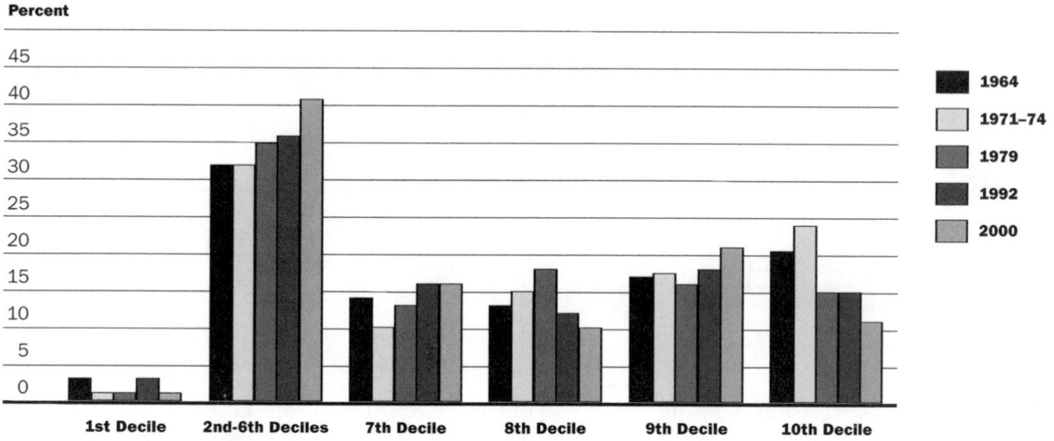

Percent

Legend: 1964, 1971–74, 1979, 1992, 2000

(Bar chart with vertical axis from 0 to 45 in increments of 5; horizontal axis categories: 1st Decile, 2nd–6th Deciles, 7th Decile, 8th Decile, 9th Decile, 10th Decile)

Source: Sean P. Corcoran, William N. Evans, and Robert M. Schwab, "Women, the Labor Market, and the Declining Relative Quality of Teachers," *Journal of Policy Analysis and Management* 23, no. 3 (2004): 455, 465. Data for 1964 are from the Wisconsin Longitudinal Survey; data for 1971–74, from Project Talent; data for 1979, from the National Longitudinal Study of the Class of 1972; data for 1992 from the High School and Beyond survey; and data for 2000, from the National Educational Longitudinal Survey.

were severely constrained by discrimination. As a result, among the available alternatives, teaching was a relatively high-status occupation for both women and people of color—a situation that helped guarantee a steady flow of academically talented women and minorities into the teaching profession. Changes in the occupational choices of black college graduates illustrate this trend. In the late 1960s, six out of every ten black college graduates entered teaching within five years of graduation; by the early 1980s, that figure was one in ten.[63]

As labor market opportunities for women and minorities have expanded, their opportunity costs have risen—and have risen most sharply for those with stronger academic abilities. Research by Sean Corcoran, William Evans, and Robert Schwab shows that from 1964 to 2000 the average ability level of entering female teachers declined only slightly, but the share of young female teachers from the top decile of their high school class fell from 20 percent to 11 percent.[64] Figure 4,

which is excerpted from their work, illustrates these trends.

In summary, improved labor market opportunities for women and minorities have forced education to compete increasingly with other occupations for talented college graduates. And as figure 4 indicates, education is losing this competition. Part of the explanation is that other occupations reward strong academic skills more than education does.[65] Using data from the National Center for Education Statistics' 1993–2003 Baccalaureate and Beyond Longitudinal Survey, Dan Goldhaber and Albert Liu found that unlike teaching salaries, nonteaching salaries for recent female college graduates rewarded college selectivity, technical majors, and high GPAs.[66]

Working Conditions. In the past two decades, teachers' working conditions have improved in some ways and deteriorated in others. On the one hand, as noted, both class sizes and student-teacher ratios have fallen.[67] On the other hand, NCLB and state accountability systems have increased pressure on teachers to improve student test scores. The pressure is particularly great on teachers working in schools that serve high shares of disadvantaged students. For instance, one 2004 study found that after the implementation of a statewide accountability system, teachers in North Carolina were more likely to leave

---

International comparisons also reveal considerable variation in teachers' working conditions, even among nations with strong systems of public education.

---

schools with low test scores and those that were labeled "low-performing."[68]

Another trend in working conditions is the movement to differentiate the traditionally flat teaching career. Historically, the main option for teachers who wanted to advance professionally was to stop teaching and become administrators.[69] The 1980s saw efforts to create career ladders that would generate leadership opportunities for teachers. But many of these initiatives faltered because some teachers saw them as threats to the egalitarian nature of the profession.[70] Today a similar trend toward differentiation of teaching roles appears to have two distinct rationales. One is the belief that peer-to-peer professional development will help teachers raise student achievement.[71] The other is the belief that more opportunities for advancement will mitigate attrition among new teachers, some of whom report wanting up-

ward job mobility.[72] Among today's new positions are mentors, who assist new teachers; peer coaches, who provide instructional guidance to colleagues; and peer reviewers, who evaluate their colleagues' instruction.[73] Little systematic data, however, exist on how widespread these roles are or whether they improve instruction or increase teacher retention.[74]

What's True Internationally

In most countries, salaries, class size policies, curriculum requirements, and licensure standards are set at the national level; in the United States, they are set at local and state levels. Nevertheless, the problem of inequitable distribution of effective teachers across schools is not unique to the United States. For example, teacher surpluses in the north of England coexist with teacher shortages in more populous, diverse areas such as London and the southeast.[75] Research in Norway has also shown that teachers are more likely to leave schools with high shares of minority or special needs students.[76] The inequitable distribution of effective teachers poses a troubling challenge for policymakers worldwide—a challenge that may take on even greater proportions in industrialized nations as Europe continues to become more ethnically diverse.

International comparisons also reveal considerable variation in teachers' working conditions, even among nations with strong systems of public education. In Singapore, whose students scored first among the forty-nine nations that participated in the 2003 Trends in International Mathematics and Science Study (TIMSS), the central government prescribes the curriculum and places a heavy emphasis on students' performance on standardized tests.[77] In Finland, whose students scored first on the Program for International

Student Assessment (PISA) in 2000 and 2003, teachers have high levels of curricular autonomy, and student assessments tend to be individualized and diagnostic.[78] These differences in working conditions between nations with high-performing educational systems suggest the need for caution in thinking about the types of working conditions that will foster a highly effective teaching workforce in the United States.

Policy Responses

Several policies have been proposed to increase the supply of effective teachers and distribute them more equitably. We briefly summarize three categories of responses, leaving detailed discussions to other articles in this volume.

Increase Salaries Uniformly

Given that shortages of effective teachers result when the quantity demanded exceeds the quantity supplied at a given wage, one oft-proposed policy solution has been across-the-board increases in teachers' salaries.[79] The rationale is that in the short term, salary increases draw reserve-pool teachers into classrooms, and in the long term they make the profession more attractive to young people considering teaching careers. By increasing the number of applicants for teaching positions, salary increases would allow schools to be more selective in their hiring decisions.

On the other side of the ledger, across-the-board salary hikes are likely to increase the number of ineffective as well as effective teachers who want to enter and remain in public schools.[80] Consequently, salary increases will improve the teaching force only if schools are able to make wise decisions about whom they hire and retain. Because schools typically lack the information they need to identify effective teachers at the

point of hiring and often have difficulty terminating ineffective teachers they have already employed, across-the-board salary increases are unlikely, by themselves, to improve the effectiveness of the teaching force.

Reduce Barriers to Entry

One way to increase the number of people willing and able to teach at the going wage is to reduce or eliminate restrictions on who is allowed to teach. In 2005, forty-seven states offered some form of alternative program that enabled people to become licensed quickly, with minimal preparation time and expense.[81] But these alternative programs vary enormously in terms of their selectivity, their management, and the training they provide, making it difficult to generalize about their effectiveness.[82]

Still, there is evidence that teachers who enter the profession through competitive alternative licensure programs, such as Teach for America or the New York City Teaching Fellows Program, are as effective as those who enter teaching through traditional routes and that some alternative certification programs (for example, the New York City Teaching Fellows) are better than traditional programs at recruiting minority teachers.[83] Nevertheless, critics argue that the brief summer training programs offered by several of these alternative programs cannot adequately prepare new teachers to work with disadvantaged students whose backgrounds and learning experiences often differ markedly from their own. Critics also warn that the short-term commitments required by some alternative certification programs, such as the two years required by Teach for America, help ensure that the least-advantaged students are constantly taught by a stream of novices.[84] Further evidence on alternative licensure is presented in the article by Donald Boyd, Daniel Goldhaber, Hamilton Lankford, and James Wyckoff in this volume.

Make Teacher Compensation More Flexible

A third response to the teacher quality challenge is to replace the uniform salary schedule that rewards only academic degrees and years of experience with more flexible pay structures. One form of flexible compensation is pay for performance, or merit pay—in which a portion of teachers' compensation is based on estimates of their effectiveness at raising student achievement. Pay-for-performance schemes have been attempted in thousands of U.S. school districts over the past century, only to be dropped within five years in most cases, mainly because of reduced incentives for teamwork, the inability of administrators to defend subjective evaluations, the wariness of administrators to give poor ratings to teachers who could not be easily terminated, and the unpredictability of awards from year to year.[85] Nevertheless, such schemes have recently enjoyed a resurgence in popularity. Denver undertook a comprehensive, union-approved merit pay program in 2006.[86] And other localities such as Houston are following suit.[87] A more thorough examination of pay-for-performance systems is presented in the article by Victor Lavy in this volume.

Other forms of flexible compensation reward teachers according to their opportunity costs or according to the characteristics of the schools in which they teach. Some researchers advocate higher pay for teachers (for example, in math and science) whose skills command a premium in the labor market, arguing that such policies would mitigate subject-specific shortages.[88] In fact, some schools already differentiate informally, by placing teachers in high-demand subjects at higher steps on the salary schedule than their experience would otherwise warrant.[89]

Certain state and federal programs also provide incentives for those who teach in shortage subject areas or in schools with difficult working conditions. For instance, the federal Perkins Loan program offers 100 percent loan forgiveness over a five-year period to those who teach in shortage subject areas or in low-income schools, and a similar incentive was implemented for federal Stafford Loans in 1998.[90] Although such programs target the distribution problem by improving the financial incentives for working in low-income schools, most do not specifically target the most effective or academically accomplished teachers.[91]

What's True Internationally

As we have shown, the United States is hardly alone among industrialized nations in its desire to staff public schools with effective teachers and to see that those teachers work in schools where they are most needed. It is therefore not surprising that a number of the policy incentives that are being tried in the United States have also been undertaken abroad. While articles elsewhere in this volume describe some of these initiatives in greater detail, we highlight a few noteworthy examples.

Salaries. In most industrialized nations, teacher salary schedules are similar in structure to those in the United States. That is, the schedules primarily reward experience and educational attainment.[92] Yet industrialized nations vary in the relative attractiveness of teachers' salaries and in the size of the salary increases associated with additional teaching experience. In some countries, including Korea, Japan, and Portugal, average salaries of experienced teachers far exceed those of inexperienced teachers ($75,000 versus $27,000 in Korea in 2002), meaning that experience carries considerable financial rewards. In contrast, other countries, especially those in Scandinavia, offer starting salaries that are close to those at the top of the scale ($19,000 versus $22,000 in Iceland in 2002), meaning that teachers enjoy only minimal earnings growth as they advance through their careers. The United States falls somewhere in between, with average high and low salaries of $52,000 and $29,000, respectively, in 2002.[93]

Barriers to Entry. Many industrialized nations also resemble the United States in terms of barriers to entering the teaching profession. Most countries require teachers to obtain licenses through coursework, examinations, and student teaching, though the details of these requirements vary by country. Still, a few countries, including England and Wales, have responded to teacher shortages by creating alternative routes into the profession.[94]

Researchers for the Organization for Economic Cooperation and Development note that licensure requirements "are more likely to exist" in countries "where the provision of teacher education is diverse and perceived to be of variable quality."[95] From this perspective, government-issued licensure requirements are seen as important quality controls in countries like the United States, where teacher education programs are not tightly regulated and where the quality of such programs varies markedly.[96]

Flexible Compensation. Several countries are also experimenting with forms of pay for performance. In a few nations, such as Chile and Mexico, performance is defined partly in terms of gains in student achievement.[97]

Such policies and their outcomes are described in greater detail in the article by Emiliana Vegas in this volume. In other nations, such as England, Portugal, and Switzerland, teachers can receive salary increases if they volunteer to have their pedagogy assessed against national teaching standards.[98] Because such assessments take into account teachers' curriculum vitae and work portfolios, they are in some ways comparable to national board certification in the United States.

One country that is notably different is Sweden. In 1995, Sweden abandoned the experience-based salary schedule to give schools more flexibility in what they paid each teacher. But subsequent research has shown that teachers' salaries in Sweden have become more rather than less uniform.[99]

Finally, several countries use compensating wage differentials to attract teachers to hard-to-staff schools and geographic regions. Australia, for example, offers geographic hardship incentives to encourage people to teach in its sparsely inhabited central desert area.[100]

Conclusion

If the United States is to equip its young people with the problem-solving and communication skills that are essential in the new economy, it is more important than ever to recruit and retain high-quality teachers. In recent years, the demand for quality teachers has increased as enrollments have risen, class sizes have fallen, and a large share of the teacher workforce has begun to retire. At the same time, because women and minorities have more career options today than ever before, it is increasingly difficult to attract and retain the many high-quality teachers that are needed. Moreover, schools are often limited in their ability to identify and reward the most effective teachers. As a result of these challenges, schools now face high turnover and hiring problems in subjects with high opportunity costs and in the schools with the most difficult working conditions.

The unequal distribution of effective teachers is perhaps the most urgent problem facing American education. Poor children and children of color are disproportionately assigned to teachers who have the least preparation and the weakest academic backgrounds, and this pattern is long-standing. It is no wonder teacher turnover is high in schools that serve large shares of poor or nonwhite students. The work in these schools is difficult, and the teachers who attempt to do it are often the least equipped to succeed and often lack the working conditions necessary to succeed.

In response to these challenges, a number of policy instruments have been proposed. Some focus on increasing the supply of effective teachers; others, on correcting the inequitable distribution of effective teachers across schools. Though several of these policy proposals are already being tried, few are being rigorously evaluated.

Puzzles and Unanswered Questions

U.S. policymakers have tried many approaches to attracting and retaining high-quality teachers, but the effectiveness of these approaches remains largely unknown. Today, long-term databases that link teachers to students in states like Florida, North Carolina, and New York offer new opportunities to evaluate these policy interventions. In time, the data-keeping requirements of the accountability movement should provide researchers with additional data sets that can be used to analyze teachers' effectiveness in raising student achievement. An unresolved question is how to make constructive use of measures of teachers' value added.

There is also much to be learned by looking beyond U.S. borders to understand how teacher labor markets work in other countries. It would be naive to assume that policies rooted in one nation's culture can be easily and quickly transplanted into another, but it is important to consider what challenges other countries face, what policies they are using to deal with these challenges, and how effective the policies have been in attracting and retaining skilled teachers and in improving student achievement.

A final, critical need is to accumulate knowledge. States and school districts are trying a variety of strategies to attract skilled teachers to high-need schools and subject areas. Yet few of these initiatives have been designed in a way that makes it possible to evaluate their effectiveness rigorously.

It is also important to think broadly about the types of incentives that matter to teachers. Paying large financial bonuses to teachers to do impossible jobs will not help children. An essential part of the solution to the distribution problem is to find ways to make schools supportive and humane places for teachers and the students with whom they work.

Notes

1. Thomas S. Dee, "Are There Civic Returns to Education?" Working Paper 9588 (Cambridge, Mass.: National Bureau of Economic Research, 2003).

2. Richard J. Murnane and others, "How Important Are the Cognitive Skills of Teenagers in Predicting Subsequent Earnings?" *Journal of Policy Analysis and Management* 19, no. 4 (2000): 547–68.

3. National Center for Education Statistics, *NAEP: 2004 Long-Term Trend Summary Data Tables*, nces.ed.gov/nationsreportcard/ltt/results2004/2004_sdts.asp (July 23, 2005).

4. Frank Levy and Richard J. Murnane, *The New Division of Labor: How Computers Are Creating the Next Job Market* (New York: Russell Sage Foundation, 2004).

5. Dan Goldhaber and Daniel Player, "What Different Benchmarks Suggest about How Financially Attractive It Is to Teach in Public Schools," *Journal of Education Finance* 30, no. 3 (2005): 211–30.

6. In a longitudinal study of teachers in Michigan and North Carolina, Richard Murnane and colleagues found that chemistry and physics teachers exited from the profession more rapidly than teachers of other subjects and were less likely to return, and that teachers with higher scores on the National Teacher Examination left the profession more rapidly than those with lower test scores. See Richard J. Murnane and others, *Who Will Teach? Policies That Matter* (Harvard University Press, 1991). In the United Kingdom, Arnaud Chevalier and colleagues used surveys of five cross-sections of university graduates from 1960 to 1990 to demonstrate that a 10 percent increase in teachers' relative wages would result, on average among the five cohorts, in a 5.4 percentage point increase in the probability of teaching six years later. See Arnaud Chevalier, Peter Dolton, and Steven McIntosh, *Recruiting and Retaining Teachers in the UK: An Analysis of Graduate Occupation Choice from the 1960s to the 1990s* (London: Centre for the Economics of Education, 2002). In Australia, Andrew Leigh used salary data from Australia's Graduate Destination Surveys and national data on undergraduates' entrance rankings and courses of study to estimate that a 1 percent increase in teachers' pay relative to the pay in alternative professions is associated with a 0.8 point increase in the mean percentile rank of undergraduates entering teacher education courses. See Andrew Leigh, *Teacher Pay and Teacher Aptitude* (Australian National University, Social Policy Evaluation, Analysis and Research Centre, 2005).

7. Susan Moore Johnson, Jill Harrison Berg, and Morgaen L. Donaldson, *Who Stays in Teaching and Why: A Review of the Literature on Teacher Retention* (Washington: NRTA, 2005).

8. Eric A. Hanushek, John F. Kain, and Steven G. Rivkin, "Why Public Schools Lose Teachers," *Journal of Human Resources* 39, no. 2 (2004): 326–54. See also Todd R. Stinebrickner, Benjamin Scafidi, and David L. Sjoquist, *Race, Poverty, and Teacher Mobility*, Research Paper Series 06-51 (Andrew Young School of Policy Studies, 2005).

9. For evidence of the correlation between school facilities and teachers' intent to remain in their current schools, see Jack Buckley, Mark Schneider, and Yi Shang, "Fix It and They Might Stay: School Facility Quality and Teacher Retention in Washington, D.C.," *Teachers College Record* 107, no. 5 (2005): 1107–23.

10. Two such initiatives are the Chancellor's District in New York City and the School Improvement Zone in the Miami-Dade County Public Schools. For a discussion of the first, see Deinya Phenix and others, "A Forced March for Failing Schools: Lessons from the New York City Chancellor's District," *Education Pol-*

icy Analysis Archives 13, no. 40 (2005). For a discussion of the second, see Center for Educational Performance and Accountability, *Can Miami-Dade Schools Teach Florida a Lesson?* www.floridataxwatch.org/resources/pdf/ StudentAchievementinMiamiDadeSchoolsRelease.pdf (August 5, 2006).

11. David Tyack and Larry Cuban, *Tinkering toward Utopia: A Century of Public School Reform* (Harvard University Press, 1995).

12. John Wirt and others, *The Condition of Education 2005* (Washington: National Center for Education Statistics, 2005).

13. National Center for Health Statistics, *Health, United States, 2005, with Chartbook on Trends in the Health of Americans* (Hyattsville, Md., 2005).

14. Patrick Rooney and others, *The Condition of Education 2006* (Washington: Institute of Education Sciences, National Center for Education Statistics, 2006).

15. U.S. Census Bureau, *Statistical Abstract of the United States, 2004–05* (2005).

16. Thomas S. Dee, "Teachers, Race, and Student Achievement in a Randomized Experiment," *Review of Economics and Statistics* 86, no. 1 (2004): 195–210. See also Eric A. Hanushek and others, *The Market for Teacher Quality*, Working Paper 11154 (Cambridge, Mass.: National Bureau of Economic Research, 2005).

17. C. Emily Feistritzer, *Profiles of Teachers in the US 2005* (Washington: National Center for Education Information, 2005).

18. CSR Research Consortium, *Class Size Reduction in California: The 1998-99 Evaluation Findings*, www.classize.org/summary/98-99/#1 (September 4, 2005).

19. National Center for Education Statistics, *Digest of Education Statistics, 2004* (Washington, 2004).

20. Dale Ballou, *The Condition of Urban School Finance: Efficient Resource Allocation in Urban Schools* (Amherst, Mass.: University of Massachusetts, Amherst, 1998).

21. U.S. Department of Education, *Individuals with Disabilities Education Act,* www.ed.gov (October 16, 2005).

22. Eric A. Hanushek, *The Evidence on Class Size* (Rochester, N.Y.: W. Allen Wallis Institute of Political Economy, 1998).

23. See, for instance, Steven G. Rivkin, Eric A. Hanushek, and John F. Kain, "Teachers, Schools, and Academic Achievement," *Econometrica* 73, no. 2 (2005): 417–58; Jonah E. Rockoff, "The Impact of Individual Teachers on Student Achievement: Evidence from Panel Data," *American Economic Review* 94, no. 2 (2004): 247–52; Daniel Aaronson, Lisa Barrow, and William Sander, *Teachers and Student Achievement in the Chicago Public Schools*, WP-2002-28 (Chicago: Federal Reserve Bank of Chicago, 2003).

24. Richard Hofstadter, *Anti-Intellectualism in American Life* (New York: Vintage Books, 1963). For an example of the value some schools place on athletic coaching, see H. G. Bissinger, *Friday Night Lights: A Town, a Team, and a Dream* (Reading, Mass.: Addison-Wesley, 1990). For examples of preferential hiring based on familial connections, see Gretchen McKay, "Nepotism Loosely Regulated by State, School Districts," *Pittsburgh Post-Gazette,* February 5, 2003, www.post-gazette.com/localnews/20030205nepotism0205p9.asp (January 18, 2006).

25. Richard M. Ingersoll, "The Problem of Underqualified Teachers in American Secondary Schools," *Educational Researcher* 28, no. 2 (1999): 26–37.

26. Rivkin, Hanushek, and Kain, "Teachers, Schools, and Academic Achievement" (see note 23). See also Aaronson, Barrow, and Sander, *Teachers and Student Achievement in the Chicago Public Schools* (see note 23).

27. For evidence on verbal aptitude scores, see Eric A. Hanushek, "Teacher Characteristics and Gains in Student Achievement: Estimation Using Micro Data," *American Economic Review* 61, no. 2 (1971): 280–88. For evidence on ACT scores, see Ronald F. Ferguson and Helen F. Ladd, "How and Why Money Matters: An Analysis of Alabama Schools," in *Holding Schools Accountable: Performance-Based Education Reform*, edited by Helen F. Ladd (Brookings, 1996), pp. 265–98. And for evidence on college selectivity, see Ronald G. Ehrenberg and Dominic J. Brewer, "Do School and Teacher Characteristics Matter? Evidence from High School and Beyond," *Economics of Education Review* 13, no. 1 (1994): 1–17; as well as Anita Summers and Barbara Wolfe, "Do Schools Make a Difference?" *American Economic Review* 67, no. 4 (1977): 639–52.

28. Murnane and others, *Who Will Teach?* (see note 6).

29. Dale Ballou and Michael Podgursky, "Recruiting Smarter Teachers," *Journal of Human Resources* 30, no. 2 (1995): 326–38.

30. See, for instance, Donald Boyd and others, "How Changes in Entry Requirements Alter the Teacher Workforce and Affect Student Achievement," Working Paper 11844 (Cambridge, Mass.: National Bureau of Economic Research, 2005); Paul T. Decker, Daniel P. Mayer, and Steven Glazerman, *The Effects of Teach for America on Students: Findings from a National Evaluation* (Princeton, N.J.: Mathematica Policy Research, 2004); Thomas J. Kane and Douglas O. Staiger, *Using Imperfect Information to Identify Effective Teachers* (Cambridge, Mass.: National Bureau of Economic Research, 2005); Thomas J. Kane, Jonah E. Rockoff, and Douglas O. Staiger, *Identifying Effective Teachers in New York City* (Cambridge, Mass.: National Bureau of Economic Research, 2005); Linda Darling-Hammond and others, "Does Teacher Preparation Matter? Evidence about Teacher Certification, Teach for America, and Teacher Effectiveness," paper presented at the annual meeting of the American Educational Research Association, Montreal, Canada, 2005.

31. Dan Goldhaber and Emily Anthony, *Can Teacher Quality Be Effectively Assessed?* (Seattle: Center on Reinventing Public Education, 2005).

32. U.S. Department of Education, *Highly Qualified Teachers and Paraprofessionals*, www.ed.gov/admins/tchrqual/learn/hqt/hqteachers.pdf, 2002 (July 23, 2006).

33. Kati Haycock, "Closing the Achievement Gap in America's Public Schools: The No Child Left Behind Act," Testimony before the U.S. House of Representatives, Committee on Education and the Workforce, 2005.

34. A. Paige Baker, Dengke Xu, and Ethel Detch, *The Measure of Education: A Review of the Tennessee Value Added Assessment System* (Nashville, Tenn.: Office of Education Accountability, 1995).

35. Lana C. Selvers, *Tennessee Plan for Implementing the Teacher and Paraprofessional Quality Provisions of the No Child Left Behind Act of 2001* (Nashville, Tenn.: Tennessee State Department of Education, 2005).

36. James Scott, *Teacher Tenure*, www.ericdigests.org/pre-925/tenure.htm (August 5, 2006).

37. Kane and Staiger, *Using Imperfect Information to Identify Effective Teachers* (see note 30).

38. Brian A. Jacob and Steven D. Levitt, "Rotten Apples: An Investigation of the Prevalence and Predictors of Teacher Cheating," *Quarterly Journal of Economics* 118, no. 3 (2003): 843–77.

39. Organization for Economic Cooperation and Development (OECD), *Education at a Glance* (Paris, 2004).

40. Naoko Moriyoshi, "Teacher Preparation and Teachers' Lives in Japan," in *Contemporary Research in the United States, Germany, and Japan on Five Education Issues: Structure of the Education System, Standards in Education, the Role of School in Adolescents' Lives, Individual Differences among Students, and Teachers' Lives*, edited by Harold W. Stevenson, Shin-Ying Lee, and Roberta Nerison-Low (U.S. Department of Education, 2003), pp. 410–38.

41. Phillip McKenzie and Paulo Santiago, *Teachers Matter: Attracting, Developing, and Retaining Effective Teachers* (Paris: OECD, 2005).

42. Torberg Falch and Bjarne Strom, "Teacher Turnover and Non-Pecuniary Factors," *Economics of Education Review* 24, no. 6 (2004): 611–31.

43. McKenzie and Santiago, *Teachers Matter* (see note 41).

44. Richard M. Ingersoll, "Teacher Turnover and Teacher Shortages: An Organizational Analysis," *American Educational Research Journal* 38, no. 3 (2001): 499–534.

45. David Grissmer and Sheila Nataraj Kirby, "Teacher Turnover and Teacher Quality," *Teachers College Record* 99, no. 1 (1997): 45–56.

46. Richard M. Ingersoll, *Is There Really a Teacher Shortage?* (Philadelphia: Consortium for Policy Research in Education and Center for the Study of Teaching and Policy, 2003).

47. Murnane and others, *Who Will Teach?* (see note 6).

48. Ibid.

49. Ingersoll, *Is There Really a Teacher Shortage?* (see note 46).

50. Hamilton Lankford, Susanna Loeb, and James Wyckoff, "Teacher Sorting and the Plight of Urban Schools: A Descriptive Analysis," *Educational Evaluation and Policy Analysis* 24, no. 1 (2002): 37–62.

51. Goldhaber and Anthony, *Can Teacher Quality Be Effectively Assessed?* (see note 31).

52. Charles T. Clotfelter, Helen F. Ladd, and Jacob L. Vigdor, "Who Teaches Whom? Race and the Distribution of Novice Teachers," *Economics of Education Review* 24, no. 4 (2005): 377–92.

53. Decker, Mayer, and Glazerman, *The Effects of Teach for America on Students* (see note 30).

54. Howard S. Becker, "Role and Career Problems of the Chicago Public School Teacher" (University of Chicago Press, 1951).

55. See, for example, Jonathan Kozol, *Savage Inequalities: Children in America's Schools* (New York: Crown, 1991).

56. Ingersoll, "Teacher Turnover and Teacher Shortages" (see note 44). Note that because the Teacher Follow-Up Survey interviews only those who leave their schools, it is not possible to compare their responses to those who stayed in those schools.

57. Donald Boyd and others, "The Draw of Home: How Teachers' Preferences for Proximity Disadvantage Urban Schools," Working Paper 9953 (Cambridge, Mass.: National Bureau of Economic Research, 2003).

58. Susan Moore Johnson and others, "The Support Gap: New Teachers' Early Experiences in High-Income and Low-Income Schools," *Education Policy Analysis Archives* 12, no. 61 (2005).

59. Ballou, *The Condition of Urban School Finance* (see note 20).

60. E. Henderson, N. Protheroe, and S. Porch. *Developing an Effective Substitute Teacher Program* (Arlington,Va.: Educational Research Service, 2002).

61. Ismat Abdal-Haqq, *Not Just a Warm Body: Changing Images of the Substitute Teacher* (Washington: ERIC Clearinghouse on Teaching and Teacher Education, 1997).

62. Susan Moore Johnson and the Project on the Next Generation of Teachers, *Finders and Keepers: Helping New Teachers Survive and Thrive in Our Schools*, Jossey-Bass Education Series (San Francisco: Jossey-Bass, 2004).

63. Murnane and others, *Who Will Teach?* (see note 6).

64. Sean P. Corcoran, William N. Evans, and Robert M. Schwab, "Women, the Labor Market, and the Declining Relative Quality of Teachers," *Journal of Policy Analysis and Management* 23, no. 3 (2004): 449–70.

65. Caroline M. Hoxby and Andrew Leigh, "Pulled Away or Pushed Out? Explaining the Decline of Teacher Aptitude in the United States," *American Economic Review* 93, no. 2 (2004).

66. Dan Goldhaber and Albert Yung-Hsu Liu, "Teacher Salary Structure and the Decision to Teach in Public Schools: An Analysis of Recent College Graduates," paper presented before the American Education Finance Association, 2003.

67. Hanushek, *The Evidence on Class Size* (see note 22).

68. Charles T. Clotfelter and others, "Do School Accountability Systems Make It More Difficult for Low-Performing Schools to Attract and Retain High-Quality Teachers?" *Journal of Policy Analysis and Management* 23, no. 2 (2004): 251–71.

69. For a thorough sociological analysis of the traditionally flat teaching career, see Dan C. Lortie, *Schoolteacher: A Sociological Study,* 2nd ed. (University of Chicago Press, 1975).

70. See, for example, Ann Weaver Hart, "Creating Teacher Leadership Roles," *Educational Administration Quarterly* 30, no. 4 (1994): 472–97. See also Susan J. Rosenholtz, "Education Reform Strategies: Will They Increase Teacher Commitment?" *American Journal of Education* 95, no. 4 (1987): 534–62.

71. Barbara Neufeld and Dana Roper, *Coaching: A Strategy for Developing Instructional Capacity: Promises and Practicalities* (Washington: The Aspen Institute Program on Education and The Annenberg Institute for School Reform, 2003). See also Susan M. Poglinco and others, *The Heart of the Matter: The Coaching Model in America's Choice Schools* (Philadelphia: Center for Policy Research in Education, 2003).

72. Heather G. Peske and others, "The Next Generation of Teachers: Changing Conceptions of a Career in Teaching," *Phi Delta Kappan* 83 (2001): 304–11.

73. Morgaen L. Donaldson and others, "'Hot Shots' and 'Principal's Pets': How Colleagues Influence Second-Stage Teachers' Experience of Differentiated Roles," paper presented at the annual meeting of the American Educational Research Association, Montreal, Canada, 2005.

74. Regarding trends in mentoring and induction programs for new teachers, Smith and Ingersoll, using data from the 1990–91 and 1999–2000 NCES Schools and Staffing Survey, found that the share of new public schoolteachers receiving induction or mentoring rose from just under 51 percent to 83 percent between 1990 and 1999. They also found that the odds that a teacher mentored by a teacher of the same subject would leave teaching at the end of the first year were 0.7 times the odds of other teachers, though there was no effect on a teacher's movement between schools. The findings cannot be interpreted as causal, however, and they do not address the question of whether there is a retention effect for the *mentors*. See Thomas M. Smith and Richard M. Ingersoll, "What Are the Effects of Induction and Mentoring on Beginning Teacher Turnover?" *American Educational Research Journal* 41, no. 3 (2004): 681–714.

75. Peter Dolton, "The Supply of Teachers," in *Handbook of the Economics of Education*, edited by Eric A. Hanushek and Finis Welch (Dordecht, The Netherlands: Elsevier, 2006).

76. Torberg Falch and Bjarne Strom, "Teacher Turnover and Non-Pecuniary Factors," *Economics of Education Review* 24, no. 6 (2004): 611–31.

77. Robert B. Kozma, *National Policies That Connect ICT-Based Education Reform to Economic and Social Development* (Menlo Park, Calif.: Center for Technology in Learning, SRI International, 2005).

78. Ibid.

79. See, for example, Dave Eggers, Ninive Calegari, and Daniel Moulthrop, "Reading, Writing, Retailing," *New York Times,* June 27, 2005, www.nytimes.com/2005/06/27/opinion/27eggers.html?ex=1277524800&en=fa0e123be439de5a&ei=5088&partner=rssnyt&emc=rss (June 27, 2005).

80. Ballou and Podgursky, "Recruiting Smarter Teachers" (see note 29).

81. C. Emily Feistritzer, *Alternative Certification: A State-by-State Analysis* (Washington: National Center for Education Information, 2005).

82. Susan Moore Johnson, Sarah E. Birkeland, and Heather G. Peske, *A Difficult Balance: Incentives and Quality Control in Alternative Certification Programs* (Cambridge, Mass.: Project on the Next Generation of Teachers, Harvard Graduate School of Education, 2005).

83. For evidence on the ability of traditionally licensed teachers versus alternate-route teachers to raise student achievement, see the following studies: Decker, Mayer, and Glazerman, *The Effects of Teach for America on Students* (see note 30); Linda Darling-Hammond and others, "Does Teacher Preparation Matter?" (see note 30); Kane and Staiger, *Using Imperfect Information to Identify Effective Teachers* (see note 30); Kane, Rockoff, and Staiger, *Identifying Effective Teachers in New York City* (see note 30). For evidence on the demographic traits of teachers entering NYC schools through various licensure routes, see Kane, Rockoff, and Staiger (see note 30).

84. Linda Darling-Hammond, "Who Will Speak for the Children? How 'Teach for America' Hurts Urban Schools and Students," *Phi Delta Kappan* 76, no. 1 (1994): 21–33.

85. Richard J. Murnane and David K. Cohen, "Merit Pay and the Evaluation Problem: Why Most Merit Pay Plans Fail and a Few Survive," *Harvard Educational Review* 56, no. 1 (1986): 1–17.

86. Nancy Mitchell, "Denver Teachers Opt for Merit Pay," *Rocky Mountain News* (Denver, Colo.), December 29, 2005, www.rockymountainnews.com/drmn/education/article/0,1299,DRMN_957_4348741,00.html (December 30, 2005).

87. Connie Sadowski, *Houston District OKs Teacher Merit Pay Plan,* www.heartland.org/Article.cfm?artId= 18637 (July 23, 2006).

88. Joseph A. Kershaw and Roland N. McKean, *Teacher Shortages and Salary Schedules* (New York: Mc-Graw-Hill, 1962).

89. Murnane and others, *Who Will Teach?* (see note 6).

90. Beginning in 1998, up to $5,000 of an individual's Stafford Loans could be forgiven at the end of a five-year teaching spell in a low-income school. In 2004, the maximum forgiveness allowance was raised to $17,500 for teachers of math, science, or special education. For information on Stafford Loan forgiveness, see U.S. Department of Education, *Teacher Loan Forgiveness Program—FFEL and Direct Loan Programs,* studentaid.ed.gov/PORTALSWebApp/students/english/cancelstaff.jsp?tab=repaying (January 3, 2006). For information on Perkins Loan forgiveness, see U.S. Department of Education, *Student Aid on the Web: Perkins Loan Cancellation,* studentaid.ed.gov/PORTALSWebApp/students/english/cancelperk.jsp?tab=repaying (September 21, 2005).

91. For summaries of loan forgiveness and related incentives across the United States, see American Federation of Teachers, *Loan Forgiveness and Teacher Scholarship Programs,* www.aft.org/teachers/jft/loanforgiveness.htm (January 10, 2006).

92. OECD, *Education at a Glance* (see note 39).

93. McKenzie and Santiago, *Teachers Matter* (see note 41).

94. Ibid.

95. Ibid., p. 114.

96. Marilyn Cochran-Smith, "Taking Stock in 2005: Getting Beyond the Horse Race," *Journal of Teacher Education* 56, no. 1 (2005): 3–7.

97. OECD, *Education at a Glance* (see note 39).

98. McKenzie and Santiago, *Teachers Matter* (see note 41).

99. Annelie Strath, *Teacher Policy Reforms in Sweden: The Case of Individualized Pay* (International Institute for Educational Planning and UNESCO, 2004).

100. McKenzie and Santiago, *Teachers Matter* (see note 41).

The Effect of Certification and Preparation on Teacher Quality

Donald Boyd, Daniel Goldhaber, Hamilton Lankford, and James Wyckoff

Summary

To improve the quality of the teacher workforce, some states have tightened teacher preparation and certification requirements while others have eased requirements and introduced "alternative" ways of being certified to attract more people to teaching. Donald Boyd, Daniel Goldhaber, Hamilton Lankford, and James Wyckoff evaluate these seemingly contradictory strategies by examining how preparation and certification requirements affect student achivement.

If strong requirements improve student outcomes and deter relatively few potential teachers, the authors say, then they may well be good policy. But if they have little effect on student achievement, if they seriously deter potential teachers, or if schools are able to identify applicants who will produce good student outcomes, then easing requirements becomes a more attractive policy.

In reviewing research on these issues, the authors find that evidence is often insufficient to draw conclusions. They do find that highly selective alternative route programs can produce effective teachers who perform about the same as teachers from traditional routes after two years on the job. And they find that teachers who score well on certification exams can improve student outcomes somewhat. Limited evidence suggests that certification requirements can diminish the pool of applicants, but there is no evidence on how they affect student outcomes. And the authors find that schools have a limited ability to identify attributes in prospective teachers that allow them to improve student achievement.

The authors conclude that the research evidence is simply too thin to have serious implications for policy. Given the enormous investment in teacher preparation and certification and given the possibility that these requirements may worsen student outcomes, the lack of convincing evidence is disturbing. The authors urge researchers and policymakers to work together to move to a more informed position where good resource decisions can be made.

www.futureofchildren.org

Donald Boyd is deputy director of the Center for Policy Research at the University at Albany, SUNY; Daniel Goldhaber is research associate professor at the University of Washington; Hamilton Lankford is professor of economics at the University at Albany, SUNY; and James Wyckoff is professor of public administration at the University at Albany, SUNY. The authors benefited from comments by Paul Decker, Pamela Grossman, Susanna Loeb, and participants at the Future of Children Conference on Excellence in the Classrooms. They appreciate very good research assistance from Kristy Michel, Noelle Ellerson, and Brian Pack. All errors are attributable to the authors.

Donald Boyd, Daniel Goldhaber, Hamilton Lankford, and James Wyckoff

In the United States individual states regulate the teaching profession through teacher certification programs that serve as gateways into the teaching profession. Every state has its own procedures for certifying teachers, and every public school is expected to hire teachers certified by the state. Certification always involves exams, often in both general knowledge and teaching skills, and it nearly always involves coursework and practice teaching. Ideally certification keeps poor teachers out of the classroom, while giving people with the potential to be good teachers the skills and experience they need to do their jobs well. But certification may also have an unintended consequence. Because the path to certification can be arduous, it may reduce the appeal of teaching for some people who could potentially become good teachers.

The renewed focus of U.S. education policy on the quality of classroom teachers and teaching is raising new questions about how the nation prepares and certifies its teachers. The commitment of the 2001 No Child Left Behind Act (NCLB) to school accountability and to improving educational outcomes for all students, together with improved monitoring of student achievement, has heightened public awareness of long-standing sociodemographic gaps in student achievement. Dramatic disparities in the qualifications of teachers across schools and newly documented disparities in teachers' ability to influence student achievement mean that poor, minority, and low-performing students are much more likely to have teachers who are inexperienced, uncertified, and less academically able than their higher-performing peers. The achievement of these students suffers as a result.

But improving the quality of the teacher workforce is a challenge. Increased school enrollment, high rates of teacher attrition (particularly in the most difficult-to-staff schools), and the retirement of baby-boom teachers complicates efforts to hire high-quality teachers. Policymakers have addressed these issues of teacher quality and quantity in a variety of ways. Some states have tightened regulation of teacher preparation and certification—for example, extending course requirements for teachers and imposing more entry exams. Many states have also tried to attract more and different people to teaching by reducing entry requirements and introducing "alternative certification" programs. Although the two approaches are seemingly at odds, each could potentially either improve or reduce the quality of the pool of potential teachers. The precise effect of each depends on how it interacts with complicated labor market dynamics driven by teachers' preferences, local school systems' hiring decisions, and economic fluctuations.

We begin our analysis by describing the traditional and alternative routes that teachers follow to enter the profession. We then survey research that examines the relationship between teacher preparation and student achievement, between certification exams and student achievement, between certification requirements and the supply and qualifications of people pursuing teaching careers, and between the hiring decisions of school administrators and the qualifications of teachers. We conclude by offering some recommendations for policy.

Routes into Teaching
Traditionally most U.S. school districts have hired graduates of teacher preparation programs operated by schools of education in the nation's colleges and universities. Successful completion of such programs is by far the most common route to teacher certifica-

tion. But many difficult-to-staff urban and rural schools, unable to hire enough teachers from traditional preparation programs, especially in subject areas such as math, science, and special education, are forced to hire uncertified teachers, who thus become concentrated in schools with the lowest-performing students. For example, Lankford and several colleagues find that in New York State, teachers in elementary schools with 20 percent or more of fourth graders in the lowest performance group on English language arts exams were five times more likely to be uncertified to teach any of their current assignments than teachers in schools with fewer than 5 percent of fourth graders in the lowest performance group.[1] Other research finds similar sorting in other schools.[2]

No Child Left Behind aims to change this landscape by requiring states to ensure that all teachers are "highly qualified." The legislation considers new teachers highly qualified if they receive state certification and demonstrate content knowledge of the material they teach, either by passing a subject-area exam or by having an undergraduate major in that subject, or both. Veteran teachers can meet NCLB's "highly qualified" teacher standard either by passing subject-area exams or through a process known as the High Objective Uniform State Standard of Evaluation (HOUSSE), defined separately within each state.[3] The "highly qualified" requirements are not particularly stringent, but many states and districts have nevertheless had to struggle to meet them.

States have thus implemented incentive programs to attract people into teaching, particularly in difficult-to-staff subject areas and difficult-to-staff schools. They have also introduced new routes into teaching that have fewer up-front requirements. These alternate routes and programs have become an important source of supply for many schools, especially those that are difficult to staff.

Comparing the preparation and qualifications of teachers entering the profession through these two routes is not easy. Little systematic information is available about either the structure or the content of their

---

States have thus implemented incentive programs to attract people into teaching, particularly in difficult-to-staff subject areas and difficult-to-staff schools.

---

preparation or about how effective these teachers are in the classroom. Nor are there systematic national, or even state, databases on the content of teacher preparation programs generally. No national database collects information on the coursework or other aspects of the preparation of individual teachers, though some studies of particular school districts or states are beginning to develop such data.[4] There does not even appear to be a repository for information about the various requirements of schools of education. It is possible, however, to get data on state certification requirements, and these varying requirements give at least some sense of the range of preparation that teachers receive. Many programs may exceed the minimum requirements for certification and many individuals within these programs likely exceed the minimum program requirements. Moreover, there is considerable variation in the content of purportedly similar courses and experiences.

States set their certification requirements independently, subject only to the NCLB requirements for highly qualified teachers. In practice, many states have similar certification requirements. All states require teachers either to complete an approved preparation program or to pass one or more certification exams. The vast majority of states require both. States do vary somewhat in the knowledge and skills they consider important for teachers, what kind of education they require, and the timing of that education relative to when people begin teaching. As observers are increasingly aware, there is more variation within certification programs than across them.[5] Thus traditional preparation in some states may look very similar to alternative preparation in others.

In the remainder of this section we summarize the certification requirements of both the traditional teacher preparation route and the alternate route to give some sense of how the minimum threshold for teacher preparation varies among the states. We discuss other credentials that some teachers pursue and then examine the certification exam requirements for teachers.

Traditional Preparation

Traditional teacher preparation programs are the primary source of teacher supply in most states. These programs are shaped by a combination of state regulations, the criteria of accreditation groups, and the choices made by individual programs and institutions. States approve teacher education programs, enabling them to offer degrees. Would-be teachers who successfully complete approved programs need only pass any required certification exams to become licensed. States assume that by completing the state-approved preparation program, teachers have met the preparation component of certification, including required course content and field experiences. Required course content falls into three broad areas: foundational courses (for example, learning and development, philosophy or history of education, multicultural education); pedagogical courses (for example, methods of teaching or classroom management); and content or subject-matter knowledge. Programs also require candidates to complete field experiences, where they link their education to teaching experiences. Many preparation programs supplement these three areas with additional coursework, or present existing courses within a framework that addresses a specific orientation or mission, such as urban education, though information about such aspects of the programs is largely anecdotal.

Table 1 describes several key state requirements for teacher preparation as of 2006.[6] One important requirement addresses the content knowledge of subject-area teachers. Twenty-five states require high school teachers both to have a major in their subject area and to pass a content-knowledge exam. Six states require teachers only to have a major in their subject area, while eighteen other states require them only to pass a content-knowledge exam in their area.[7] Within these requirements, however, the content knowledge that constitutes a major or that must be demonstrated on certification exams varies widely.

Most traditional teacher preparation programs devote significant resources to teaching pedagogy, the skills that enable teachers to structure and communicate material to students; and most states also require teachers to demonstrate knowledge of pedagogy through exams or coursework. Pedagogy includes knowledge of instructional methods, learning theories, measurement and testing,

Table 1. Illustrative Attributes of Teacher Preparation Programs Required for State Certification

State	Content knowledge			Pedagogy			Field experience
	Subject-area requirements for beginning teachers		Percent of secondary teachers who majored in their core academic subjects in 2000	Nature of students' learning process	Subject-area pedagogy	Classroom manage-ment	Minimum student teaching (weeks)
	High school	Middle school					
Alabama	Major	Major	65	E, M, S	E, M, S	E, M, S	15[a]
Alaska			53	No	No	No	
Arizona			52	No	No	No	
Arkansas			64	E, M, S	No	E, M, S	12
California	Major[b]		59	E, S	E, S	E, S	9
Colorado	Major[c]		62	. . .	. . .	. . .	13[d]
Connecticut	Major	Minor	64	. . .	. . .	E, M, S	10
Delaware			55	No	No	. . .	
District of Columbia			81	E, M, S	M, S	E, M, S	
Florida			67	E, M, S	E, M, S	E, M, S	10
Georgia	Major[c]		61	E, M, S	E, M, S	E, M, S	
Hawaii			62	. . .	. . .	. . .	
Idaho	Major and minor		56	E, S	E, S	No	6 sem. hrs.
Illinois	Major[c]		64	E, M, S	E, M, S	E, M, S	
Indiana	Major[e]		73	E, M, S	M, S	E, M, S	9
Iowa	Major[e]		69	E, M, S	M, S	. . .	12
Kansas	Major[c]	Major[c]	64	E, M, S	E, M, S	E, M, S	12
Kentucky			60	No	No	No	12
Louisiana	Major and minor	Minor	48	E, M, S	E, M, S	E, M, S	9[a]
Maine	Minor		58	. . .	. . .	. . .	15
Maryland	Major[c]		68	E, M, S	E, M, S	E, M, S	20[a]
Massachusetts			70	E, M, S	E, M, S	E, M, S	5[a]
Michigan	Major and minor		54	E, S	E, S	. . .	6
Minnesota			86	E, M, S	E, M, S	E, M, S	10
Mississippi	Major[e]		58	. . .	. . .	. . .	12
Missouri	Major	Minor	61	. . .	. . .	. . .	8 sem. hrs.
Montana	Major and minor		62	No	No	No	
Nebraska	Major		71	E, M, S	E, M, S	E, M, S	14
Nevada	Major[e]		57	. . .	. . .	. . .	8 sem. hrs.
New Hampshire	Major		72	. . .	. . .	. . .	15[a]
New Jersey	Major	Minor	74	. . .	. . .	. . .	15[a]
New Mexico	Minor	Minor	48	E, M, S	E, M, S	E, M, S	14
New York	Major		74	E, M, S	E, M, S	E, M, S	8[a]
North Carolina	Major[b]	Major[b]	76	. . .	. . .	. . .	10
North Dakota	Major[e]		65	. . .	. . .	. . .	10
Ohio	Major[c]		61	E, M, S	E, M, S	E, M, S	
Oklahoma	Major	Minor	53	. . .	. . .	. . .	12
Oregon			58	E, M, S	E, M, S	E, M, S	15
Pennsylvania	Major[c]		72	E, M, S	E, M, S	No	12
Rhode Island	Major		77	E, M, S	E, M, S	. . .	
South Carolina			74	E, M, S	E, M, S	E, M, S	12

continued on next page

Table 1. Illustrative Attributes of Teacher Preparation Programs Required for State Certification—*Continued*

	Content knowledge			Pedagogy			Field experience
	Subject-area requirements for beginning teachers		Percent of secondary teachers who majored in their core academic subjects in 2000	Nature of students' learning process	Subject-area pedagogy	Classroom manage-ment	Minimum student teaching (weeks)
State	High school	Middle school					
South Dakota	Major[c,e]		57	. . .	. . .	. . .	10
Tennessee	Major[c]		57	E, M, S	E, M, S	M, S	15
Texas			53	. . .	. . .	. . .	12
Utah	Major and minor		61	E, S	E, S	E, S	
Vermont	Major	Minor	65	E, M, S	E, M, S	E, M, S	12
Virginia	Major	Minor	66	E, M, S	E, M, S	. . .	5[a]
Washington			53	E, M, S	E, M, S	E, M, S	
West Virginia	Minor		59	. . .	. . .	. . .	12
Wisconsin	Major[c]	Minor	79	E, M, S	E, M, S	E, M, S	15[a]
Wyoming			64	. . .	. . .	. . .	8

Source: Data are from "Quality Counts at 10: A Decade of Standards Based Education," *Education Week* 25, no. 17 (2006): 86–87, except for pedagogy data, which are taken from the National Association of State Directors of Teacher Education and Certification. In pedagogy columns, E indicates elementary school requirement; M, middle school requirement; S, secondary school requirement; a blank cell indicates that no data have been submitted by the state.

a. The Editorial Projects in Education (EPE) Research Center converted requirements given in terms of hours, days, or semesters into weeks.

b. State requires teacher candidates to demonstrate subject-matter competency either by majoring in the subject taught or by passing a content test.

c. State does not stipulate how much coursework constitutes a major.

d. Colorado requires 800 hours of student teaching and other kinds of clinical experience. The EPE Research Center therefore based its estimate of minimum number of weeks required for student teaching on 400 hours.

e. State requires a major in the subject taught, but teachers can receive additional content-area endorsements if they obtain at least a minor in the subject.

and classroom management. Such material can be offered in free-standing courses or, when it is specific to a particular subject area, woven into a subject-matter course. Based on states' certification requirements there is substantial uniformity in many areas of pedagogy. As table 1 shows, 84 percent of states require preparation programs to present material on classroom management, and 83 percent require them to address subject-area pedagogy. Only four states have no specific pedagogy requirements. Nevertheless, pedagogy is a contentious area of teacher preparation. Some observers believe teacher preparation programs and state certification requirements place too much emphasis on pedagogy.[8] Others debate how to deliver

pedagogic knowledge to teachers to have the greatest effect on student outcomes—either in the classroom or in field experiences, where prospective teachers can practice their skills.[9]

Thirty-eight states require beginning teachers to have field experiences, such as student teaching. But as the table indicates, state requirements on student teaching vary substantially. Some states require as few as five weeks, while others require fifteen to twenty weeks. Many observers believe that field experience is a crucial component of teacher preparation, especially when teachers are being prepared to teach in an environment with which they are not familiar.

Table 2. Illustrative Attributes of Alternative Route Programs and Assessment Required for State Certification

| State | Attributes of programs | | | Written tests required for initial license in 2005–06 | | | |
| | Program for candidates with a B.A. in 2005–06 | Pre-service training | | Subject knowledge | | | Subject-specific pedagogy |
		Minimum duration[a]	Practice teaching or fieldwork	Basic skills	High school	Middle school	
Alabama	Yes[b]			Yes	Yes	Yes[c]	
Alaska	Yes[b]			Yes			
Arizona	Pilot	4 weeks			Yes		
Arkansas	Yes	2 weeks		Yes	Yes	Yes[c]	Yes
California	Yes	120 hours		Yes	Yes[d]	Yes[d]	Yes
Colorado	Yes				Yes		
Connecticut	Yes	8 weeks	Yes	Yes	Yes	Yes	Yes
Delaware	Yes	120 hours	Yes	Yes	Yes		Yes
District of Columbia	Yes[b]	7 weeks	Yes	Yes	Yes		Yes
Florida	Yes			Yes	Yes	Yes[c]	
Georgia	Yes	4 weeks	Yes	Yes	Yes	Yes	Yes
Hawaii	Yes		Yes	Yes	Yes	Yes	Yes
Idaho	Yes	9 credits and 30 hours			Yes		
Illinois	Yes		Yes	Yes	Yes	Yes[c]	Yes[e]
Indiana	Yes	18 credit hours	Yes	Yes	Yes		Yes
Iowa	Yes	12 credit hours	Yes				
Kansas	Yes[b]	2 credit hours			Yes	Yes	
Kentucky	Yes	8 weeks	Yes		Yes	Yes	
Louisiana	Yes	9 credit hours	Yes	Yes	Yes	Yes	Yes[e]
Maine				Yes	Yes		
Maryland	Yes	135 hours		Yes	Yes		Yes

continued on next page

Alternative Routes

Alternative routes to certification typically allow teachers to enter the classroom by postponing or bypassing many of the criteria required by traditional teacher preparation programs. As shown in table 2, forty-six states and the District of Columbia report having at least one alternate route to certification.[10] All require teachers to hold a bachelor's degree; 80 percent require teachers to demonstrate subject matter knowledge by completing coursework or passing an exam, or both.

Although some states have long used alternate routes, more than half of such programs were created in the past fifteen years and more than a third were created after 2000. Some states and school districts rely heavily on alternate routes as a source of supply. New Jersey, Texas, and California get more than a third of their new teachers in this way, and alternate routes are a rapidly growing source of supply in many other states and school districts.[11] Often the growth of alternate routes reflects a shift away from emergency and temporary certification.

The requirements of alternate route programs vary greatly across states. Many alternative certification programs have both pre-service and in-service requirements. Some require as little as two weeks of pre-service

Table 2. Illustrative Attributes of Alternative Route Programs and Assessment Required for State Certification—*Continued*

| State | Attributes of programs | | | Written tests required for initial license in 2005–06 | | | |
| | Program for candidates with a B.A. in 2005–06 | Pre-service training | | Subject knowledge | | | Subject-specific pedagogy |
		Minimum duration[a]	Practice teaching or fieldwork	Basic skills	High school	Middle school	
Massachusetts	Yes	7 weeks	Yes	Yes	Yes	Yes	Yes[e]
Michigan	Yes[b]			Yes	Yes		
Minnesota	Yes			Yes	Yes	Yes	
Mississippi	Yes	90 hours		Yes	Yes		Yes
Missouri	Yes	2 weeks		Yes	Yes	Yes	Yes
Montana	Yes	6 credit hours					
Nebraska	Yes[b]			Yes			
Nevada	Yes[b]	3 weeks		Yes	Yes		Yes
New Hampshire	Yes	1 week		Yes	Yes		
New Jersey	Yes	4 weeks	Yes		Yes	Yes	
New Mexico	Yes			Yes	Yes	Yes	
New York	Yes[b]	200 credit hours	Yes	Yes	Yes	Yes[c]	
North Carolina	Yes	2 weeks		Yes	Yes[d]	Yes[d]	Yes
North Dakota				Yes	In 2006–07	In 2006–07	In 2006–07
Ohio	Yes	6 credit hours	Yes		Yes	Yes	
Oklahoma	Yes			Yes	Yes		Yes
Oregon	Yes[b]			Yes	Yes	Yes[c]	
Pennsylvania	Yes[b]			Yes	Yes	Yes	Yes
Rhode Island							Yes
South Carolina	Yes	2 weeks		Yes	Yes	Yes	Yes
South Dakota	Yes	9 credit hours			Yes		
Tennessee	Yes[b]			Yes	Yes		Yes
Texas	Yes				Yes	Yes[c]	Yes
Utah	Yes				. . .[f]		
Vermont				Yes	Yes		
Virginia	Yes	180 hours	Yes	Yes	Yes	Yes	Yes[e]
Washington	Yes		Yes[g]	Yes	Yes		
West Virginia	Yes			Yes	Yes	Yes	Yes
Wisconsin	Pilot		Pilot[g]	Yes	Yes	Yes[c]	
Wyoming	Yes	9 credit hours					Yes

Source: See table 1.

a. Column indicates the minimum pre-service requirement for one or more of the state's alternative routes. States may have other alternative routes that require longer pre-service components.

b. At least one of the state's alternative routes requires participants to complete a traditional teacher preparation program while teaching.

c. At least some of the state's middle school teachers may pass one test that covers all core academic content areas, instead of tests specific to each subject area.

d. State requires teacher candidates to demonstrate subject-matter competency either by obtaining a major in the subject or by passing a content test.

e. States require only teachers of certain subjects, such as reading or technology, to pass subject-specific pedagogy tests.

f. Utah requires teachers to pass a content test to move from a Level 1 license to a Level 2 license, but prospective teachers need only take, not pass, content tests for initial licensure.

g. In Washington State and Wisconsin, participants in alternative routes are required to teach with their mentor teachers for at least a semester.

preparation, while others effectively require an academic year. More typically, pre-service ranges from four to twelve weeks during the summer before the new teacher enters the classroom and often includes pedagogy, methods of teaching, and field experiences. Fewer than half the states require practice teaching or fieldwork. In-service preparation typically involves coursework or mentoring, or both. Requirements for courses in education are common, but the nature and quantity of those courses vary widely.

A brief description of several alternate route programs illustrates some of the differences. Texas offers nearly 100 programs, of which ITeachTexas is typical. A statewide web-based program, it requires no onsite pre-service meetings. Eligible applicants must have a bachelor's degree with at least a 2.5 grade point average and must prove competency in reading, writing, and math either through coursework or minimum scores on standardized tests such as the ACT, SAT, or GRE. Once accepted, candidates have two years to meet the requirements for a standard teaching certificate. They must first complete a ten-part computer module, after which they are eligible to begin teaching. Finally, they must pass certification tests, including the appropriate subject-area test, complete the two-semester field experience, and secure recommendations from their mentor and campus administrator.[12]

The New York City Teaching Fellows Program, established in 2000, is the largest alternative route in the country. Only one in eight applicants becomes a teaching fellow. Applicants must have a bachelor's degree with at least a 3.0 grade point average. The summer before the school year begins, fellows must attend an intensive seven-week training session in which they observe and assist veteran teachers. Fellows must pass the basic skills and content-specialty certification exams before they can begin teaching. Once assigned a teaching position, they must begin an approved master's degree program that will qualify them for continuing certification in their subject area. Fellows now supply about 25 percent of new hires in New York City.

A relatively new approach to certification is the Passport to Teaching program of the American Board for Certification of Teacher Excellence (ABCTE). Initiated in 2004, the passport to teaching requires a professional teaching-knowledge exam and a subject-area exam. It is now recognized as a valid certification route by five states: Florida, Idaho, New Hampshire, Pennsylvania, and Utah.[13] Because it affords relatively low-cost access to the profession, it can increase supply significantly, but it puts heavy reliance on exams to ensure that applicants are qualified.

Alternative routes can alter substantially the composition of the teacher workforce, as the Teaching Fellows Program in New York City illustrates. In 2001 about half of all new teachers hired in New York City were uncertified; by 2004 that share had fallen below 10 percent, and it continues to fall. In short, New York City's uncertified teachers have been largely replaced by the teaching fellows.[14] Moreover, the teaching fellows' certification exam scores, undergraduate college rankings, and SAT scores on average substantially exceed those both of unlicensed teachers and of teachers prepared in traditional programs.[15] Teaching fellows are also on average a more diverse group than traditionally prepared teachers, with relatively more men and half again as many Hispanics and blacks. And the teaching fellows are more likely than traditionally prepared teachers to work in more difficult-to-staff schools.

Additional Certification

Of thirty-eight states responding to a survey by the National Association of State Directors of Teacher Education and Certification (NASDTEC), 82 percent offer second-stage certification, and 68 percent require it.[16] State requirements for second-stage certification vary. Eighty percent of the states that require such certification require additional teaching experience, 15 percent require teachers to have a master's degree, while 12 percent require some other form of additional coursework. Twelve percent require teachers to pass a state assessment.

In addition, forty-nine states recognize certification by the National Board for Professional Teaching Standards (NBPTS). Although no state requires national board certification, thirty-seven states provide financial incentives to encourage teachers to pursue the rigorous program, which is generally recognized as a standard nationwide for evaluating the knowledge and teaching skills of teachers.[17]

Certification Exams

States began testing teachers as a condition of employment during the 1960s. Since then, they have increasingly used exams to assess whether teachers have the minimum skills needed to enter teaching. States give four different types of tests: basic skills, liberal arts general knowledge, subject-matter knowledge, and pedagogic skills; some tests cover combinations of these topic areas. Of the states responding to the NASDTEC survey, 71 percent require a basic skills exam; 90 percent, a subject-matter exam; and 65 percent, a pedagogy exam. Fewer than 25 percent require a general knowledge exam. Most states requiring exams use the Praxis exam administered by Educational Testing Services (ETS). Typically, each type of test covers areas that reflect different skills identified

as important for teachers. For example, the ETS professional knowledge test examines knowledge of how to plan instruction, implement instruction, evaluate instruction, and manage the learning environment.

States have different standards as to what constitutes a passing score on the exams. Even within states, passing scores change over time. Passing scores are typically determined by a panel of education experts who relate the minimum content knowledge and teaching knowledge required of a beginning teacher to knowledge demonstrated on the exam. Pass rates are typically in the 70–90 percent range, which is high relative to licensure exams in professions such as law, accounting, or medicine. Moreover, teachers typically may take the exam as many times as they choose—which raises the question of how many applicants the exam ultimately screens out.

How Preparation and Certification Affect Student Achievement

Depending on the path they take, people who enter teaching may meet many or few educational and testing requirements. In most states the route to teaching through traditional preparation programs can be arduous. In some states alternative routes may impose a lighter burden. What is the evidence regarding the effectiveness of these varying requirements in improving classroom teaching and student performance? Whether the varied components of teacher preparation or certification improve student outcomes depends on the relationship of these components to improved teaching and on the teacher hiring decisions that would be made in the absence of minimum requirements.

Teacher preparation and certification could improve student outcomes by several different paths. They could improve outcomes directly, by improving teaching, or indirectly, by providing information about teachers that is related to achievement. For example, requiring teachers to have more subject-area knowledge in math could enable them to teach math more effectively, thus improving student assessments in math. But that same requirement could also identify difficult-to-measure attributes, such as motivation and persistence, that are related to becoming a more effective teacher. Certification requirements could improve student outcomes if they delineate minimally qualified teachers and if, in their absence, hiring authorities would not hire the best candidates. The requirements thus constrain districts to hire at least minimally qualified teachers.

But because teacher preparation represents a substantial cost to individuals, both in terms of expenses, such as tuition, and in terms of the time needed for coursework, which could have been used for other activities, such as employment, it may reduce the supply of teachers. Preparation in state-approved programs does indeed provide some evidence that a teaching candidate has a minimal set of knowledge and skills. But if hiring authorities can determine independently which teaching candidates can most improve student achievement, then eliminating the requirement for teacher preparation could improve student outcomes by expanding the pool of candidates. Thus the net effect depends on a trade-off: the gain in student outcomes that results from teacher preparation weighed against the loss in student outcomes that results when authorities cannot hire people who have not met preparation requirements but who could nonetheless be effective teachers.

A similar argument holds for certification exams. These exams put a floor under the measured knowledge individuals must have to become certified. If the exams identify good teachers more effectively than hiring authorities can in the absence of the exams, then they could improve student achievement. But if the exams make distinctions based on knowledge that is not closely related to student outcomes, or if they classify individuals erroneously, they could exclude applicants who would be more effective teachers, thereby reducing student outcomes.

As a final note, the effect of preparation requirements and certification exams on teaching and student outcomes will be felt most directly in the most difficult-to-staff schools. Abundant evidence that teachers are sorted by their certification requirements across schools indicates that schools with the poorest or lowest-performing students have the least qualified teachers.[18] Higher-performing suburban schools will be relatively unaffected by the differential effect of preparation and exam requirements.

Assessing How Preparation and Certification Affect Student Achievement

The extent to which teacher preparation and certification improve the quality of teaching is an empirical question. Answering it requires focusing on questions in four key areas: teacher preparation, certification exams, teacher supply, and hiring.

First, to what extent do the knowledge and skills provided in teacher preparation programs improve teachers' ability to raise achievement for students? Some aspects of preparation, such as content knowledge, may be more important for student outcomes than others. What is the evidence for each of the components of preparation?

Second, how effective are certification exams in distinguishing between teachers who are adequate and those who are inadequate at improving student outcomes? Are the knowledge and skills tested on certification exams the same as those that raise student achievement? If so, to what extent do the exams reliably test that information and distinguish among candidates?

One reliable way to identify the effects of certification and teacher preparation on students' educational gains is through experiments in which teachers are randomly assigned to students.

Third, does the requirement that teachers be certified, with all that entails, deter some people from becoming teachers who could have improved student outcomes? If so, to what extent?

And finally, how effective are local hiring authorities in recognizing the attributes that will make applicants effective teachers? First, to what extent are hiring authorities assisted by the information about teacher quality provided by teacher preparation and certification? Second, to what extent do certification requirements constrain hiring authorities who would otherwise have hired less competent teachers?

Interpreting evidence on how teacher preparation and certification affect student achievement requires care. First, as noted, relatively little is known about the specific content or quality of teacher preparation programs. Most of the empirical work is thus based on proxies, which at times may not be closely linked to the concept of interest. Second, the usual caution in social science not to interpret correlational relationships as causal relationships warrants particular attention in this instance, because of the well-documented and systematic sorting of students and teachers, with the least-qualified teachers teaching the lowest-performing students within and across school districts.[19] Because more qualified teachers are much more likely to teach students who perform well, researchers must be careful in attributing better student outcomes to the high qualifications of teachers. For example, if teachers in schools where students perform best in math are more likely to be certified in math, one might be tempted to conclude that being certified to teach math contributes to higher student achievement. But in reality the teachers may be in schools where students perform well in math because these teachers prefer to teach good students and because employers want to staff their courses with in-field certified teachers. Finally, the forces that lead some states to have more rigorous certification policies may also cause those states to have accountability programs for students and teachers that could also affect student outcomes. Unless they take these other factors into account, analysts might mistakenly conclude that student achievement is being affected by certification, when instead it reflects some other effects.

One reliable way to identify the effects of certification and teacher preparation on students' educational gains is through experiments in which teachers are randomly assigned to students. Although experimental design is increasingly popular in education research, few such experiments have addressed the issues raised in this review.[20] As an alternative, researchers can rely on quasi-experiments. In certain cases, for example, a real situation comes close to random assignment. In other cases, statistical methods can control for teacher and student sorting. Although a complete description of the research methods that address the issue of teacher and student selection is beyond the scope of this article, suffice it to say that using rigorous standards of causal modeling calls into question much of the research on the effects of teacher certification and teacher preparation on student outcomes. However, there are some notable exceptions. For example, as described in greater detail below, recent research using extensive administrative data and sophisticated methods isolates the effects of teacher certification requirements on student value added.

Several analysts have recently reviewed research on whether and how teacher certification and preparation affect student outcomes.[21] We organize the evidence drawn from these reviews around questions in the four areas set out above: preparation, certification exams, teacher supply, and hiring.

Preparation

Research insights regarding the effects of graduate degrees and specific coursework on teachers' ability to improve students' outcomes have improved in recent years, but in general good evidence remains limited. Furthermore, the value of teacher preparation may well differ depending on the grade level or types of students being taught—issues to which typically little attention is paid.

Many studies find that the students of teachers with a graduate degree perform no better than those of teachers with only a bachelor's degree.[22] Other studies find both positive and negative effects of teachers' graduate degrees on student achievement.[23] More nuanced research examines the relationship between the field of graduate work and the subject matter taught and tested. For example, achievement in high school math is greater for students whose teacher has a graduate degree in mathematics than for students whose teacher either has no graduate degree or a degree in another subject.[24] Although it is plausible that subject-area graduate education could have such an effect, it is unclear whether the stronger performance of teachers with advanced degrees in math reflects their greater knowledge of math or simply their interest in math, which presumably predated and led them to graduate study and would have affected student performance even if they had no master's degree. Researchers have uncovered no evidence of similar effects of graduate work in English or science.

Because both graduate and undergraduate degrees can mask wide variation in subject-specific courses, several studies have focused on the number of subject-specific courses that teachers took. One such study finds no relationship between the number of college math courses a teacher took and the math gains of his fourth-grade students.[25] Others find that students of teachers with more math courses do have greater high school math gains, but the effects are generally small.[26] It could well be that the additional math courses make a difference for high school students but not for elementary school students. Similar research on the number of science courses is inconclusive, and researchers have not yet focused on other subject areas.[27] Thus the evidence provides some small support for the value of subject-specific coursework and graduate degrees, at least for teachers of high school mathematics. Given this research base, the graduate coursework requirements in some states' certification systems, which impose large costs on teachers, and the incentives for graduate coursework in most school districts' salary schedules, which impose substantial costs on the districts, deserve greater scrutiny.[28]

The evidence for other areas of teacher preparation is even more tentative. As noted,

---

Although research suggests that knowledge and skills regarding how to teach can influence student achievement, no study identifies either which of these skills are important or the best way for aspiring teachers to develop them.

---

an important component of virtually all certification and traditional teacher preparation programs is training in pedagogy. Most traditional teacher preparation programs contain multiple courses on aspects of pedagogy. Nearly all routes into teaching include some field experience, like student teaching, where pedagogical skills may be learned and practiced. And the first years of teaching provide important lessons on what works. Identifying the best way to prepare teachers to convey subject knowledge to various student audiences is complex and a matter of some dispute.[29] Research examining how students learn, together with the frequently replicated empirical observation that teachers' effectiveness improves over the first few years of

their careers, offers at least indirect evidence that pedagogy is important.[30] Because pedagogy covers a number of distinct areas, it should be possible to discern the relative importance of various aspects of pedagogy by identifying the relationship of sub-scores on pedagogy exams or of specific coursework to student achievement.

To our knowledge, however, no research focuses on the relationship between certification exams in pedagogy and student achievement. Of the few studies that examine the relationship between pedagogy coursework and student achievement, none finds causal evidence and only a few provide even general correlational evidence. For example, one study finds that content-related pedagogy coursework in mathematics is positively linked with student achievement and is more closely linked with higher gains than is additional content coursework.[31] Although research suggests that knowledge and skills regarding how to teach can influence student achievement, no study identifies either which of these skills are important or the best way for aspiring teachers to develop them. Given the substantial investment most teacher preparation programs make in pedagogy, well-designed research in this area could be important.

Many close observers of teacher education believe that field experiences exert an important influence on teacher preparation. Once again, however, there is only limited research documenting any relationship between field experiences and student achievement, and none sorts out what particular content and duration of field experiences are most influential. As summarized by several studies, evaluations of field experiences typically focus on teachers' perceptions of how experiences are structured or self-identified changes in beliefs or practice.[32]

Numerous studies explore whether easily measured attributes of teacher preparation, such as having a master's degree, make a difference in student achievement. But the evidence on whether particular features of teacher preparation, such as the area of study or the extent and nature of content courses, affect student outcomes is much more limited. For policy at the state, school district, or teacher education program level to be informed, rigorous research examining the effectiveness of specific attributes of teacher preparation is essential. There is room for some optimism here, as several large-scale studies are now attempting to examine these relationships.[33] But what is most remarkable today is the lack of evidence on the effect of almost any aspect of teacher preparation on the performance of students.

Certification Exams

Certification exams are typically developed by a panel of experts who determine the passing level, or cut score, by relating minimum levels of content and teaching knowledge for beginning teachers to what is measured on the various exams. Two issues must be kept in mind in using such exams to assess the quality of teachers. First, the tests are not directly linked to student outcomes and thus may not be a good measure of how well a teacher will perform in the classroom. Second, the tests are designed to distinguish knowledge around the cut score and probably perform less well as a proxy for skills and knowledge as scores move away from that point. Because cut points for certification exams differ from state to state, it is possible to assess how scores, especially around the cut point, might affect student achievement. Moreover, in many states teachers who fail certification exams are allowed to teach as uncertified teachers, offering another opportunity to examine how the knowledge and skills measured by the exams affect student achievement.

A growing body of research is evaluating the extent to which certification exams are good signals of teacher effectiveness by examining the relationship between teachers' exam scores and the achievement gains of their students.[34] In general, this research finds that exam scores are positively linked to teacher effectiveness, but the size of the effect varies widely—probably because data were aggregated to different levels and because the studies failed to account for the sorting of teachers and students that may bias these effects.

Three recent studies address these issues with strong research designs and good data.[35] In both North Carolina and New York City, these studies find, performance on required certification exams is predictive of teachers' abilities to increase student achievement, especially in math, but exam scores affect student achievement less than, for example, teacher experience does. Thus the exams do distinguish among teachers, but only relatively weakly.

Overall, research suggests that requiring certification exams does not result in a higher proportion of "good" teachers' being selected but does reduce overall participation in teacher preparation.[36] Teachers in states with exam requirements have similar academic qualifications to teachers in states without them, although the qualification measures are limited and it is unclear whether unobserved attributes might differ. Research on how requiring the exam affects pursuit of education degrees is limited to a single cohort of teachers, and the effect is identified from differences across states, so this finding should be treated with care. These exams do tend to disproportionately screen out minority teacher applicants.[37]

Teacher Supply

The problem in assessing whether requiring certification deters potentially effective teachers from entering the profession is observing what social scientists call the counterfactual—in this case, how the size and composition of the pool of teacher candidates would have differed without certification. All states certify teachers, and even in states where certification is least rigorous, the requirements can be meaningful. One study uses the variation across state certification requirements to examine whether the requirements reduce the likelihood that college graduates are education majors. It finds that more stringent certification course requirements do reduce the share of education majors, all else equal.[38] But this evidence, while suggestive, must be viewed with caution, given that the study observes the effect of differences in course requirements at a single point in time. These differences may be correlated with other differences across states that influence the likelihood of becoming an education major. In short, direct evidence on how certification affects the supply of teachers is lacking.

The extent to which alternative routes may affect teacher supply by producing teachers who perform well is one of the most pressing policy issues related to teacher preparation. Until recently, research on alternate routes did not compare the effects on student outcomes of teachers who reached the profession by different routes. Several such analyses, though, are now available.

One insight into how more lenient certification requirements might expand teacher supply comes from comparing the attributes of alternatively certified and traditionally prepared teachers. Nearly all alternative certification programs lower the cost of becoming a teacher, either by reducing the requirements that teachers must fulfill or by allowing teachers to complete requirements while earning a salary as a teacher, or both. Much of alternative certification is focused on attracting people into teaching who did not major in education and might never have been interested in doing so. Some alternative certification programs have been able to recruit teachers with stronger qualifications than those of traditionally prepared teachers. For instance, in 2003 Teach for America (TFA) had 16,000 applicants for 1,800 available slots and was therefore able to be highly selective in terms of teacher qualifications.[39] But even in the districts where TFA has its greatest presence, its teachers are a small fraction of the entering teaching workforce. Can alternate routes attract a significant share of entering teachers with strong qualifications?

As noted, teachers recruited in recent years to teach in New York City public schools through the New York City Teaching Fellows Program constitute about a quarter of all new teachers and have qualifications (for example, certification exam scores, undergraduate college rankings, and SAT scores) that on average substantially exceed those of teachers from traditional preparation programs.[40] But these mere facts are far from an analysis of how supply would be affected in the absence of certification. On one hand, New York City Teaching Fellows are given a stipend to subsidize their graduate education, likely inducing an increased interest independent of the reduced entry requirements. On the other hand, they must complete the same requirements as other teachers to receive their second-stage certification, likely dampening interest in the program, since requirements have been delayed but not eliminated.

What is the evidence on the relative effectiveness of alternate route teachers? Because Teach for America places teachers in several states it is one of the most widely known alternative route programs, and several studies have analyzed differences in achievement among students taught by Teach for America teachers, traditionally certified teachers, and unlicensed teachers.[41] Their findings are similar, but differ somewhat depending on specification and the school districts examined. The most persuasive evidence suggests that, on average, students of entering TFA teachers perform at least as well in math as those of other entering teachers, including those from traditional preparation programs, but slightly worse in English language arts. With two or three years of experience, TFA teachers have student gains that are somewhat better than those of other teachers in math, and about the same in English language arts. Findings for the New York City Teaching Fellows are similar. New York requires alternatively certified teachers to complete a master's program in education, thus the TFA teachers and New York City Teaching Fellows are enrolled in education courses during their first three years of teaching. These evaluations bundle two characteristics of teachers—their general ability and their preparation to teach. As noted, TFA and the New York City Teaching Fellows Program strongly emphasize recruitment and selection, and their teachers have better general qualifications but receive substantially less pre-teaching preparation to teach. Thus, these findings may mean that the higher general qualifications of TFA and Teaching Fellow teachers initially offset the more substantial preparation of teachers following the traditional route.

It is important to note that to date, all the studies that have examined the effects of teacher preparation on student achievement have compared one program with another and they do not indicate performance in an absolute sense. Thus, all programs may be doing a fine job or all may be producing relatively weak gains in achievement. One study finds wide variation among teachers within each pathway, suggesting that much remains

---

Thus, these findings may mean that the higher general qualifications of TFA and Teaching Fellow teachers initially offset the more substantial preparation of teachers following the traditional route.

---

to be learned about what knowledge and skills in teachers best produce student achievement gains.[42]

Hiring

Requiring state certification of teachers constrains local hiring to candidates who at least meet the certification requirements. Whether it improves or diminishes the quality of teachers hired depends on the ability and incentives of hiring authorities.

The degree to which localities discern teacher quality and act on that information depends on the ability of hiring authorities to identify teacher qualifications that signal ability to improve student outcomes. It also depends on the capacity of their human resource departments and the incentives they have to improve students' academic achievement. In many districts certification may have no effect at all in schools that teachers find attractive because these schools have an ample supply of applicants who would easily meet most certification requirements. Difficult-to-staff schools, though, have no such supply and have in the past hired many uncertified teachers. Enforcing certification requirements would force these schools to alter their hiring patterns. Thus, a promising research strategy is to examine hiring decisions in difficult-to-staff schools, where this effect is likely most keenly felt, especially under increased accountability for student outcomes.

Surprisingly little evidence is available on whether school systems make good selections among teacher applicants, and that evidence is mixed. One research study finds that teacher applicants who attend above-average colleges are significantly less likely to be hired than applicants who attend below-average colleges and that attributes such as undergraduate GPA and subject specialties have only a small effect on an applicant's probability of being hired.[43] But that research examines the attributes only of teachers who ultimately take jobs and does not distinguish between the attributes that employers value and look for in job candidates and the attributes of teachers who are willing to accept jobs. Highly qualified candidates may simply not be willing to teach in schools where less-qualified candidates accept jobs. Other research finds that employers prefer to hire teachers with better academic qualifications, such as higher scores on certification exams and a degree from a better undergraduate college.[44] Employers' weightings of job candidates are strongly related to higher scores on the teacher certification exam, especially in the range just above the exam cut score.

But recent evidence suggests that districts rely more on interviews and teacher credentials in making hiring decisions than on observations of teachers in the classroom. On the whole, new teachers report having had relatively few interactions with school-based personnel in the hiring process.[45] In addition, teachers were more frequently asked to submit transcripts, letters of reference, and resumes than portfolios and writing samples.[46] In many school districts, then, the hiring process is not likely to be good at distinguishing high-quality teachers, much less at providing a guarantee of hiring the best available teachers. Moreover, recently implemented accountability systems within each state may well change the incentives that school districts face to hire and retain the teachers most likely to improve student achievement. In sum, it is not possible to judge whether school districts' hiring decisions are helped or hurt by the constraint of being able to hire only certified teachers.

Policy Implications

In theory, strong teacher preparation and certification requirements can either improve or worsen student outcomes, depending on how well these requirements distinguish among more able teachers, on how they affect the supply of potential candidates, and on the ability and motivation of local hiring authorities. If more stringent requirements improve student achievement and deter relatively few potential teachers, then the requirements may well be good policy. Reduced certification requirements become more attractive as the effect of these requirements on student outcomes diminishes, the pool of prospective teachers who are deterred by the requirements grows, and the ability of schools to identify applicants who will produce good student outcomes increases. What evidence have researchers produced to make it possible to evaluate these issues?

In the area of teacher preparation, substantial evidence suggests that general graduate preparation does little to improve student performance. Content knowledge in math contributes to student achievement in math, but little is known about other subject areas or about the quantity or focus of content knowledge that is relevant. Subject matter pedagogy may improve student achievement, but no evidence exists on most other aspects of pedagogy. Nor have researchers produced evidence that teacher field experiences affect student outcomes, although most teachers and other close observers see a strong link between the two. There is, however, evidence that highly selective alternative route programs can be a good source of qualified teachers.

As to certification exams, there is good evidence that teachers' scores on the exams have a modest positive effect on their students' achievement, with the best evidence of an effect in math. But without evidence on the supply effects of certification exams, the net effect remains in doubt.

In the area of teacher supply, there is modest evidence that teacher certification requirements shrink the pool of people who pursue teaching careers but virtually no evidence on whether shrinking the pool has had a meaningful effect on student outcomes.

And finally, in the area of hiring, the evidence suggests that schools have limited ability to identify in prospective teachers the attributes that allow them to improve student outcomes.

What are the policy implications of this research? In a few areas, evidence of how preparation and certification affect student achievement is relatively firm. In others, although little is known, circumstantial evidence provides some insights. In too many areas, though, the evidence is just too thin to have implications for policy. The lack of evidence should not, however, be interpreted to mean that potentially large effects do not exist. Given the enormous investment that is

If more stringent requirements improve student outcomes and deter relatively few potential teachers, then the requirements may well be good policy.

made by would-be teachers, education schools, school districts, and states in preparing and certifying teachers, and given the possibility that these requirements may reduce student achievement, the lack of convincing evidence in most of these areas is disturbing. The lack of an evidentiary base is important and has implications for both researchers and policymakers.

The cost of ill-informed policy can be enormous. Consider, for example, a policy that requires all new teachers to have three credit hours (about forty-two classroom hours) of training in X before entering teaching. Based on estimates of the number of new teachers and the average wages of teachers, the cost of such a policy would exceed $250 million a year. If X can be shown to sufficiently improve outcomes for the students of these teachers after accounting for any reductions in supply, it is likely a good investment. If not, these are resources that could well have been put to much better use. Compare the cost of this seemingly small policy intervention with the structure of teacher preparation and certification as a whole and it quickly becomes clear that better evidence could have an enormous effect on the use of scarce resources.

How are researchers and policymakers to move from the current state of knowledge of the effects of teacher preparation and certification to a more informed position from which good resource decisions can be made? Although there are hopeful signs that rigorous research developing causal connections between interventions and student outcomes is becoming more common, too often both researchers and policymakers fall short. Researchers often find it too costly, either in time or money, to develop data needed for convincing causal analysis. Policymakers often implement policy in ways that make evaluation difficult, if not impossible. Because most policies are developed and implemented by states and school districts, state and school officials should work much more closely with researchers as policies are contemplated. Both researchers and policymakers must thus change the ways they typically go about their work.

Notes

1. See H. Lankford and others, "Teacher Sorting and the Plight of Urban Schools: A Descriptive Analysis," *Educational Evaluation and Policy Analysis* 24, no. 1 (2002): 37–62.

2. See, for example, H. Peske and Kati Haycock, *Teaching Inequality: How Poor and Minority Students Are Shortchanged on Teacher Quality* (Washington: Education Trust, 2006).

3. "No State Meeting Teacher Provision of 'No Child' Law," *Education Week* 25, no. 38 (2006): 1, 16.

4. Research projects in Ohio, New York City, Louisiana, and Texas are collecting data on the structure and content of teacher preparation programs in those states.

5. See, for example, T. Kane and others, "What Does Certification Tell Us about Teacher Effectiveness? Evidence from New York City," unpublished paper (Harvard University, March 2006); and D. Boyd and others, "How Changes in Entry Requirements Alter the Teacher Workforce and Affect Student Achievement," *Education Finance and Policy* 1, no. 2 (2006): 176–216.

6. Information regarding traditional preparation program certification requirements is drawn from "Quality Counts at 10: A Decade of Standards Based Education," *Education Week* 25, no. 17 (2006): 85–86; and the online compilation of the National Association of State Directors of Teacher Education and Certification (NASDTEC) at www.nasdtec.org. The information in table 1 is illustrative; both Quality Counts and the NASDTEC site also show requirements for other certification components.

7. "Quality Counts" (see note 6).

8. See, for example, D. Goldhaber, "The Mystery of Good Teaching," *Education Next* (2002), no 1: 50–55.

9. See, for example, "Scholars Eye 'Signature' Method of Teacher Training," *Education Week* 25, no. 7 (2005): 8.

10. Ibid.

11. See the website of the National Center for Alternative Certification, *Teach-Now*, www.teach-now.org.

12. This material is drawn from the ITeach Texas website, www.iteachtexas.com/Timeline.cfm.

13. "ABCTE Study Finds Links between Tests and Student GPAs," *Education Week* 25, no. 37 (2006): 14.

14. Boyd and others, "How Changes in Entry Requirements Alter the Teacher Workforce and Affect Student Achievement" (see note 5).

15. Ibid.

16. These and the following statistics regarding second-stage certification are taken from the NASDTEC website, www.nasdtec.org.

17. "Quality Counts" (see note 6).

18. See Lankford and others, "Teacher Sorting and the Plight of Urban Schools" (see note 1).

19. Ibid. See also C. Clotfelter and others, "Teacher-Student Matching and the Assessment of Teacher Effectiveness," Working Paper 11936 (Cambridge, Mass.: National Bureau of Economic Research, 2004); D. Goldhaber, "Everyone's Doing It, but What Does Teacher Testing Tell Us about Teacher Effectiveness?" manuscript (University of Washington, 2006).

20. Below we discuss S. Glazerman and others, "Alternative Routes to Teaching: The Impacts of Teach for America on Student Achievement and Other Outcomes," *Journal of Policy Analysis and Management* 25, no. 1 (2006): 75–96. In addition, Mathematica Policy Research is currently using an experimental design to evaluate teacher induction programs.

21. See, for example, S. Wilson and others, *Teacher Preparation Research: Current Knowledge, Gaps, and Recommendations* (Seattle, Wash.: Center for the Study of Teaching Policy, 2001); A. Wayne and P. Youngs, "Teacher Characteristics and Student Achievement Gains: A Review," *Review of Educational Research* 73, no. 1 (2003): 89–122; M. Allen, *Eight Questions on Teacher Preparation: What Does the Research Say?* (Denver, Colo.: Education Commission of the States, 2003); M. Cochrane-Smith and K. Zeichner, eds., *Studying Teacher Education: The Report of the AERA Panel on Research and Teaching Education* (Mahwah, N.J.: Lawrence Erlbaum Associates, 2005).

22. For a summary of these studies, see E. A. Hanushek, "Assessing the Effects of School Resources on Student Performance: An Update," *Educational Evaluation and Policy Analysis* 19, no. 2 (1997): 141–64.

23. See R. Ferguson and H. F. Ladd, "How and Why Money Matters: An Analysis of Alabama Schools," in *Holding Schools Accountable: Performance Based Reform in Education,* edited by H. F. Ladd (Brookings, 1996), pp. 265–98; R. G. Ehrenberg and D. J. Brewer, "Do School and Teacher Characteristics Matter? Evidence from High School and Beyond," *Economics of Education Review 13* (1994): 1–17.

24. See D. D. Goldhaber and D. J. Brewer, "Does Teacher Certification Matter? High School Teacher Certification Status and Student Achievement," *Educational Evaluation and Policy Analysis* 22, no. 2 (2000): 129–45; D. D. Goldhaber and D. J. Brewer, "Evaluating the Effect of Teacher Degree Level on Educational Performance," in *Developments in School Finance,* edited by W. J. Fowler (National Center for Education Statistics, U.S. Department of Education, 1997), pp. 197–210; B. Rowan and others. "Using Research on Employees' Performance to Study the Effects of Teachers on Students' Achievement," *Sociology of Education* 70, no. 4 (1997): 256–84.

25. R. Eberts and J. Stone, *Unions and Public Schools: The Effect of Collective Bargaining on American Education* (Lexington, Mass.: Lexington Books, 1984).

26. D. H. Monk and J. A. King, "Multilevel Teacher Resource Effects in Pupil Performance in Secondary Mathematics and Science: The Case of Teacher Subject Matter Preparation," in *Choices and Consequences: Contemporary Policy Issues in Education,* edited by R. G. Ehrenberg (Ithaca, N.Y.: ILR Press, 1994), pp. 29–58; D. H. Monk, "Subject Matter Preparation of Secondary Mathematics and Science Teachers and Student Achievement," *Economics of Education Review* 13, no. 2 (1994): 125–45.

27. A small but growing literature examines the effects of teacher professional development on student achievement. Much of this literature finds positive effects, and some finds large positive effects; see J. Angrist and J. Guryan, "Teacher Testing, Teacher Education, and Teacher Characteristics," *American Economic Review* 94, no. 2 (2004): 241–46. Other research suggests the effects may be insignificant; see B. Jacob and L. Lefgren, "The Impact of Teacher Training on Student Achievement: Quasi-Experimental Evidence from School Reform Efforts in Chicago," *Journal of Human Resources* 39, no. 1 (2004).

28. There is limited research on the cost of graduate degrees for teachers. Knapp and others estimate that the cost of a master's degree to a full-time student is more than $42,000; see J. L. Knapp and others, "Should a Master's Degree Be Required of All Teachers?" *Journal of Teacher Education* 41, no. 2 (1990): 27–37.

29. P. Grossman, "Research on Pedagogical Approaches in Teacher Education," in *Studying Teacher Education: The Report of the AERA Panel on Research and Teaching Education,* edited by M. Cochrane-Smith and K. Zeichner (Mahwah, N.J.: Lawerence Erlbaum Associates, 2005), pp. 425–76.

30. See, for example, S. G. Rivkin and others, "Teachers, Schools, and Academic Achievement," *Econometrica* 73, no. 2 (2005); D. Boyd and others, "Complex by Design: Investigating Pathways into Teaching in New York City Schools," *Journal of Teacher Education* 57, no. 1 (2006): 156–66.

31. Monk, "Subject Matter Preparation of Secondary Mathematics and Science Teachers and Student Achievement" (see note 26). It should be noted that this analysis includes no controls for students other than the pre-test. Given that subsequent research has documented substantial sorting of teachers to particular student populations and that these student groups have substantial differences in achievement gains, the results should be interpreted with care.

32. Wilson and others, *Teacher Preparation Research* (see note 21); R. Clift and P. Brady, "Research on Methods Courses and Field Experiences," in *Studying Teacher Education: The Report of the AERA Panel on Research and Teaching Education,* edited by M. Cochrane-Smith and K. Zeichner (Mahwah, N.J.: Lawrence Erlbaum Associates, 2005).

33. For research under way in New York City, see D. Boyd and others, "Complex by Design: Investigating Pathways into Teaching in New York City Schools," *Journal of Teacher Education* 57, no. 1 (2006): 156–66; and www.teacherpolicyresearch.org. For research in Ohio, see T. Lasley and others, "A Systematic Approach to Enhancing Teacher Quality: The Ohio Model," *Journal of Teacher Education* 57, no. 1 (2006): 13–21; and http://tqp.mvnu.edu. Research is just beginning in Louisiana and Florida.

34. See R. F. Ferguson, "Paying for Public Education: New Evidence on How and Why Money Matters," *Harvard Journal on Legislation* 28, no. 2 (1991): 465–98; R. F. Ferguson, "Teachers' Perceptions and Expectations and the Black-White Test Score Gap," in *The Black-White Test Score Gap,* edited by C. Jencks and M. Phillips (Brookings, 1998), pp. 273–317; Ferguson and Ladd, "How and Why Money Matters" (see note 23); R. P. Strauss and E. A. Sawyer, "Some New Evidence on Teacher and Student Competencies," *Economics of Education Review* 5, no. 1 (1986), pp. 41–48; Goldhaber, "Everyone's Doing It" (see note 19); Clotfelter and others, "Teacher-Student Matching and the Assessment of Teacher Effectiveness" (see note 19); C. Clotfelter and others, "How and Why Do Teacher Credentials Matter for Student Achievement?" working paper, Duke University (2006).

35. Goldhaber, "Everyone's Doing It" (see note 19); Clotfelter and others, "How and Why Do Teacher Credentials Matter for Student Achievement?"(see note 34); D. Boyd and others, "The Narrowing Gap in New York City Teacher Qualifications and Its Implications for Student Achievement in High-Poverty Schools," working paper, University at Albany, SUNY (2006).

36. See Angrist and Guryan, "Teacher Testing, Teacher Education, and Teacher Characteristics" (see note 27); E. Hanushek and R. Pace, "Who Chooses to Teach and Why?" *Economics of Education Review* 14, no. 2 (1995): 101–17.

37. Karen J. Mitchell and others, eds., *Testing Teacher Candidates: The Role of Licensure Tests in Improving Teacher Quality,* National Research Council (Washington, D.C.: National Academy Press, 2001); Angrist and Guryan, "Teacher Testing, Teacher Education, and Teacher Characteristics" (see note 27).

38. Hanushek and Pace, "Who Chooses to Teach and Why?" (see note 36).

39. Ashindi Maxton, Teach for America, e-mail communication, October 8, 2003.

40. D. Boyd and others, "How Changes in Entry Requirements Alter the Teacher Workforce and Affect Student Achievement" (see note 5).

41. M. Raymond and others, *Teach for America: An Evaluation of Teacher Differences and Student Outcomes in Houston, Texas* (Stanford, Calif.: Hoover Institution, Center for Research on Education Outcomes, 2001); L. Darling-Hammond and others, "Does Teacher Preparation Matter? Evidence about Teacher Certification, Teach for America, and Teacher Effectiveness," *Education Policy Analysis Archives* 13, no. 42 (2005): 1–47; Glazerman and others, "Alternative Routes to Teaching" (see note 20); Boyd and others, "How Changes in Entry Requirements Alter the Teacher Workforce and Affect Student Achievement" (see note 5); T. Kane, J. Rockoff, and D. Staiger, "What Does Certification Tell Us about Teacher Effectiveness? Evidence from New York City," manuscript, National Bureau of Economic Research (March 2006).

42. Kane, Rockoff, and Staiger, "What Does Certification Tell Us about Teacher Effectiveness?" (see note 41).

43. D. Ballou, "Do Public Schools Hire the Best Applicants?" *Quarterly Journal of Economics* 111, no. 1(1996): 97–134.

44. D. Boyd and others, "Analyzing the Determinants of the Matching of Public School Teachers to Jobs: Estimating Compensating Differentials in Imperfect Labor Markets," manuscript, University of Albany, SUNY (2005).

45. R. P. Strauss and others, "Who Should Teach in Our Public Schools? Implications of Pennsylvania's Teacher Preparation and Selection Experience," *Economics of Education Review* 19, no. 4 (2000): 387–414; E. Liu and S. Johnson, "New Teachers' Experiences of Hiring: Late, Rushed and Information-Poor," Next Generation of Teachers Working Paper (Harvard Graduate School of Education, 2003).

46. Liu and Johnson, "New Teachers' Experiences of Hiring" (see note 45); D. Balter and W. Duncombe, "Staffing Classrooms: Do Teacher Hiring Practices Affect Teacher Qualifications?" manuscript, Syracuse University, Center for Policy Analysis (2005).

Pay, Working Conditions, and Teacher Quality

Eric A. Hanushek and Steven G. Rivkin

Summary

Eric Hanushek and Steven Rivkin examine how salary and working conditions affect the quality of instruction in the classroom. The wages of teachers relative to those of other college graduates have fallen steadily since 1940. Today, average wages differ little, however, between urban and suburban districts. In some metropolitan areas urban districts pay more, while in others, suburban districts pay more. But working conditions in urban and suburban districts differ substantially, with urban teachers reporting far less administrator and parental support, worse materials, and greater student problems. Difficult working conditions may drive much of the difference in turnover of teachers and the transfer of teachers across schools.

Using rich data from Texas public schools, the authors describe in detail what happens when teachers move from school to school. They examine how salaries and student characteristics change when teachers move and also whether turnover affects teacher quality and student achievement. They note that both wages and student characteristics affect teachers' choices and result in a sorting of teachers across schools, but they find little evidence that teacher transitions are detrimental to student learning.

The extent to which variations in salaries and working conditions translate into differences in the quality of instruction depends importantly on the effectiveness of school personnel policies in hiring and retaining the most effective teachers and on constraints on both entry into the profession and the firing of low performers.

The authors conclude that overall salary increases for teachers would be both expensive and ineffective. The best way to improve the quality of instruction would be to lower barriers to becoming a teacher, such as certification, and to link compensation and career advancement more closely with teachers' ability to raise student performance.

www.futureofchildren.org

Eric A. Hanushek is senior fellow at the Hoover Institution of Stanford University, research associate of the National Bureau of Economic Research, and chairman of the executive board of the Texas Schools Project of the University of Texas at Dallas. Steven G. Rivkin is professor of economics at Amherst College, research associate of the National Bureau of Economic Research, and associate director for research of the Texas Schools Project of the University of Texas at Dallas. The authors thank John Guryan and the editors for helpful comments on early drafts. The research was supported by the Packard Humanities Institute.

Eric A. Hanushek and Steven G. Rivkin

How best to attract and retain good teachers is perhaps the most important policy issue in education today. Few observers dispute the premise that good schools require good teachers in the classrooms. But agreement about how public policy can best facilitate the hiring and retention of effective teachers is far more elusive. In this article we examine aspects of the teacher labor market to shed light on how salaries and working conditions affect the quality of instruction.

Our underlying presumption is that the proof of high-quality instruction is in the pudding—teacher quality must be addressed in terms of how much students actually learn. In other words, teacher quality should be measured by the contribution of a teacher to student learning, typically measured by test scores, and not by characteristics such as possession of an advanced degree, experience, or even scores on licensing examinations.

Assessing how salary and working conditions affect teaching quality is complicated. Because traditionally accepted measures of teacher quality, such as experience and years of schooling, are only weakly linked with student achievement, they are not reliable proxies for effective teaching. An attractive alternative is to use student test score gains as measures of teacher effectiveness. While recent accountability systems have increased the availability of such test scores, researchers must still sort out how much measured student achievement reflects the performance of teachers and how much it reflects family and other influences.

Likewise, because objective measures of working conditions, such as administrator and parental support, safety, and ease of commuting, are lacking, researchers frequently use student demographic characteristics as proxies. As an alternative they sometimes rely on teacher self-reports, which have their own drawbacks. Teachers' perspectives, for example, may differ systematically by community type—cutting class or theft by students may not be regarded in the same way by all teachers—and views about working conditions may be influenced by their own job performance, making these measures unreliable.

Finally, certain aspects of the current market for teachers—including licensing restrictions, tenure, and various contractual requirements—play a role in how salary and working conditions affect the quality of instruction. For example, an increase in teacher salaries might have one effect on student achievement in the current market, with its significant barriers to entry, such as certification requirements, and quite a different effect in a more open market.

We begin by surveying variations in salaries and working conditions in U.S. public schools by region and community type. We also chart changes over time in how teacher salaries compare with salaries in other occupations. We then focus on teacher turnover, describing how teachers move from school to school, examining how salaries and working conditions change when teachers move and whether turnover affects teacher quality and student achievement. We move on to consider more generally how salary and working conditions affect the quality of instruction. We review research on how teacher experience and education, the primary determinants of compensation for public school teachers, affect student outcomes and then turn to direct evidence on how salary and working conditions affect student achievement. Having surveyed the evidence, we examine its implications for teacher policies. We conclude that the best way to improve the quality of instruction would be to lower barriers to becoming a teacher and to link compensation and career advancement more closely with performance.

Salaries and Working Conditions

As primary determinants of teacher supply, salaries and working conditions are potentially important in determining the quality of instruction, though the extent of their influence depends on the effectiveness of district personnel decisions. Because variations in salaries and working conditions can contribute to unequal school quality, they are the focus of much concern on the part of policymakers, legislators, and the courts.

Variations in Salaries and Working Conditions in 1999–2000

Tables 1 and 2 use information from the nationally representative Schools and Staffing Survey (SASS) for the 1999–2000 academic year to show variations in teacher salaries and working conditions, respectively, by region and community type (urban, suburban, and rural) that potentially contribute to unequal instructional quality.[1] Although we discuss differences among community types within specific regions, the tables report only average differences by community type for the nation as a whole.

Table 1 reveals wide variation in both starting salaries and salary growth, including patterns that contradict some widely held beliefs about salary differences by community type, such as that suburban areas pay systematically more than urban areas. Average salaries are highest in the much more urbanized Northeast, largely because average salaries in small town and rural school districts are much lower in all regions. Among new teachers in rural districts, almost one-fourth in the Northeast, one-third in the South and West, and more than 40 percent in the Midwest earned salaries of less than $25,000 a year, roughly double the shares of urban and suburban teachers in this category. Even for teachers in their tenth year, the median salary in rural districts was less than $45,000 in the Northeast and West and less than $35,000 in the South and Midwest.

Variation in urban and suburban teacher salaries is far less—and far less systematic. In the Northeast both starting and experienced urban teachers earn more, on average, than their suburban counterparts. In the South this pattern is reversed, with suburban teachers earning more than urban teachers; and in both the Midwest and West the ordering differs for starting and experienced teachers. In other words, in some metropolitan areas urban districts pay more. In others, suburban districts pay more. In no region does the urban-suburban salary gap approach the gap between metropolitan (that is, urban and suburban) and rural salaries.

The relatively small average salary difference between urban and suburban schools does not imply that the typical urban school is able to attract as large a pool of teacher applicants as the typical suburban school. As in all occupations, teachers value working conditions as well as salary. Examining differences in working conditions gives a more complete picture of differences in the average attractiveness of different types of districts.

In table 2, which surveys school working conditions as reported by teachers, urban districts stand apart from all others in almost all respects. Be it parental or administrator support or the adequacy of materials, far higher

Table 1. Share of Teachers Earning Selected Salaries in Their Starting and Tenth Years, by Region and Community Type, School Year 1999–2000

Percent

Region and community type	Average salary (dollars)				
	<25K	25–30K	30–35K	35–45K	>45K
Starting year					
Region					
Northeast	10.1	17.10	30.70	29.20	12.80
Midwest	27.2	34.20	15.60	14.90	8.20
South	20.1	34.20	25.30	15.90	4.50
West	17.6	22.70	24.70	24.00	11.00
Community type					
Urban	15.2	29.20	26.50	19.40	9.80
Suburban	15.4	26.30	26.60	22.50	9.20
Rural	34.6	35.00	14.70	12.90	2.80
All	19.4	28.9	24.0	19.6	8.0
Tenth year					
Region					
Northeast	0.8	1.9	10.4	30.8	56.1
Midwest	8.5	10.3	13.5	32.6	35.2
South	4.6	14.7	24.8	38.9	17.0
West	3.8	6.0	11.6	28.4	50.2
Community type					
Urban	2.3	6.0	14.8	32.7	44.3
Suburban	3.5	6.2	13.1	32.8	44.5
Rural	9.5	20.0	26.2	36.5	7.8
All	4.5	9.3	16.5	33.6	36.1

Source: National Center for Education Statistics, Schools and Staffing Survey, 1999–2000.

shares of urban teachers report problems in all regions. Not surprisingly, urban teachers are less likely to report general satisfaction with their jobs.

Taken together, tables 1 and 2 show the complexity of variations in salary and other job characteristics and therefore suggest that any links between these factors and quality of teaching are likely to be complex. Although the similarity in average salaries may appear to suggest that urban districts should be able to attract teachers almost as well as suburban

districts can, the pronounced differences in working conditions suggest otherwise. In the case of rural schools, the tables indicate that relatively better working conditions may compensate for lower salaries.

Trends over Time in Aggregate Salaries

In competitive labor markets, people will sort across occupations and industries according to their skills, the salaries being offered, and working conditions. As long as working conditions are roughly comparable, higher salaries should attract more able people. If

Table 2. Share of Teachers Reporting Strongly Negative Views of Various Working Conditions, by Region and Community Type, School Year 1999–2000

Percent

Region and community type	Administration is supportive	Parents are supportive	Adequate materials	Generally satisfied
Region				
Northeast	9.4	16.2	10.1	3.3
Midwest	7.4	12.6	6.1	2.1
South	7.2	17.7	8.6	3.3
West	7.5	15.9	9.5	2.7
Community type				
Urban	9.2	22.1	12.4	4.1
Suburban	7.2	13.7	7.6	2.5
Rural	7.4	13.1	5.7	2.4
All	7.8	15.8	8.5	2.9

Source: See table 1.

the relative attractiveness of working conditions in teaching and in other occupations changes little over time, salary changes in teaching should provide a good measure of changes in average teacher quality and should therefore provide an important benchmark for considering policies related to teacher quality.

Figure 1 shows changes in the share of nonteachers with at least a bachelor's degree who earned less than the average teacher between 1940 and 2000.[2] Over the period, the salaries of all young teachers relative to those of college-educated nonteachers fell, though gender differences were substantial. For men, relative salaries fell between 1940 and 1960 but then remained roughly constant. For women, relative salaries began high—above the median for college-educated women— but fell continuously. The changes are easiest to see for young teachers, but they hold for teachers of all ages, meaning that growth in late-career salaries did not offset the decline in salaries for younger teachers. Among the explanations for the relative salary decline

are technological change, expanded opportunities for women, and growth in international trade—all of which increased the demand for and earnings of highly skilled workers outside of teaching.[3]

The long decline in teachers' relative earnings has likely led to a drop-off in average teacher quality. As professional opportunities for women increased between 1960 and 1990, for example, measured achievement declined noticeably for those entering teaching.[4] But the extent of any decline in teacher quality is unclear and depends in large part on the correlation between teaching skills and the skills rewarded in the nonteacher labor market. In a simple one-dimensional skill framework in which nonpecuniary factors play no role and districts hire the best available teachers, the substantial decline in relative salary would be expected to lead to a large drop in teacher quality. But in a more complex and realistic framework, in which the skills of teachers differ from those of other professionals and in which district personnel policies lead to suboptimal hiring and

Figure 1. Percent of College-Educated Non-Teachers Earning Less than the Average Teacher, by Gender and Age, 1940–2000

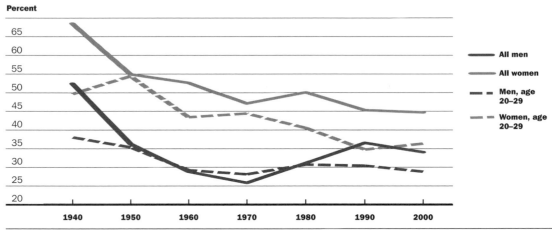

Source: Authors' calculation from U.S. Census data for 1940–2000.

retention decisions, the quality response to salary changes could be more muted. For example, if teaching places greater emphasis on a particular set of communication and interpersonal relation skills than the general labor market does, relative teacher salaries may not be a particularly good index of teacher quality. In addition, the link between relative salaries and quality may be different today than it was during the 1960s and 1970s, when the rapidly expanding opportunities for women and dramatic social changes may have greatly altered perceptions of a career in teaching.

Teacher Turnover

So far, we have shown substantial variation in salaries across districts and over time, as well as perhaps even greater variation in working conditions. The extent to which these differences affect teacher quality depends on, among other things, how much teachers care about salaries and working conditions when making career decisions. Some of the best research assessing the importance of these factors examines teachers' turnover decisions. In this section we describe in some detail the re-

lationships among turnover, salary, and working conditions using unusually rich data from Texas public schools.

Teacher Turnover in Texas

Each year many teachers in Texas move within or between school districts or leave public schools entirely. As table 3 shows, overall 82 percent remain in the same school, while 7 percent exit the public schools, 6.5 percent change schools within districts, and 5 percent switch districts. This turnover is remarkably close to national averages: between 1994 and 1995, 86 percent of all teachers remained in the same school, while 6.6 percent left teaching.[5]

Transitions differ sharply by number of years of teaching.[6] As the table shows, new teachers (zero to two years of experience) are almost twice as likely as prime-age teachers (eleven to thirty years' experience) to exit Texas public schools and almost four times as likely to switch districts. As would be expected, mobility picks up again as teachers near retirement age: almost one-fifth of teachers with more than thirty years of expe-

Table 3. Year-to-Year Transitions of Texas Public Elementary and Middle School Teachers, by Experience, 1993–96

Percent, except as indicated

| | Teachers who | | | | |
Teacher experience	Remain in same school	Change schools within district	Switch districts	Exit Texas public schools	Number of teachers
0–2 years	73.6	7.5	9.3	9.6	73,962
3–5 years	77.7	7.2	6.6	8.5	56,693
6–10 years	82.4	6.8	4.5	6.3	75,284
11–30 years	86.9	5.7	2.5	4.9	165,873
More than 30 years	77.0	4.0	0.7	18.3	6,978
All	81.8	6.5	4.8	6.9	378,790

Source: Eric A. Hanushek, John F. Kain, and Steven G. Rivkin, "Why Public Schools Lose Teachers," *Journal of Human Resources* 39, no. 2 (2004).

rience leave the Texas public schools each year. Again, national data on mobility show a similar pattern.

When we look more closely to see where teachers' transitions begin and end, we find only weak support for a widely held belief that teachers commonly leave urban districts for suburban positions. Though most urban teachers who switch districts do relocate to suburban schools, less than 2 percent of all teachers in large urban school districts switch to suburban districts each year. Indeed, the absolute number of teachers moving into urban districts is only slightly smaller than the number moving out.

How Salary and Working Conditions Affect Teacher Choices in Texas

By delving more deeply into these data to explore why teachers choose to make these transitions we can shed light on how salary and other factors work together to determine the attractiveness of a specific teaching job. Although the Texas data contain neither teacher nor administrator reports on working conditions, they do contain information on student demographics, which we use as prox-

ies for working conditions. The Texas data also do not specify a teacher's reason for exiting a school, in particular whether the exit is voluntary. Although anecdotal evidence suggests that the vast majority of transitions are voluntary, it is certainly not correct to assume that all are. Because voluntary moves would tend to lead to greater improvements in salary and working conditions, the data likely understate implied teacher preferences.

Table 4 reports changes in salaries and average student demographics for teachers changing district, by experience and gender. On average, new teachers improve their salaries, with men gaining 1.2 percent, women gaining 0.7 percent.[7] The average salary gain declines with experience for both women and men and is actually negative (roughly –0.1 percent) for women with three to nine years of experience.[8] The average gain for all movers with less than ten years of experience is slightly more than 0.4 percent of annual salary, or roughly $100.

These averages, however, mask considerable variation, some of which appears to relate systematically to the types of schools from

Table 4. Average Change in Salary and Characteristics of District Students for Texas Public Elementary and Middle School Teachers Who Change Districts, by Gender and Experience

Teacher salary and student characteristics	Men by experience		Women by experience	
	0–2 years	3–5 years	0–2 years	3–5 years
Base year salary (percent change)	1.2% (0.003)	0.7% (0.003)	0.7% (0.001)	–0.1% (0.001)
Student test score	0.05 (0.008)	0.05 (0.011)	0.08 (0.004)	0.08 (0.006)
Percent Hispanic	–4.8 (0.6%)	–3.4 (1.0%)	–4.8 (0.3%)	–4.6 (0.5%)
Percent black	–0.7 (0.4%)	–0.9 (0.5%)	–2.6 (0.2%)	–2.5 (0.3%)
Percent subsidized lunch	–4.7 (0.6%)	–3.8 (0.9%)	–7.0 (0.3%)	–5.8 (0.4%)

Source: See table 3. Average test score is the district average of mathematics and reading score on Texas Assessment of Academic Skills exams, normalized to mean 0 and standard deviation 1.

and to which teachers move. For example, teachers who move from large urban to suburban schools have average nominal salary losses of 0.7 percent. This is not to say that teachers who move to suburban schools prefer lower salaries. Instead, other advantages of suburban schools appear to make up for their lower salaries. Other things being equal, teachers would gravitate toward higher-salary districts and schools. Indeed, a study by Hanushek, Kain, and Rivkin indicates that central city schools would have to undertake substantial salary increases to reduce teacher turnover to the level observed in the typical suburban school.[9] For new teachers and teachers with three to five years of experience, the central city school would have to offer women an average salary increase of 25–43 percent. Men appear to be considerably more responsive and would require salaries around 10 percent higher.

For those teachers who move, the type of students changes far more than their salaries do. As table 4 shows, teachers who move systematically favor higher-achieving, nonminority, non-low-income students. The find-

ings for student achievement are clearest and most consistent: for the average mover, the district average achievement rises by roughly .07 standard deviation, or 3 percentile points on the state distribution. The shares of students who are black, Hispanic, and eligible for a subsidized lunch fall. On average, black and Hispanic compositions of districts decline 2 and 4.4 percent, respectively, and the share eligible for free or reduced-price lunch falls almost 6 percent. Particularly for women (who make up three-quarters of the teaching force), salary differences are far smaller than changes in student characteristics.

It should be noted that the share of black students declines primarily for white teachers. Black teachers, on average, move to schools with more minority students. Although the declining share of black students for white teachers may reflect a difference in preferred working conditions, it may also simply reflect travel distance to school. Housing patterns (either because of choice or because of discrimination) may lead black teachers to live nearer to schools with a higher share of black students than do white teachers. In fact, some evidence shows that taking into account travel distance to school eliminates the difference in apparent preferences regarding school racial composition between black and white teachers.[10]

Another sign of the potential importance of working conditions is the fact that private school salaries are systematically lower than public school salaries. Moreover, as Michael Podgursky demonstrates, this holds for nonsectarian private schools and therefore is not simply a reflection of the unique financial status of nuns and other religious professionals. His interpretation is that the salary differential reflects both better behaved and easier to teach students and other working conditions.[11]

Other researchers have used teacher self-reports in place of or in addition to student demographics to investigate how working conditions affect turnover. Susanna Loeb and Linda Darling-Hammond find that self-reported working conditions significantly affect the probability that administrators regard turnover as a serious problem, as well as their difficulty in filling vacancies and also the share of teachers in their first year.[12] Richard Ingersoll finds that most teachers exit for reasons other than dissatisfaction with their current job—retirement, for example, or personal reasons, or the pull of other jobs. According to Ingersoll's analysis, the roughly one-quarter of teachers who leave schools because they are dissatisfied cite low salaries, lack of support from the school administration, student discipline problems, and lack of teacher influence over decisionmaking.[13]

How Turnover Affects Student Achievement in Texas Data

We now turn to the question of how teacher turnover affects student outcomes. Schools in urban districts serving disadvantaged students do have higher turnover generally, leading to their having a greater share of teachers with little or no experience—clearly a cost to these schools, as inexperienced teachers tend to be less effective.[14] But the cost would be markedly reduced if the teachers leaving these schools tended to be the least effective teachers. To address that issue, we compare the overall effectiveness of teachers who exit a large urban district in

---

For those teachers who move, the type of students changes far more than their salaries do.

Texas with the effectiveness of those who remain, to learn more about systematic differences in quality. We measure quality by teacher value added to achievement. Specifically, we investigate the mathematics performance of students in fourth through eighth grades on state tests in each grade, between 1996 and 2001. These students are linked to each of their mathematics teachers. The measure of quality assigned to each teacher is the gain in standardized achievement scores that is attributable to each teacher.

Table 5 compares teachers who stay in their urban school with those who move to go to another school in the same district, to go to another district, or to leave teaching altogether. All comparisons give the estimated value both of the movers and the stayers in terms of standard deviations of the average student test score gains. The first column compares moving teachers with all other teachers in the district, and the second com-

Table 5. Estimates of Mean Differences in Teacher Quality, by Transition Status, for Elementary and Middle School Teachers in a Large Texas Urban School District

Transition status	All nonmovers in district	Nonmovers within school and year
Change campus	−0.089 (3.96)	−0.054 (2.59)
Change district	−0.011 (0.36)	−0.023 (0.78)
Exit public schools	−0.044 (1.90)	−0.072 (3.53)

Source: Eric A. Hanushek and others, "The Market for Teacher Quality," Working Paper 11154 (Cambridge, Mass.: National Bureau of Economic Research, 2005).

Note: All specifications include full sets of dummy variables for experience, year, and grade. The second estimates also include student fixed effects. The sample size is 230,000. Comparisons are to teachers remaining in same school; absolute value of *t* statistics in parentheses.

pares them with nonmovers in the same school and year. Those who exit teaching, it turns out, are significantly less effective, on average, than those who stay. Teachers who switch campuses within the same district are also significantly less effective, while those who switch districts do not appear to differ much from the stayers. Thus, in this large district in Texas, the teachers who stay are not lower in quality, on average, than those who leave.

How Salary and Working Conditions Affect Student Achievement

Having examined in detail how salary and working conditions interact in teacher turnover in Texas, we now review evidence that researchers have assembled generally on the causal effects of salary and working conditions on the quality of instruction.

We begin by focusing on how teachers' experience and education, the characteristics traditionally rewarded in teacher salary schedules, affect student achievement. Then we

turn to direct comparisons of how salary and working conditions affect student outcomes. Efforts to produce a valid estimate of that direct relationship are complicated by the fact that working conditions, family income, and other factors affect both salary and outcomes.

How Teacher Education and Experience Affect Quality of Instruction

Because experience and teacher education are the primary determinants of a teacher's position in a district's salary schedule, it is often assumed that higher salaries raise quality because more experienced and highly educated teachers earn more and are more effective. Yet the structure of a salary schedule does not constitute evidence, and even such conceptually appealing assumptions require empirical validation.

Teacher experience and graduate education explain much of the overall variation in teacher compensation.[15] Dale Ballou and Michael Podgursky estimate that on average 17 percent of the teacher wage bill reflects extra payments for experience and an additional 5 percent reflects payments for a master's degree, though the premium for a postgraduate degree varies substantially.[16] These premiums tend to compare favorably with those in private industries, which typically lack the strong employment rights enjoyed by many tenured teachers. The experience and education "pay parameters" are commonly used in empirical analyses of teacher performance in the classroom, partly because experience and education would be expected to improve teacher skills and also because they are readily measured and virtually always available in administrative data sets.

Skepticism about how important education and experience are for teacher quality can be traced back to 1966, when a major federal government study by James Coleman suggested that common measures of teacher and school quality seemed to have little effect on student achievement.[17] Sharp criticism of the Coleman Report generated a massive research effort on teacher quality, but subsequent findings have tended to reinforce the initial report.[18]

Analysts investigating teacher quality in the wake of the Coleman Report have tried to estimate the relationship between student achievement, on the one hand, and quantifiable characteristics of teachers and schools, along with measures of family background, on the other. They have inferred teacher quality from the way teacher education and experience affect student performance. But education and experience simply do not appear to have a strong effect on student achievement. Research has found little or no evidence of a systematic relationship between teacher value added to student achievement and a graduate education (master's degrees and above).[19] The few studies that find that a teacher's postgraduate education improves student outcomes are balanced by others that find just the opposite, that it lowers student achievement. And extensive investigation of the effects of teacher experience has resulted in widely different findings and also raised methodological concerns. One key issue is the extent to which experienced teachers select particular students. Many teacher contracts explicitly allow more experienced teachers to choose their school.[20] Because teachers prefer to teach in schools where student achievement is high, more experienced teachers tend to be at schools with higher-achieving students.[21] That finding, however, does not mean that more experienced teachers produce greater gains in student achievement than less experienced teachers do. Indeed, it could mean

just the opposite—that higher student achievement "causes" teacher experience in the sense that schools with easier-to-educate students attract experienced teachers. The studies that most clearly identify the importance of teacher experience find that the quality of instruction tends to increase substantially during the first few years of teaching but not in subsequent years.[22]

Research has found little or no evidence of a systematic relationship between teacher value added to student achievement and a graduate education (master's degrees and above).

If education and experience are not good overall measures of teacher quality, does that mean that salary does not affect teacher quality or even that teacher performance is not an important determinant of student outcomes? The answer is no on both counts. First, as table 1 documents, much of the substantial salary variation across districts at the entry level is not explained by experience or by teacher education (most entering teachers do not have a postgraduate degree). Second, even a finding that quality is not systematically related to compensation does not mean that teacher performance has little overall impact on outcomes.

Teacher Salaries and Quality of Instruction

Many studies have pursued the question of whether more highly paid teachers generate higher student achievement. Some of these studies can be difficult to interpret, in part because they tend to confuse differences in the level of salaries with the differences in compensation for experience and education discussed above. In addition, as Susanna Loeb and Marianne Page point out, many fail to account for the ways in which differences in working conditions help to pinpoint the causal effect of salary.[23] For example, teachers likely require higher pay to take a job at a

---

As a whole, there is little evidence to suggest that more highly paid teachers are systematically more effective, but methodological problems may limit the value of many studies.

---

dangerous school or one where the teaching requirements are more onerous, and it is difficult to separate the effect of such working conditions from that of salary.[24]

As a whole, there is little evidence to suggest that more highly paid teachers are systematically more effective, but methodological problems may limit the value of many studies. Two studies, however, attempt to circumvent problems resulting from the purposeful sorting of families and teachers among schools and the difficulty of accounting for working conditions.

Loeb and Page find that higher salaries significantly improve students' educational attainment. They use the average differences across states and time in the salaries of nonteachers as a way to identify the causal effects

of salaries, the idea being that salaries of nonteachers affect the ability of schools to hire teachers but otherwise have no direct effect on the probability that a student remains in high school. The paper provides evidence that the observed relationship between student achievement and salary is quite sensitive to controls for alternative earnings opportunities and other factors that affect both teacher labor market decisions and student achievement.[25]

Hanushek and several colleagues use a sample of teachers who move from a large Texas central city school district to other Texas districts to examine whether districts appear to use higher salaries and more generally desirable student demographic characteristics to attract higher-quality teachers. They measure quality by teacher value added to student achievement in the urban district before moving.[26] They find little or no evidence that the teachers who move to schools with higher salaries or higher-achieving students, higher-income students, and lower shares of minority students are of systematically higher quality as measured by value added to student achievement. The lack of a systemic link between quality, on the one hand, and salary and working conditions, on the other, suggests that districts may have difficulty measuring the quality of potential hires or that they do not place great weight on instructional effectiveness relative to other characteristics.

Teacher Policy
In conclusion, we explore the policy implications of the evidence on how pay and working conditions affect teacher quality. At the outset of our discussion, we emphasize the crucial importance of teacher quality to student outcomes. A string of good teachers can help offset the deficits of home environment or

push students with good preparation even farther.

As the relative pay of teachers has slipped over the past half-century, many observers have begun to call for increasing teachers' overall pay. Improving teacher quality, they assert, requires making salaries competitive. Some even propose a "grand bargain." The idea is that if districts raise overall pay—say, to the level of that of accountants—teachers and their unions will agree to more flexible pay arrangements and work rules.[27] But holding all parties to such a bargain would be difficult, because wage setting is a political activity, not a market activity.

Simply raising all salaries would not only be expensive; it would also be inefficient. Although it could attract a new group of teachers into the profession and retain teachers who would otherwise leave, it would not necessarily improve the quality of teachers in the short term.[28] Retaining teachers would be beneficial if they were the high-quality ones, but there is no strong reason to expect this to be the case. Although higher salaries appear to reduce the departure rates of teachers with graduate degrees—teachers who would thus have higher salaries in other professions—graduate degrees are not a good predictor of teacher effectiveness.[29] Moreover, as noted, movers are on average less effective than stayers, at least for our large urban district.

It is possible, but by no means certain, that higher-quality movers would be more sensitive to salary. Higher salaries would certainly tend to increase the pool of potential teachers, but how that would affect overall teacher quality depends on the ability of principals and human resource teams to hire and, more important, retain the better teachers. Exist-

ing evidence, while not definitive, suggests that schools are not very effective at choosing the best teachers.[30]

With few exceptions, advocates of across-the-board salary increases pay too little heed to teachers' classroom performance and to administrators' personnel decisions. A better policy approach is to focus much more on student performance and administrator accountability, while increasing the supply of potential teachers. The idea is to loosen up on prescribed schooling and training requirements and focus on potential and actual effectiveness in the classroom, rather than "potential."

Our position is simple: if student performance is the issue, policy should emphasize student performance. Researchers have found wide variation in teacher quality, even among teachers with similar education and experience. The variation appears to spring from differences in teacher skill and effort, inadequate personnel practices (particularly in retention but also in hiring) in many schools and districts, and differences in the number and quality of teachers willing to work, by subject and working conditions. That final source of variation may well justify substantial flexibility in pay schedules, promotion opportunities, and rigorous retention standards, and more should be learned about the consequences of differentiated pay and job classifications. The variation in skill and effort raises the most difficult set of issues for policymakers, because regulations, including but not limited to certification requirements, are not likely to get at the crux of the issue.

Rather, the evidence strongly suggests to us that principals and superintendents should make decisions about teacher hiring, retention, promotion, and pay based on their evaluation of teachers' potential and actual effectiveness in raising student achievement and other outcomes, and not on a set of teacher characteristics such as education and experience. Principals do in fact know who the better teachers are.[31] Their demonstrated ability to identify teachers at the top and bottom of the quality distribution could almost certainly be extended toward the middle ranges, par-

---

Unless those who make personnel decisions have a strong incentive, they are unlikely to make difficult, high-stakes choices regarding teacher pay, promotion, and employment.

---

ticularly if good tests of student achievement are administered regularly. But other aspects of personnel management, including tenure, promotion, and pay decisions, leave tremendous room for improvement.[32]

Researchers to date have not found most performance-based teacher pay plans effective.[33] But experiments in performance-based pay, though numerous, have been limited in the size and character of their incentive schemes.[34] Of particular importance to the success of such pay programs, and to school

effectiveness more generally, is the accountability of administrators. Unless those who make personnel decisions have a strong incentive, they are unlikely to make difficult, high-stakes choices regarding teacher pay, promotion, and employment. Such choices are often difficult and uncomfortable, and the path of least resistance is to grant tenure to virtually all teachers except in extreme cases and to avoid making decisions about compensation. Because such accountability is not common in education today, there is little to build on in implementing administrator accountability. A variety of institutional structures may provide appropriate incentives; schools nationwide are experimenting with different organizational arrangements, including charter schools, school report cards, merit schools, school vouchers, and public school choice.

Finally, our analysis of teacher mobility showed that salary affects mobility patterns less than do working conditions, such as facilities, safety, and quality of leadership.[35] Compensation alone, it seems clear, is but a partial measure of the returns to work. But school policy discussions give remarkably little attention to working conditions. Research has linked teachers' negative perceptions of working conditions with their exit from schools, but it has not closely tied poor working conditions to the quality of teachers in the classroom. An important agenda item, both for research and for policy, is to learn which working conditions are most important for teachers.

Notes

1. The description of working conditions follows closely the work of Susanna Loeb and Linda Darling-Hammond, "How Teaching Conditions Predict Teacher Turnover in California Schools," *Peabody Journal of Education* 80, no. 3 (2005): 44–70.

2. Note that salaries for teachers include all earnings, regardless of source. Thus, any summer or school year earnings outside of teaching are included. No adjustments are made, however, for any differences in the length of the school day or in number of days worked during the year. Nor is any calculation of employer-paid fringe benefits made. A clear discussion of the importance of each of these, along with interpretation of the overall salary differences, can be found in Michael Podgursky, "Fringe Benefits," *Education Next* 3, no. 3 (2003). For the time-series comparisons, these omitted elements of compensation are most relevant if there have been relative changes in their importance between teachers and nonteachers over time. We currently have few data on any such changes.

3. Fredrick Flyer and Sherwin Rosen, "The New Economics of Teachers and Education," *Journal of Labor Economics* 15, no. 1, pt. 2 (1997), describe a more formal model of changing female opportunities and their impact on the teaching profession. Darius Lakdawalla, "The Economics of Teacher Quality," *Journal of Law and Economics* 94, no. 1 (2006): 285–329, and Darius Lakdawalla, "Quantity over Quality," *Education Next* 2, no. 3 (2002), extend this to concentrate on the role of productivity changes in competing industries.

4. Marigee P. Bacolod, "Do Alternative Opportunities Matter? The Role of Female Labor Markets in the Decline of Teacher Quality" (University of California, Irvine, Department of Economics, 2005).

5. National Center for Education Statistics, *Digest of Education Statistics, 2001* (U.S. Department of Education, 2002).

6. Todd R. Stinebrickner, "An Analysis of Occupational Change and Departure from the Labor Force," *Journal of Human Resources* 37, no. 1 (2002), provides comparisons across occupations and finds that teacher job and occupational changes are below those elsewhere in the economy, but that teachers are much more likely to exit entirely from the labor force.

7. Because women teachers are more likely to be married or have children than men of the same age, the smaller gains of women may reflect the fact that more transitions are precipitated by family considerations. However, we have no explicit information on reason for moving or family status. In our analysis we also provide "adjusted" salary measures that allow for features of the schools.

8. We present the analysis in terms of teacher experience, but tenure within the district may also have separate implications for salary and other factors that affect satisfaction and mobility.

9. Eric A. Hanushek, John F. Kain, and Steven G. Rivkin, "Why Public Schools Lose Teachers," *Journal of Human Resources* 39, no. 2 (2004).

10. Don Boyd and others, "The Draw of Home: How Teachers' Preferences for Proximity Disadvantage Urban Schools," *Journal of Policy Analysis and Management* 24, no. 1 (2005).

11. Podgursky, "Fringe Benefits" (see note 2).

12. Loeb and Darling-Hammond, "How Teaching Conditions Predict Teacher Turnover in California Schools" (see note 1).

13. See the review and evidence in Richard M. Ingersoll, "Teacher Turnover and Teacher Shortages: An Organizational Analysis," *American Educational Research Journal* 38, no.3 (2001): 499–534.

14. See, for example, Charles T. Clotfelter, Helen F. Ladd, and Jacob L. Vigdor, "Who Teaches Whom? Race and the Distribution of Novice Teachers," *Economics of Education Review* 24, no. 4 (2005): 377–92.

15. The central compensation component of most teacher contracts is a matrix that indicates the salary for a teacher based on years of experience and amount of education. This salary schedule seldom varies by other, apparently natural, factors such as field of teaching or demonstrated results in the classroom.

16. See Dale Ballou and Michael Podgursky, "Returns to Seniority among Public School Teachers," *Journal of Human Resources* 37, no. 4 (2002): 892–912. They provide comparisons showing that teacher wage growth, at least over the first fifteen years of a career, is comparable to that in other white collar professions. Podgursky, "Fringe Benefits" (see note 2), does provide evidence that salaries in private schools tend to rise faster earlier in the career than do those in public schools.

17. James S. Coleman and others, *Equality of Educational Opportunity* (U.S. Government Printing Office, 1966).

18. The various criticisms of the Coleman Report centered largely on the statistical methodology and the biases introduced by the analytical approach. They did not, however, provide an alternative view of what factors were important in determining student achievement. See, for example, Samuel Bowles and Henry M. Levin, "The Determinants of Scholastic Achievement—An Appraisal of Some Recent Evidence," *Journal of Human Resources* 3, no. 1 (1968); Glen G. Cain and Harold W. Watts, "Problems in Making Policy Inferences from the Coleman Report," *American Sociological Review* 35, no. 2 (1970); and Eric A. Hanushek and John F. Kain, "On the Value of 'Equality of Educational Opportunity' as a Guide to Public Policy," in *On Equality of Educational Opportunity*, edited by Frederick Mosteller and Daniel P. Moynihan (New York: Random House, 1972).

19. Summaries of research related to teacher education and to other measures of teacher characteristics can be found in Eric A. Hanushek, "The Failure of Input-Based Schooling Policies," *Economic Journal* 113, no. 485 (2003); and Eric A. Hanushek and Steven G. Rivkin, "How to Improve the Supply of High Quality Teachers," *Brookings Papers on Education Policy 2004.*

20. The impact of teacher experience on teacher mobility and school choices was first noted by David Greenberg and John McCall, "Teacher Mobility and Allocation," *Journal of Human Resources* 9, no. 4 (1974); and Richard J. Murnane, "Teacher Mobility Revisited," *Journal of Human Resources* 16, no. 1 (1981).

21. See Hanushek, Kain, and Rivkin, "Why Public Schools Lose Teachers" (see note 9).

22. The source of this experience effect is important to understand. The simplest explanation is that the teacher learns classroom management, solidifies subject matter knowledge, and develops pedagogical skills during the first year or two on the job. Another interpretation of teacher experience is that it is not really that teaching skills improve over time but that teacher experience merely indicates something about those who elect to stay in teaching. Direct investigation of this question finds that both learning and selection are relevant, though in the first two years, the dominant effect is learning to teach better. Two early investigations of experience effects and their interpretation are Richard J. Murnane and Barbara Phillips, "What Do Effective Teachers of Inner-City Children Have in Common?" *Social Science Research* 10, no. 1 (1981); and Richard J. Murnane and Barbara R. Phillips, "Learning by Doing, Vintage, and Selection: Three Pieces of the Puzzle Relating Teaching Experience and Teaching Performance," *Economics of Education Review*

1, no. 4 (1981). More recent analyses finding that any experience effects are concentrated in the early years include Jonah E. Rockoff, "The Impact of Individual Teachers on Student Achievement: Evidence from Panel Data," *American Economic Review* 94, no. 2 (2004); Steven G. Rivkin, Eric A. Hanushek, and John F. Kain, "Teachers, Schools, and Academic Achievement," *Econometrica* 73, no. 2 (2005); Eric A. Hanushek and others, "The Market for Teacher Quality," Working Paper 11154 (Cambridge, Mass.: National Bureau of Economic Research, 2005); Don Boyd and others, "How Changes in Entry Requirements Alter the Teacher Workforce and Affect Student Achievement," Working Paper 11844 (Cambridge, Mass.: National Bureau of Economic Research, 2005); and Thomas J. Kane, Jonah E. Rockoff, and Douglas O. Staiger, "What Does Certification Tell Us about Teacher Effectiveness? Evidence from New York City" Working Paper 12155 (Cambridge, Mass.: National Bureau of Economic Research, 2006).

23. Susanna Loeb and Marianne E. Page, "Examining the Link between Teacher Wages and Student Outcomes: The Importance of Alternative Labor Market Opportunities and Non-Pecuniary Variation," *Review of Economics and Statistics* 82, no.3 (2000): 393–408.

24. One justification for reducing class size even if class size has no direct impact on teachers is that teachers like smaller classes and therefore would have to be paid less to work with them, thus offsetting the costs of class size reduction. But little evidence supports this hypothesis; see Eric A. Hanushek and Javier A. Luque, "Smaller Classes, Lower Salaries? The Effects of Class Size on Teacher Labor Markets," in *Using What We Know: A Review of the Research on Implementing Class-Size Reduction Initiatives for State and Local Policymakers*, edited by Sabrina W. M. Laine and James G. Ward (Oak Brook, Ill.: North Central Regional Educational Laboratory, 2000), pp. 35–51.

25. Loeb and Page, "Examining the Link" (see note 23).

26. Hanushek and others, "The Market for Teacher Quality" (see note 22). A growing number of researchers have investigated whether some teachers tend to get larger achievement gains than others. These analyses invariably show very large differences in the achievement associated with individual teachers. The historical development of this body of work can be traced from Eric A. Hanushek, "Teacher Characteristics and Gains in Student Achievement: Estimation Using Micro Data," *American Economic Review* 60, no. 2 (1971); Eric A. Hanushek, "The Trade-Off between Child Quantity and Quality," *Journal of Political Economy* 100, no. 1 (1992); Richard J. Murnane, *Impact of School Resources on the Learning of Inner City Children* (Cambridge, Mass.: Ballinger, 1975), David J. Armor and others, *Analysis of the School Preferred Reading Program in Selected Los Angeles Minority Schools* (Santa Monica, Calif.: Rand Corp., 1976); and Murnane and Phillips, "What Do Effective Teachers of Inner-City Children Have in Common?" (see note 22); through Daniel Aaronson, Lisa Barrow, and William Sander, "Teachers and Student Achievement in the Chicago Public High Schools" (Federal Reserve Bank of Chicago, 2003); Rockoff, "The Impact of Individual Teachers on Student Achievement" (see note 22); and Rivkin, Hanushek, and Kain, "Teachers, Schools, and Academic Achievement" (see note 22).

27. An early statement of this is found in Carnegie Forum on Education and the Economy, *A Nation Prepared: Teachers for the 21st Century* (New York, 1986). This proposal became the foundation of the pay and contract changes of the "Rochester plan," whose unfortunate demise was chronicled in Ray Marshall and Marc Tucker, *Thinking for a Living: Education and the Wealth of Nations* (New York: Basic Books, 1992).

28. See Dale Ballou and Michael Podgursky, *Teacher Pay and Teacher Quality* (Kalamazoo, Mich.: W. E. Upjohn Institute for Employment Research, 1997), on this point.

29. Richard J. Murnane and others, *Who Will Teach? Policies That Matter* (Harvard University Press, 1991); Peter J. Dolton and Wilbert van der Klaauw, "Leaving Teaching in the U.K.: A Duration Analysis," *Economic Journal* 105 (1995); Peter J. Dolton and Wilbert van der Klaauw, "The Turnover of Teachers: A Competing Risks Explanation," *Review of Economics and Statistics* 81, no. 3 (1999).

30. Dale Ballou, "Do Public Schools Hire the Best Applicants?" *Quarterly Journal of Economics* 111, no. 1 (1996); Ballou and Podgursky, *Teacher Pay and Teacher Quality* (see note 28); Hanushek and others, "The Market for Teacher Quality" (see note 22).

31. See Armor and others, *Analysis of the School Preferred Reading Program* (see note 26), and Murnane, *Impact of School Resources on the Learning of Inner City Children* (see note 22), who identify total teacher effects as discussed above and relate them to principals' evaluations. A recent analysis goes further, to survey teachers on their evaluations; Brian A. Jacob and Lars Lefgren, "Principals as Agents: Subjective Performance Measurement in Education," mimeo (John F. Kennedy School of Government, 2005); Brian A. Jacob and Lars Lefgren, "When Principals Rate Teachers," *Education Next* 6, no. 2 (2006).

32. Note that the issues of hiring and retaining district administrators are very similar to those for teachers. While less studied, there is little evidence that current requirements for certification are closely related to the effectiveness of administrators. One relevant study is Ronald G. Ehrenberg, Randy A. Ehrenberg, and Richard P. Chaykowski, "Are School Superintendents Rewarded for 'Performance'?" in *Microlevel School Finance: Issues and Implications for Policy*, edited by David H. Monk and Julie Underwood (Cambridge, Mass.: Ballinger, 1988). A recent policy statement, Broad Foundation and Thomas B. Fordham Institute, "Better Leaders for America's Schools: A Manifesto" (Washington, 2003), also makes policy recommendations on administrators that parallel the thoughts about teachers presented here. Such proposals are also similar to those developed in more detail in Marci Kanstoroom and Chester E. Finn Jr., eds., *Better Teachers, Better Schools* (Washington: Thomas B. Fordham Foundation, 1999). In addition, they encapsulate the current experiments being fostered in the Teacher Advanced Program; see Lowell Milken, "Growth of the Teacher Advancement Program: Teaching as the Opportunity 2002" (Santa Monica, Calif.: Milken Family Foundation, 2002).

33 See the article by Victor Lavy in this volume. See also David K. Cohen and Richard J. Murnane, "Merit Pay and the Evaluation Problem: Understanding Why Most Merit Pay Plans Fail and a Few Survive," *Harvard Educational Review* 56, no. 1 (1986).

34. For consideration of the available evidence on teacher merit pay, see Elizabeth Lueder Karnes and Donald D. Black, *Teacher Evaluation and Merit Pay: An Annotated Bibliography* (New York: Greenwood Press, 1986); Cohen and Murnane, "Merit Pay and the Evaluation Problem" (see note 33); David K. Cohen and Richard J. Murnane, "The Merits of Merit Pay," *Public Interest* 80 (1985); Ballou and Podgursky, *Teacher Pay and Teacher Quality* (see note 28); Dale Ballou and Michael Podgursky, "Teachers' Attitudes toward Merit Pay: Examining Conventional Wisdom," *Industrial and Labor Relations Review* 47, no. 1 (1993); Elchanan Cohn, "Methods of Teacher Remuneration: Merit Pay and Career Ladders," in *Assessing Educational Practices: The Contribution of Economics*, edited by William E. Becker and William J. Baumol (MIT Press, 1996); and James A. Brickley and Jerold L. Zimmerman, "Changing Incentives in a Multitask Environment: Evidence from a Top-Tier Business School," *Journal of Corporate Finance* 7 (2001).

35. If the teacher movements do not reflect a correlation with working conditions, the observed movements would suggest that racial preferences per se have a big influence on teachers. The policy implications of such a perspective would obviously be much more complicated.

Using Performance-Based Pay to Improve the Quality of Teachers

Victor Lavy

Summary

Tying teachers' pay to their classroom performance should, says Victor Lavy, improve the current educational system both by clarifying teaching goals and by attracting and retaining the most productive teachers. But implementing pay for performance poses many practical challenges, because measuring individual teachers' performance is difficult.

Lavy reviews evidence on individual and school-based incentive programs implemented in recent years both in the United States and abroad. Lavy himself evaluated two carefully designed programs in Israel and found significant gains in student and teacher performance. He observes that research evidence suggests, although not conclusively, that pay-for-performance incentives can improve teachers' performance, although they can also lead to unintended and undesired consequences, such as teachers' directing their efforts exclusively to rewarded activities.

Lavy also offers general guidelines for designing effective programs. He emphasizes that the system must measure true performance in a way that minimizes random variation as well as undesired and unintended consequences. It must align performance with ultimate outcomes and must be monitored closely to discourage gaming if not outright fraud in measured output. Goals should be attainable. Incentives should balance individual rewards with school incentives, fostering a cooperative culture but not at the expense of free riding. All teachers should be eligible for the incentive offered, but only a subset of teachers should be rewarded in practice. If too many teachers are rewarded, teachers may not need to exert much extra effort to benefit.

Many of the practical challenges faced by performance-related pay, Lavy says, can be addressed through careful design of the system. He emphasizes that setting up a performance-related pay system that works is not a one-time task. Even with the best preparation, initial implementation is likely to be problematic. But if the effort is seen as ongoing, it should be possible to make progress gradually in developing incentives that motivate the desired teaching behaviors and that will be perceived by teachers as fair and accurate.

www.futureofchildren.org

Victor Lavy is professor of economics at the Hebrew University of Jerusalem and a research associate at the National Bureau of Economc Research and the Centre for Economic Policy Research.

Interest in improving public education is growing not only in the United States but worldwide. One reason for the heightened public attention is the key role played by education in determining both individual earnings and broader economic growth. Another is widespread dissatisfaction with the education sector's performance of late: substantial increases in spending on public schools have failed to bring corresponding increases in student achievement.[1]

The quest to improve public education has led policymakers and researchers to focus on how to increase teachers' effectiveness. One obvious means is compensation. According to many observers, the traditional basis for teacher pay—years of service and education—provides little incentive for excellence. To make teachers more effective, these critics argue, pay should be tied to performance. And some school districts, here and abroad, are undertaking reforms to test those ideas. In November 2005, for example, Denver voters approved a $25 million tax increase to fund a form of "merit pay" to reward elementary and secondary school teachers along a variety of dimensions, including their own demonstrated knowledge and skills and student academic growth. Whether Denver's new merit pay system will improve student achievement remains uncertain; an earlier pilot study in Denver found mixed results.[2]

In this article I examine academic and policy analysis of performance-based reward programs for primary and secondary school teachers. I stress, in particular, several questions. What are the pros and cons of implementing teachers' pay incentives in schools? What criteria are to be applied in designing optimal teacher incentives? How much is performance affected by incentives offered to practicing teachers? How will incentives affect the composition of applicants to teacher-training institutions and to teaching positions in the schools? What policy measures can remedy existing distortions in teachers' compensation? My intent is not to review exhaustively what is known about performance-based pay in education, but rather to summarize selected key findings, highlight some guidelines for designing effective teacher incentives schemes, and identify areas requiring additional evidence. My objectives are to present the theoretical benefits of performance-based pay as well as some of the practical obstacles to its effective implementation, to review critically the empirical evidence, and to draw policy conclusions.

Teachers' Compensation

Pay for performance is meant to solve the twofold problem of motivating high teacher performance while attracting and retaining good teachers under conditions where their effort or ability is not readily measured or observed. In the teaching profession, earnings are based primarily on input (that is, skills and time worked), rather than on output. Such a basis, critics say, is not "results-oriented." Moving to an earnings structure that ties pay—at least partially—to some performance indicators should thus improve the current system. In theory, the idea makes good sense. But implementing pay for performance poses many practical challenges. In the teaching profession effort and output are difficult to define and measure because the work is generally complex, unique, and often results from team efforts, with any one teacher's effort difficult to disentangle from that of the others on the team. One key goal of education is to give students the skills needed to ensure a productive career and sustain their economic well-being. Yet, because it takes years for the adult earnings of a student to materialize, it is impossible to tie a teacher's wages to his students' earnings. Recent studies do in fact suggest that students' test scores are strongly corrrelected with their future earnings, but using test scores to measure a teacher's performance presents practical problems.[3] Peer or principal evaluations are yet another way to measure performance, given the drawbacks of testing and the many teachers for whom testing would not apply. But these approaches also have drawbacks.

Performance-Based Pay

Pay based on performance usually involves some objective assessment of schools' or teachers' efforts or success or some measure of their students' performance. Performance-based pay schemes have many variable features. They can compensate teachers only for their own performance or they can be structured as a team incentive program, with group performance determining the total incentive payment, which is then divided among team members regardless of individual performance. The group can include all of the school's teachers or a subgroup, such as the teachers of a given grade or a specific subject. Performance-based pay schemes can, but need not, involve sanctions for below-threshold performance. Although monetary rewards are the most common incentive in performance-related pay, other incentives can include reduced teaching load, promotion, and public recognition of outstanding teachers. The reward can be just a one-time event or it can be ongoing, leading to a permanent salary increase. It can be based on a relative criterion (for example, the average test score gain of a teacher's class relative to the classes of other teachers) or on an absolute criterion (such as the class average test score being higher than a predetermined threshold). The reward may be a fixed sum

that is equal for all winners, or it can vary and increase with the winner's level of achievement. The total amount of awards may be predetermined (for example, only a certain number of teachers can win an award) or it may be open. The performance criteria can include outcomes for the teachers themselves, such as measures of absenteeism or

---

Pay based on performance usually involves some objective assessment of schools' or teachers' efforts or success or some measure of their students' performance.

---

performance on a test. They can also include measures of the teacher's students' performance, such as attendance, grade retention, dropout rates, or performance on tests. These criteria are not mutually exclusive.

The target set for determining award winners is critically important both for efficiency and for equity. For example, if schools are ranked according to how many students attain a certain level of literacy as determined by an examination, gains near the cutoff are most rewarded. But if schools or teachers are rewarded on the basis of average test scores or changes in those averages, then credit is given for gains at all parts of the achievement distribution, not just those close to the cutoff point. For example, students in the bottom 5 percent of the achievement distribution might be too far away from the literacy standard to pass the test after one or two years, but raising their test scores might be worthwhile nonetheless. A hybrid measure could target both some cutoff as well as some average. It is also possible to design a scheme that differentially weights improved test scores at different points of the achievement distribution, with the bottom weighted more than the top, the middle more than either extreme, and so forth. Finally, an important, but potentially underappreciated, part of a pay-for-performance plan is the identity of those who evaluate the teachers. The evaluators can be external to the school or can be peers, principals, or district supervisors.

Despite the almost innumerable combinations offered by these options, three prototypes of performance-based reward programs are most often implemented in education systems and are commonly examined by researchers. The first model, *merit pay*, generally involves individual incentives based on student performance. The second, *knowledge- and skill-based compensation*, generally involves individual incentives based on teacher skills. Knowledge- and skill-based pay differs from merit pay because it provides clear guidelines on what is being evaluated. The third model, *school-based compensation*, generally involves schoolwide incentives, typically based on student performance.

Potential Benefits of Performance-Based Pay

Performance-based pay in education brings with it many potential benefits but also many challenges. This section and the next present the main issues.

Productivity and Efficiency Considerations. In theory, pay based on output has two advantages over input-based pay in terms of efficiency (that is, producing "more" education for the same cost). The first, most frequently noted efficiency advantage has to do with incentives. Rewarding teachers or schools on the basis of an agreed metric aligns incentives directed at teachers or schools with those directed at students and potentially the entire society. If wages are based on student performance, for example, they provide teachers or schools with powerful signals about what is valued and what is not. Absent such signals, even well-meaning teachers may emphasize material that is obsolete or generally no longer valued by parents or the labor market. Similarly, if wages are based not only on the individual benefits of schooling to students (social scientists call these "private returns") but on the benefits to society as a whole ("social returns"), teachers or schools would take into account the social returns to education when making choices about their work. A student, for example, may want to drop out before completing high school because he feels that the costs of staying in school outweigh his individual benefits. A teacher considering only those individual benefits may not work as hard to discourage him from dropping out as would a teacher considering the costs and benefits to society as a whole.

Individual performance-based pay schemes improve efficiency by helping correct distortions in a teacher's effort that might result from gaps between her preferences and those of her students. For example, a teacher might fail to assign homework even though she knows its value for her students because correcting and grading assignments involves more work for herself. Individual performance-based pay provides some incentive for the teacher to do the "right thing."

The second efficiency advantage of output-based pay, mainly relevant for the merit pay model, involves sorting and selection. Assuming that the compensation system accurately identifies productivity, basing pay on performance will attract and retain the most productive teachers. Even if teachers are unable to alter their own behavior to enhance performance, as measured, say, by students' test scores, some people are still inherently better than others at affecting test scores. Basing pay on output also tends to discourage teachers who cannot enhance their students' performance from remaining in the profession. A related point is that output-based pay will create a market for teaching quality that will help teachers move to schools where their talent is most highly valued. Equalization between productivity and wages will result, with poorly performing teachers receiving reduced wages and lower probabilities of promotion, and more capable teachers commanding better options. Finally, if teachers are able to improve their classroom performance, linking compensation to performance will provide all teachers incentives to improve through professional development, which will therefore induce still further productivity gains.[4]

Performance-related pay based on individual or schoolwide schemes could also improve school productivity by inducing better governance. For one thing, it requires school principals to monitor closely the quality of their teachers' work.[5] It is also assumed to bring about more coherent and common teacher-management goals in addition to an improved flow of information and feedback among all school agents. This result is assumed to flow from a common interest in improved outcomes.[6]

Other Potential Benefits. Critics of traditional pay schemes that reward experience and formal qualifications instead of performance argue that these schemes are unfair to highly motivated, effective, and efficient teachers whose extra efforts are not rewarded.[7] Per-formance-based pay can thus make compensation systems more equitable.

Finally, performance-based pay may increase support for public education from politicians and members of the public who are convinced that the reform will reverse the education sector's poor reputation and perceived inefficient use of resources.[8]

Potential Drawbacks to Performance-Based Pay

Despite its theoretical benefits, performance-based pay offers many practical challenges.

Measurement Problems. Performance measurement poses two separate problems for performance-based pay. Incentive systems assume that everyone can agree on goals; they also assume that it is possible to measure accurately progress toward these goals. Agreeing on goals is particularly difficult in education because competition between public schools is rare. In the private sector, market mechanisms discipline firms into providing products that consumers value, but public schools lack market discipline. Schooling is compulsory and public, and students are simply assigned to attend their neighborhood school. Parents and students who are unhappy with what their schools offer generally have no alternative except to attend a private school or move to another neighborhood or city—alternatives that are too costly for many.[9]

The other measurement issue represents the most common claim made against performance-based pay: evaluating progress toward the goal fairly and accurately is problematic. This is especially so when evaluation is based on proxies (as it often is), such as self-reported effort and motivation.[10] Identifying precisely what one teacher contributes to a student's performance and separating his contribution from those of other teachers, the school, the principal, and the family is extremely difficult.[11] Compounding the problem is the fact that students are often deliberately assigned to specific teachers—that is, the assignment of teachers to classes is not random. A still further complication is how to identify the contributions of previous teachers, who may have been superior or inferior.

Pay based on reading and math test scores, for example, might encourage teachers to favor those subjects at the expense of, say, music and art or values and civic responsibility.

Negative Effects on Motivation and Collegiality. Another concern is that implementing individual-based incentives may create unfair competition between teachers, especially in the absence of transparent criteria, thus undermining collaboration. Even if evaluation is accurate and fair, teachers may still feel aggrieved if their competence is questioned. Evaluation may also create new hierarchies by giving administrators an additional source of power over teachers and the curriculum. Individual incentives could also undermine principal-teacher relationships because of the asymmetry in how each party views teacher evaluation: teachers use it to determine how they are performing and how they can improve, while principals use it to measure teachers' contribution to the school.[12]

Unintended Consequences. Some analysts caution that performance-based pay may have unintended consequences. Teachers, for example, may focus on the easiest way to increase the rewarded measure while ignoring measures that schools and parents ultimately want to improve.[13] Similarly, when one dimension of output is easily measured but another is not, teachers may dedicate their efforts to maximizing the measurable at the expense of the unmeasured dimension. Collectively, such efforts could even begin to constrict a school's curriculum to measurable subjects.[14] A further risk is that because test scores measure only certain skills, linking compensation to test scores might cause teachers to sacrifice the nurturing of curiosity and creative thinking to teaching the skills tested on standardized exams—a practice known as teaching to the test.[15] Pay based on reading and math test scores, for example, might encourage teachers to favor those subjects at the expense of, say, music and art or values and civic responsibility.[16] A teaching-to-the-test mentality is thus assumed to support the creation of a system where a narrow curriculum necessarily restricts student achievement in domains not tested.

Unintended consequences may also arise if teachers "game play" and develop responses that generate rewards contradicting the profession's spirit.[17] In other words, measuring student output may stimulate teachers to participate in inappropriate or deviant behavior, such as cheating. Using data from Chicago's public schools, Brian Jacob and Steve Levitt detected cheating in approximately 4 to 5 percent of the classes in their sample.[18] They also found that cheating responds swiftly to changes in teacher incentives. After standardized tests took on increased salience in Chicago's public schools in 1996, the prevalence of cheating rose sharply in low-achieving classrooms, but not in classes with average or above-average students. The prevalence of cheating also appeared to be systematically lower where the costs of cheating were higher or the benefits of cheating lower, as in classrooms where a large number of students' test scores were excluded from official calculations because they were bilingual. Other studies of unintended consequences include altering school lunch menus during testing periods in an apparent attempt to artificially increase student test scores and manipulating who takes the test.[19]

Providing financial incentives to improve performance may be counterproductive in other ways as well. First, it may demoralize teachers, resulting in reduced effort. In laboratory experiments, one study found that workers in high-powered incentive systems may become unmotivated and thus work less than they would under a flat wage regime.[20] Second, financial incentives may undermine intrinsic motivation, that is, the sense of duty or satisfaction that motivates coming to work.[21] This threat is particularly real for teachers, who, as a group, exhibit strong intrinsic motivation flowing from the value they place on interacting with children and seeing them succeed.[22]

Another potential distortion is that teachers may focus disproportionate attention on those students who are most likely to improve their test scores or to cross a designated threshold.[23] The highest- and lowest-performing students may consequently be neglected because they do not promise adequate returns on investments of teachers' quality time.

Risks Posed to Teachers Could Increase Costs. The risks posed to teachers by performance-based pay could lead them to demand high compensation, which could in turn raise the cost of education.[24] Unlike rel-

atively risk-free input-based payment, performance-based pay exposes employees to earnings variability beyond their control. If teachers, like other workers, are risk averse, inducing them to accept a risky compensation package will entail higher average pay overall.

Teachers Are Motivated by Nonfinancial Incentives. A frequent criticism of performance-based pay is that teachers, as professionals relatively immune to motivation by pecuniary rewards, will not respond to financial incentives. Monetary rewards could thus simply inflame resentment toward management and decrease employee loyalty, both of which could reduce productivity. One study suggests that nonmonetary rewards, such as additional holidays, may be better motivators.[25]

Union and Teachers' Opposition. Teacher unions worldwide strongly oppose performance-based pay.[26] Unions view wage differentiation on the basis of subject taught, as well as any sort of subjective evaluation of teachers, as threats to their collective bargaining strategies and therefore reject them outright. And union views weigh heavily: lobbying by unions has often halted efforts to legislate performance-based rewards.[27] Union objections appear to reflect opposition voiced by teachers directly.[28] Teachers see performance-based pay, supported by unfair evaluation, as a threat to their autonomy. Sanctions against poorly performing schools, which are included in some performance-based schemes, are another major source of union and teacher opposition.[29]

Disappointing Experience with Past Merit Pay Programs. The repeated failures of poorly designed and implemented merit pay programs over the past two decades have undermined the credibility of new and better-designed initiatives. A key weakness in past programs has been opaque goals, which make it hard for teachers to understand the program and undermine their support for it. Opaque goals also make it difficult for administrators to explain why some staff members receive a bonus and others do not. One study finds that even in established programs such as those implemented in Kentucky and North Carolina, many participants remain skeptical that bonuses go to qualified teachers.[30]

The High Cost of Performance-Based Pay Schemes. Finally, implementing performance-based pay is easier in small organizations, such as private schools, than in large public school systems with sizable teaching staffs. System size therefore impinges on the observed high cost of performance-related pay, making the program infeasible. One study argues that adequate evaluation of every teacher, expensive in itself, would require considerable resources if performed regularly.[31] The time alone required to administer a pay-for-performance system would have severe budgetary implications.[32] Moreover, as a research study points out, improved productivity in the private sector can generate added income to help mitigate budget problems, but enhanced productivity in public schools has no such effect.[33]

Overcoming Some of the Obstacles

Several of the many potential obstacles to implementing an effective performance-related pay system can be addressed. For example, one solution to the measurement problem is to compensate teachers on the basis of principal evaluations. Brian Jacob and Lars Lefgren compared subjective principal assessments with measures of teacher effectiveness based on gains in student achievement on standardized tests—measures often known as teacher value added—and found that principals are

quite good at identifying those teachers who produce the largest and the smallest standardized achievement gains in their schools, but far less able to distinguish between teachers in the middle of the distribution.[34] They also found that principals systematically discriminate against male and untenured faculty.[35]

A principal-based assessment system would likely result in higher student achievement than today's input-based compensation system. But Jacob and Lefgren cite an important limitation of their research. First, the principals whom they examined were not themselves evaluated explicitly on the basis of their ability to identify effective teachers. Moving to a system where principals have more authority and responsibility for monitoring teacher effectiveness might enhance a principal's capacity to identify the required characteristics. But principals may be less willing to assess teachers honestly under such a system, perhaps in response to social or political pressures. Further, the inability of principals to distinguish between teachers in a broad middle range of quality suggests caution in relying on principals for the finely tuned performance determinations that might be required under certain merit pay policies.

In response to the concern that merit pay models may hamper collaboration, one could structure the system to reward teacher cooperation, especially through group-based pay.[36] This strategy can foster both teacher interdependence and acknowledgement of that interdependence. That said, team-based incentive systems raise the risk of "free riding."[37] If each teacher's share of the team reward is small relative to the cost of effort and if effort is difficult to observe, every teacher in the team will have an incentive to shirk and free ride on the efforts of others.[38] One way to avoid this problem is to encourage peer pressure and mutual monitoring within the team.[39]

Fears that teachers would need to be highly compensated for the increased risk in a performance-based compensation system are probably overstated. If teachers are paid on the basis of student performance, and if the number of students whom teachers teach each year is high, the year-to-year variation in average class test scores is likely to be small. Furthermore, even under the most ambitious schemes only a fraction of teachers' wages would be tied to performance, thus making compensation based on incentives only a marginal component of pay. It is thus unlikely that earnings will fluctuate by more than a few percent annually around some basic trend.

The idea that teachers themselves—as reflected in the positions of their unions—oppose performance-based rewards may also be overstated. One study found that most teachers favor additional pay for additional duties per se and as a component of a career ladder where performance dictates the speed of advancement.[40] Unsurprisingly, performance-based rewards are more popular when they supplement, rather than replace, other forms of salary.

The same study found that the pay level in a school district appeared to have no influence on teachers' attitudes toward merit pay, although teachers who were paid low salaries and who belonged to ethnic minorities were more likely than others to support the program. Attitudes toward merit pay were independent of the number of students who were eligible for free lunches, suggesting that students' socioeconomic status did not affect teachers' views on merit pay. Interestingly,

private school teachers viewed performance-related pay more favorably than their public school counterparts.[41] Teachers' attitudes thus appear relatively malleable and to depend on program design.

Teachers' and union objections were overcome in some cases when specific interest groups and legislators supported perform-

---

Fears that teachers would need to be highly compensated for the increased risk in a performance-based compensation system are probably overstated.

---

ance-based pay. But political turnover makes such support fragile, particularly in times of economic recession, because the cost of performance-based pay is more visible than are the benefits of improved student achievement. [42]

Many of the practical challenges faced by performance-related pay, then, can be addressed through careful design of the system. And despite the opposition of teachers unions to performance-based compensation, it is not clear that the objections to such systems come from the teachers themselves.

Evidence on School-Based Performance Systems
In this section I review evidence on several school-based incentive programs implemented in recent years both in the United States and in other countries. The programs vary in their basic structure and details, with

some targeted at teams of teachers and others at individuals.[43]

Evidence from the United States

Although school-based performance pay theoretically has many attractive features, researchers have been able to find little causal evidence that it is effective in U.S. programs. For example, three researchers studied school-based incentive pay systems in Kentucky, North Carolina (Charlotte-Mecklenburg), and Maryland.[44] They concluded that in the Charlotte-Mecklenburg and Kentucky programs, but not in the Maryland program, both teacher motivation and student outcomes improved. But because all three studies lacked a control group, they could not establish definitively that the program itself—and not some other factor—was the cause of the improvements.[45]

Similarly Helen Ladd studied a school-based bonus program in Dallas.[46] The program, which began in the 1991–92 school year and continued through 1995, ranked schools by how well their students' test scores compared with state average scores, adjusting for students' socioeconomic status. To avoid teaching to the test or other gaming behavior, the program relied on multiple measures of student outcomes, including two tests given each year. Ladd compared gains in school-level test scores in Dallas with gains in other cities (adjusting for many school characteristics, such as racial mix and relative deprivation) to evaluate the impact of this bonus scheme. She found that pass rates appeared to increase more quickly in Dallas than in other cities. Effects were most positive for Hispanics and whites and insignificant for blacks. Although the study suggests that a school-based program can be effective, it was not conclusive. It had, for example, only a limited number of student and school charac-

teristics to adjust to make the participating schools comparable to other schools in the state. In addition, the test score gains in Dallas may have been part of a trend that started before the program was implemented.

The Dallas study also highlights some unintended consequences. In an earlier study, Charles Clotfelter and Ladd had reported that in the Dallas program, schools of low socioeconomic status rarely won awards.[47] In response, the state divided schools into five groups based on socioeconomic characteristics and rewarded the top performers in each group. But some of the lower-performing schools in the upper socioeconomic bands felt that they had been treated unfairly. Dividing the schools into socioeconomic groups also encouraged an undesired strategic response from principals who realized that their ability to gain an award was based on the socioeconomic category into which they were placed.

Finally, two studies of a South Carolina performance-based program that included both school-based and individual-based rewards found that student performance improved.[48] The studies, however, may overstate the incentive effects because teachers could choose whether to apply for an award. If, as would be expected, only the most productive teachers chose to apply, then part of the student gains may be attributable not to the incentives but to the fact that participants were better teachers in the first place.

International Evidence

One of the stronger examples of a school-based incentive program comes from Israel. In February 1995, Israel announced a competition for a monetary bonus for secondary schools and teachers based on their students' performance.[49] The objectives were to reduce dropout rates and improve scholastic achievement. The three performance measures were average number of credits per student, share of students receiving a matriculation diploma, and school dropout rate.

Sixty-two schools were initially selected for the program, with several schools added later. In 1996, participating schools competed for about $1.5 million in awards. Schools were ranked according to their annual improvement, adjusting for the socioeconomic background of the students. Only the top third of performers won awards. The distribution of cash incentives among the award-winning schools was determined solely by their ranking in terms of relative improvement (in 1996, the highest-scoring winner won $105,000; the lowest-scoring, $13,250). Teachers received 75 percent of the award as a salary bonus (proportional to gross income); the remainder was used to improve faculty facilities, such as teachers' common rooms. In 1996, the bonuses ranged from 1 to 3 percent of average teacher salary. The combined performance of a team determined the total incentive payment, which was split among individuals regardless of performance.[50]

The student outcomes rewarded included most of those that can be affected by teachers, thereby reducing the dilemma teachers are assumed to face regarding how to allocate their time between rewarded and nonrewarded activities. School averages of all three performance measures were based on the size of the graduating cohort while in ninth grade rather than in twelfth grade. This procedure was adopted to discourage schools from gaming the incentive system—by encouraging weak students to transfer or drop out or by placing them in the nonmatriculation track. To encourage schools to direct more effort toward weak students, only the first 22 credit

units taken by each student were counted in computing the school's mean to determine its rank in the bonus program.

Two years after the program was implemented, I compared the program schools with a control group and found significant gains in student performance in the former.[51] Average credits were 0.7 unit higher, the share of students sitting for matriculation examinations increased by 2.1 percent, and average scores and passing rates in these examinations improved as well. Of particular importance was the decline in the dropout rate in students' transition from middle to high school. The programs also appeared mainly to affect weaker students.

Another analysis of a school-based teachers' incentive program, this one in Kenya, examined effects on both teacher behavior and test scores.[52] The program randomly assigned fifty Kenyan primary schools to a treatment group eligible for monetary incentives (21–43 percent of monthly salary). The winning schools were determined by their average test score performance relative to other treatment schools in districtwide examinations; all teachers in the winning schools received awards. The program penalized schools for dropouts by assigning low scores to students who did not take the examination. Data were collected on many types of teacher effort—teacher attendance, homework assignments, pedagogical techniques, and holding extra test preparation sessions—and on student scores obtained after the program's conclusion.

During the two years the program was in place, student scores increased significantly in treatment schools (0.14 standard deviation above the control group). But the gain in scores was not attributable to the expected incentive-induced changes in teacher behavior. In fact, teacher attendance did not improve, and no changes were found in either homework assignment or pedagogy. Instead, teachers were more likely to conduct test preparation sessions outside regular class hours. Data collected the year after the program ended showed no lasting test score gains, suggesting that the teachers focused on improving short-term rather than long-term learning. Consistent with this hypothesis, the program had no effect on dropout rates even though examination participation rose (presumably because teachers wanted to avoid penalties for no-shows). The test score effect was also strongest in geography, history, and Christian religion, arguably subjects involving the most memorization.

Summary

Although group-based pay, either alone or combined with individual-based incentives, has the promise of overcoming some of the difficulties inherent in implementing individual-based systems, the little causal evidence of its effectiveness is mixed. The strongest evidence comes from the Israeli experience; whether it could be replicated either in the United States or abroad is unknown.

Evidence on Individual-Based Performance Systems

In this section I review evidence on several individual-based incentive programs, again both in the United States and abroad.

Evidence from the United States

Studies of individual-based incentive schemes in the United States have had some success in isolating the programs' causal effects on student outcomes. But their findings have also been quite mixed. For example, one study assessed the effect on student achievement of a merit pay scheme in Michigan that rewarded individual teachers according to student re-

tention rates and evaluation questionnaires completed by their students.[53] The scheme, which did not directly target student achievement, did improve student retention. But pass rates fell, while attendance rates and grade point averages remained unchanged. The authors concluded that "incentive systems within complex organizations such as schools may produce results that are unintended and at times misdirected."

In contrast, another study combined panel data from the U.S. National Education Longitudinal Survey of 1988 (NELS88) to estimate the effects of teacher incentives on student outcomes.[54] The authors defined incentive schemes as any merit raise or bonus awarded to any proportion of teachers in a school, although the variables did not identify whether schemes stipulated that rewards were to be tied directly to student achievement. The wealth of data in the survey enabled the authors to control for many student, teacher, school, and family characteristics to make it easier to compare students taught by treatment teachers (those in the incentive scheme) with students taught by teachers in a control group. The results were positive, particularly in public and poor (low economic status) schools. Test scores were higher when awards were higher and when awards were given only to a few teachers within a school.

Finally, a third study analyzed incentive effects on student SAT scores in the Tennessee STAR (Student Teacher Achievement Ratio) and Career Ladder Evaluation programs.[55] It controlled for student and teacher characteristics as well as for class attributes that do not change over time (by including class fixed effects based on panel data). It found that SAT scores improved, with gains varying across subjects and with teacher seniority.

One reason for the mixed evidence may be that the studies combine students at all grade levels. One analysis of merit pay reforms in South Carolina in the 1980s and 1990s suggested that merit pay might be more effective in earlier grades than in later grades. More generally, the study cautioned that the effects of performance-based pay may vary across countries, schools, population groups, or time.

International Evidence

The first international example of an individual-based program is an experiment, begun in fifty high schools in Israel in December 2000, that offered teachers a bonus based on student achievement. The experiment included all English, Hebrew, Arabic, and mathematics teachers who taught tenth- to twelfth-grade classes in preparation for matriculation examinations in these subjects in June 2001. Each teacher was ranked separately on the basis of the mean performance of each class she taught. The ranking was based on the difference between actual class performance and performance predicted on the basis of students' socioeconomic characteristics, their level of proficiency in each subject, and a fixed school-level effect. Each teacher was ranked twice, once for the students' passing rate and once for average score.

Each school submitted student enrollment lists, itemized by grade, subject, and teacher, on the program's starting date. All students on these lists were included in the class mean outcomes. Students who dropped out or did not take the exams, regardless of the reason, were imputed a score of zero to neutralize any incentive for teachers to keep poorly performing students out of the tests.

All teachers who performed better than predicted in both passing rate and average score were ranked from first to fourth place and awarded points according to ranking. The awards, based on total points, ranged from 6 to 25 percent of the average annual income of high school teachers. A teacher could win several awards if she prepared more than one class for a matriculation examination.[56] Of the 629 teachers in the program, 302 won awards.

My analysis of the program found that it significantly improved matriculation examina-

> *Although group-based pay . . . has the promise of overcoming some of the difficulties inherent in implementing individual-based systems, the little causal evidence of its effectiveness is mixed.*

tion participation rates as well as the passing rate and average test scores among those who took the test.[57] These gains accounted for about half of the improved outcomes among all students. They appear to have resulted from changes in teaching methods, after-school teaching, and increased responsiveness to students' needs, not from artificial inflation or manipulation of test scores. The evidence that the incentive program improved teacher effort and pedagogy is important in the context of concerns about the programs' unintended effects, such as teaching to the test or cheating and the manipulation of test scores, and fears that such programs do not produce real learning.

As a second example, in 1999 the United Kingdom introduced a systemwide performance-related pay policy for teachers using student progress (value added) as one key criterion.[58] Using long-term teacher data and a before-and-after comparison research design, one study evaluated the policy's effect on test scores on the important GCSE (General Certificate of Secondary Education) exams, taken by students at age sixteen at the end of compulsory education.[59] Because the incentive scheme was explicitly teacher- rather than school-based, the study followed teachers over two complete two-year teaching cycles before and after the policy was introduced. Students were linked to teachers who taught them specific subjects, making it possible to compare treatment and control group teachers. This panel data structure also made it possible to control for student and teacher unchanged characteristics (by including respective fixed effects) and to measure the scheme's target: student progress.

The study reported statistically and economically significant student progress. For instance, relative to control teachers, treatment teachers increased their value added by almost half a GCSE grade per student, equal to 0.73 standard deviation. Also significant were differences between school subjects, with treatment math teachers showing no effect from participating in the program. Although promising, again, the study is not definitive. One concern is that it applied only to teachers who had been in the profession for about eight years, so that treatment and control teachers differed systematically in experience. If teachers improve in their capacity to generate value added as they gain more experience but at a decreasing rate, then, all else being equal, one can expect to see greater improvements in progress between the two teaching cycles for the less experienced (control) group. Taking teacher experience into account in the analysis may

not solve the problem if the relationship between teachers' experience and productivity is nonlinear.

Summary

In general, the evidence suggests that well-designed individual-based incentives can significantly improve student outcomes. But the research base is small, and implementing purely individual-based programs presents many challenges.

Policy Implications of the Evidence on Teachers' Incentives

Research evidence suggests, although not conclusively, that pay-for-performance incentives can improve teachers' performance. Yet these incentives can also lead to unintended and undesired consequences growing out of their inherent structural challenges, such as measurement issues or the possibility of teachers' directing their efforts exclusively to rewarded activities. Although there are no magical cures for any of these problems, it is possible to draw lessons from the experience and evaluation of the better performance-related pay programs. In this section I offer some general guidelines for designing effective programs.

Which Outcomes to Reward

Teachers should be evaluated on the basis of their true performance, not random variation in performance. Therefore, the performance measures chosen should exhibit relatively little random variation. Because teachers are expected to direct their efforts according to the incentives provided, the performance measures should cover all outcomes of interest, including quality and quantity (relevant examples are the two outcome measures used in the Israeli pay programs—passing rate and average score). Outcome measures should be as close as possible to the ultimate outcomes, difficult to game, and easy to monitor regularly.

Monitoring

Close supervision and monitoring are needed to minimize gaming and shading the truth, if not outright fraud, in measured output. Because monitoring can be costly, an appropriate strategy should balance the trade-off between penalties and probability of detection. The matriculation examination system in Israel minimizes gaming: students are tested twice—in a school and a state examination—in each subject, and their final score is a weighted average of the two. Large gaps between the scores invite penalties. Nonrandom gaps between the two scores are audited at the class and school levels. Obviously, even the best-designed measurement and monitoring system may lead to inappropriate reallocation of effort because no single system is likely to capture all important behavior. One way to avoid this constriction in effort is to include two outcomes, for instance, test scores and processes (for example, attention directed explicitly to disadvantaged students) and teacher practices (for example, teacher absenteeism).

Reward Criteria

Teachers can be compared according to student performance levels or to some form of gain in performance. Value-added measures, in particular, are more appropriate for measuring individual teacher effectiveness and ensuring fair ranking. Such methods can substantially affect school or teacher rankings, in addition to the behaviors engaged in to game the system. Performance levels create incentives to pay greatest attention to highest-performing students; value-added criteria may increase attention to lowest-performing students. It is thus important to use performance measures that can be adjusted for contributing factors, such as student socioeconomic characteristics, but not at the cost of complex value-added measures that lack transparency and are difficult to understand and accept. In addition, goals should be attainable and not be perceived as too ambitious.

Rewarding Both Short- and Long-Term Measures

Performance-related pay programs typically focus on key short-term schooling objectives—such as increasing the number of students reading at a given grade level—rather than on long-term objectives related to postsecondary education and labor market outcomes. This emphasis is due in large part to the difficulty of measuring long-term objectives, as well as to an almost universal belief that achieving short-term goals is a necessary condition for promoting long-term goals. But medium-term outcomes, such as dropout rates, can be affected by performance-related pay. The team-based program developed in Israel demonstrates how a mix of short- and medium-term goals can be achieved simultaneously in an effective performance-related pay program.

Subjective and Objective Evaluation

Subjective evaluation invites the problem of performance measure inflation (namely, that teachers under the pressure of incentives tend to give higher than warranted scores), while objective metrics invite the problems of measurement cost and the inability to encompass all school targets and goals. Given these limitations, it may be appropriate to use both—each imperfect but still informative. For example, selective emphasis can be assigned to each subjective and objective evaluation criterion, depending on subject taught or specific task, and associated with individual, team, and school performance. The evaluation process and its results should be transparent to all parties involved.

School and Individual Incentives

Because some degree of teamwork characterizes all schools, incentives should balance individual rewards with school incentives. Design of these incentives should foster a cooperative culture, but not at the cost of an aggravated free-riding problem, a condition likely to arise when only group incentives are used.

Monetary and Other Incentives

Money is not alone in motivating performance and promotions. Improved working conditions and increased decisionmaking authority may also be attractive to teachers, especially when combined with bonuses or salary increases. The Israeli school incentive program included modest monetary bonuses but large rewards in the form of media attention and enhanced reputation for the winning schools. Recognition and prestige are, it appears, highly effective motivators.

Eligibility and Size of Awards

All teachers should be eligible for the incentive offered. Only when the majority of teachers are eligible to enjoy the benefits of hard work and improved outcomes will the incentive scheme be effective. However, only a subset of teachers should be rewarded in practice. If too many teachers are rewarded, teachers may not need to exert much effort to benefit.

Flexibility

A performance-related pay program can motivate teachers and schools even more effectively if it also allows teachers to make decisions regarding instruction, curriculum, and other aspects of schooling that contribute to attaining the desired outcomes and goals. Creativity flourishes in the absence of bu-

reaucratic constraints. The search for ways to improve teaching technology arises both because teachers and schools have a direct stake in the matter and because merit pay plans reduce the need for regulation of inputs and thus give teachers and schools more freedom. It is therefore essential that performance-related pay plans be accompanied by the increased flexibility required for their success.

Conclusions

Recent reforms in public education have in common a heightened stress on effectiveness—setting standards, measuring progress toward those standards, and imposing rewards or penalties for meeting or failing to meet them. Performance-related pay systems use monetary rewards to meet these goals. In most cases these systems involve marginal changes rather than a complete revamping of the educational system. Research evidence suggests, though not conclusively, that incentive-based compensation can generate gains in student performance and teacher effectiveness. Teachers and schools appear to respond to monetary incentives by exerting more effort, applying more creativity, and modifying their pedagogical practices. Measuring and rewarding performance are thus potentially important elements in modern public school compensation systems. They can also, theoretically, discourage poor performers and attract better performers in the medium and longer terms.

It is telling that private schools typically have more flexible pay structures than public schools and that they are more likely to use variations of performance-related pay. Dale Ballou reports that in 1993, 12 percent of U.S. public school districts had merit pay plans, as compared with 35 percent of nonsectarian private schools.[60] Merit pay can clearly be integrated and implemented in the private schools. Political or technical constraints may be impeding its success in public schools.

Implementing performance-based pay requires meeting the daunting challenge of devising a system for measuring performance. The system must measure true performance in a way that minimizes random variation, as well as undesired and unintended consequences. It must align performance with ultimate outcomes and monitor performance to discourage cheating. Clearly, setting up an effective performance-related pay system is not a one-time task, but an ongoing effort. Even with the best preparation, initial implementation is likely to be problematic. Measurements will have a random component. Teachers will find ways to game the system. Any initial system will almost certainly be flawed. But if the effort is seen as an ongoing one, it should be possible to make progress gradually in addressing each of the challenges. For example, better measurement instruments should shrink the random component in the measures, measurements can be adjusted to prevent gaming, careful monitoring can detect and therefore deter cheating. Eventually incentives will be developed that motivate the desired teaching behaviors and will be perceived by teachers as fair and accurate.

Although the suggestions above are consistent with most of the limited empirical evidence available on the effectiveness of performance-related pay strategies, researchers have much work to do. Their efforts are impeded both by the reluctance of school systems to conduct careful evaluations and by a lack of appropriate outcome measures and comparison groups. Starting now, researchers should follow closely all efforts to implement performance-based pay in public schools, tracking carefully the behavioral changes induced and the ultimate outcomes of monetary rewards given to school staff. Meeting these research challenges is critical to the design of effective performance-related pay systems in the future.

Notes

1. For example, in describing the need for fundamental reform of the system, the U.S. Department of Education noted that while real spending on K–12 education has grown substantially over the last decade, academic achievement as measured by the National Assessment of Educational Progress (NAEP) has barely budged for most student categories. Such comparisons are often used in policy debates to buttress the imposition of new forms of accountability on educators instead of continuing to "throw money at schools."

2. William J. Slotnick and Maribeth D. Smith, *Catalyst for Change: Pay for Performance in Denver Final Report* (Boston: Community Training and Assistance Center, 2004). The study found the largest gains for high school students.

3. High school test scores are significantly correlated with adult (mid-20s through mid-30s) earnings, even after controlling for background variables. See R. J. Murnane, J. B. Willett, and F. Levy, "The Growing Importance of Cognitive Skills in Wage Determination," *Review of Economics and Statistics* 77 (1995): 251–66; Derek A. Neal and William R. Johnson, "The Role of Premarket Factors in Black-White Wage Differences," *Journal of Political Economy* 104, no. 5 (1996): 869–95; J. S. Zax and D. I. Rees, "IQ, Academic Performance, Environment, and Earnings," *Review of Economics and Statistics* 84, no. 4 (2002): 600–16. Janet Currie and Duncan Thomas, "Early Test Scores, Socioeconomic Status and Future Outcomes," Working Paper 6943 (Cambridge, Mass.: National Bureau of Economic Research, 1999) present estimates based on test scores of much younger children (aged seven). They find a correlation with adult earnings, after controlling for factors such as father's socioeconomic status (SES), and father's and mother's and maternal grandfather's education. These correlations lend additional support to the assumption that increased learning—as proxied by test scores—in elementary school or high school will lead to better labor market outcomes in adulthood.

4. See, for example, Edward P. Lazear, "Paying Teachers for Performance: Incentives and Selection," Stanford University, mimeo, 2001; Lewis Solomon and Michael Podgursky, "The Pros and Cons of Performance-Based Compensation" (Pasadena, Calif.: Milken Family Foundation, 2001); and H. Tomlinson, "Proposals for Performance Related Pay in English Schools," *School Leadership and Management* 20, no. 3 (2000): 281–98.

5. There is some evidence that in performance-based systems, principals tend to evaluate teachers more critically than they would otherwise; see R. Murnane and D. Cohen, "Merit Pay and the Evaluation Problem: Why Most Merit Pay Plans Fail and a Few Survive," *Harvard Educational Review* 56, no. 1 (1986): 1–17. As a precaution, Solomon and Podgursky suggest that principals themselves become subject to schoolwide performance-based evaluation to ensure the continued objectivity of their evaluations; see Solomon and Podgursky, "The Pros and Cons" (see note 4).

6. C. Kelley, "The Motivational Impact of School-Based Performance Awards," *Journal of Personnel Evaluation in Education* 12, no. 4 (1999): 309–26.

7. See, for example, T. Hoerr, "A Case for Merit Pay," *Phi Delta Kappan* 80, no. 4 (1998): 326–27.

8. See, for example, Solomon and Podgursky, "The Pros and Cons" (see note 4); and Tomlinson, "Proposals for Performance Related Pay" (see note 4).

9. However, in the United States not only are there many options for choice within the public schools (such as citywide choice systems and magnet and charter schools), but also individuals can effectively choose where

to live based on the quality of the schools. And there is compelling evidence that school quality affects where households choose to live; see, for example, Lisa Barrow, "School Choice through Relocation: Evidence from the Washington, D.C., Area," *Journal of Public Economics* 86, no. 2 (2002): 155–89; Lisa Barrow and Cecilia E. Rouse, "Using Market Valuation to Assess Public School Spending," *Journal of Public Economics* 88, nos. 9–10 (2004): 1747–69.

10. See R. Richardson, "Performance Related Pay in Schools: An Assessment of the Green Papers," Report prepared for the National Union of Teachers (London School of Economics and Political Science, 1999).

11. See D. Evans, "No Merit in Merit Pay," *American School Board Journal* 188, no. 1 (2001): 48–50; and M. Holt, "Performance Pay for Teachers: The Standards Movement's Last Stand?" *Phi Delta Kappan* 83, no. 4 (2001): 321–28.

12. American Federation of Teachers, "Merit Pay," Working Paper (2001), www.aft.org/issues/meritpay/meritpay.html (January 15, 2003); L. Barber and K. Klein, "Merit Pay and Teacher Evaluation," *Phi Delta Kappan* 65, no. 4 (1983): 247–51; T. Cutler and B. Waine, "Mutual Benefits or Managerial Control? The Role of Appraisal in Performance Related Pay for Teachers," *British Journal of Educational Studies* 48, no. 2 (2000): 170–82; M. Holt, "Performance Pay for Teachers" (see note 11); and A. Ramirez, "How Merit Pay Undermines Education," *Educational Leadership* 58, no. 5 (2001): 16–20.

13. See Bengt Holmstrom and P. Milgrom, "Multi-Task Principal-Agent Problems: Incentive Contracts, Asset Ownership and Job Design," *Journal of Law, Economics and Organization* 7 (1991).

14. R. Chamberlin and others, "Performance-Related Pay and the Teaching Profession: A Review of the Literature," *Research Papers in Education* 17, no. 1 (2002): 31–49.

15. See, for example, Paul Glewwe, Nauman Ilias, and Michael Kremer, "Teacher Incentives," Working Paper 9671 (Cambridge, Mass.: National Bureau of Economic Research, 2003).

16. The reallocation of effort and resources toward subjects that are measured and rewarded and away from subjects that are not measured and thus not rewarded has been documented empirically. For example, teachers have reported spending more time on tested topics and less on untested topics as a result of high-stakes testing programs; see L. A. Shepard and K. C. Dougherty, "Effects of High-Stakes Testing on Instruction," paper presented at the annual meeting of the American Educational Research Association and National Council on Measurement in Education, Chicago, 1991; M. L. Smith and others, *The Role of Testing in Elementary Schools*, CSE Technical Report 321 (Los Angeles: Center for Research on Evaluation, Standards, and Student Testing, 1991); B. M. Stecher and others, *The Effects of the Washington State Education Reform on Schools and Classrooms*, CSE Technical Report 525 (Los Angeles, Calif.: Center for Research on Evaluation, Standards, and Student Testing, 2000). Teachers have also reported stressing certain formats or styles used in test items in their instruction; see D. M. Koretz and L. S. Hamilton, *Teachers' Responses to High-Stakes Testing and the Validity of Gains: A Pilot Study*, CSE Technical Report 610 (Los Angeles, Calif.: Center for Research on Evaluation, Standards, and Student Testing, 2003); J. J. Pedulla and others, *Perceived Effects of State-Mandated Testing Programs on Teaching and Learning: Findings from a National Survey of Teachers* (Boston, Mass.: National Board on Educational Testing and Public Policy, 2003); T. A. Romberg, E. A. Zarinia, and S. R. Williams, *The Influence of Mandated Testing on Mathematics Instruction: Grade 8 Teachers' Perceptions* (National Center for Research in Mathematical Science Education, University of Wisconsin-Madison, 1989). Shepard and Dougherty, for instance, found that in two districts with high-stakes writing tests, writing teachers admitted that as a result of the format of the writ-

ing test used in those districts, they emphasized student searches for mistakes in written work rather than the production of students' own writing.

17. See B. Malen, "On Rewards, Punishments, and Possibilities: Teacher Compensation as an Instrument for Education Reform," *Journal of Personnel Evaluation in Education* 12, no. 4 (1999): 387–94.

18. Brian Jacob and Steve Levitt, "Rotten Apples: An Investigation of the Prevalence and Predictors of Teacher Cheating," *Quarterly Journal of Economics* 3 (2003): 843–77.

19. David N. Figlio and J. Winicki, "Food for Thought: The Effects of School Accountability Plans on School Nutrition," Working Paper 9319 (Cambridge, Mass.: National Bureau of Economic Research, 2002); and David N. Figlio and Lawrence S. Getzler, "Accountability, Ability and Disability: Gaming the System," Working Paper 9307 (Cambridge, Mass.: National Bureau of Economic Research, 2002).

20. Ernst Fehr and Klaus M. Schmidt, "Fairness and Incentives in a Multi-Task Principal-Agent Model," *Scandinavian Journal of Economics* 106, no. 3 (2004): 453–74.

21. David Kreps, "Intrinsic Motivation and Extrinsic Incentives," *American Economic Review* 87, no. 2 (1997): 359–64.

22. This concern could be more meaningful in developing countries, where incentives are employed to increase teachers' work attendance. For example, if the incentives are based solely or primarily on presence in the classroom, teachers may come to believe that class attendance per se is more important than their performance in the classroom. Equally worrisome is the possibility that teachers who previously believed that they were required to work every day in the month might increase their absenteeism once they reached their target monthly income; Ernst Fehr and Lorenz Gotte, "Do Workers Work More If Wages Are High? Evidence from a Randomized Field Experiment," Working Paper 125 (University of Zurich, 2002).

23. Murnane and Cohen, "Merit Pay and the Evaluation Problem" (see note 5).

24. See Lazear, "Paying Teachers for Performance" (see note 4).

25. W. Firestone and J. Pennell, "Teacher Commitment, Working Conditions, and Differential Incentive Policies,'" *Review of Educational Research* 63, no. 4 (1993): 489–525.

26. See D. Ballou and M. Podgursky, "Teachers' Attitudes towards Merit Pay: Examining Conventional Wisdom," *Industrial and Labor Relations Review* 47, no. 1 (1993): 50–61; S. McCollum, "How Merit Pay Improves Education," *Educational Leadership* 58, no. 5 (2001): 21–24; H. Tomlinson, "Proposals for Performance Related Pay in English Schools," *School Leadership and Management* 20, no. 3 (2000): 281–98.

27. Recently, though, a dent has been observed in this formerly united front in the United States with the appearance of a group of teachers unions that supports the efforts of the Consortium for Research and Policy in Education (CRPE) to introduce knowledge- and skills-based pay; see A. Odden, "Paying Teachers for Performance," *School Business Affairs* (June 2000): 28–31.

28. Ballou and Podgursky, "Teachers' Attitudes towards Merit Pay" (see note 26).

29. C. Kelley, H. Heneman, and A. Milanowski, "Teacher Motivation and School-Based Performance Awards," *Education Administration Quarterly* 38, no. 3 (2002): 372–401.

30. Ibid.

31. A. Odden, "New and Better Forms of Teacher Compensation Are Possible," *Phi Delta Kappan* 81, no. 5 (2000): 361–66.

32. Cutler and Waine, "Mutual Benefits or Managerial Control?" (see note 12).

33. A. Mohrman, S. Mohrman, and A. Odden, "Aligning Teacher Compensation with Systemic School Reform: Skill-Based Pay and Group-Based Performance Awards," *Educational Evaluation and Policy Analysis* 18, no. 1 (1996): 51–71.

34. Brian Jacob and Lars Lefgren, "Principals as Agents: Subjective Performance Measurement in Education," Working Paper 11463 (Cambridge, Mass.: National Bureau of Economic Research, May 2005).

35. Several past studies in education found little correlation between principal-based teacher evaluations; see, for example, D. M. Medley and H. Coker, "The Accuracy of Principals' Judgments of Teacher Performance," *Journal of Educational Research* 80 (1987): 242–47. However, David Armor and others, *Analysis of the School Preferred Reading Program in Selected Los Angeles Minority Schools*, Report R-2007-LAUSD (Santa Monica, Calif.: RAND, 1976), found that principal evaluations of teachers predicted student achievement even after conditioning on prior student test scores and a host of other student and classroom-level demographic controls. The authors argue that these results indicate that principals *can* identify effective teachers. While these findings are suggestive, this literature has many limitations. Most of the studies involved extremely small, often nonrepresentative samples, and the methodologies used often do not account for selection and measurement error issues.

36. E. Cohn, "Methods of Teacher Remuneration: Merit Pay and Career Ladders," in *Assessing Educational Practices: The Contribution of Economics*, edited by W. Becker and W. Baumol (New York: Russell Sage Foundation, 1996); Mohrman, Mohrman, and Odden, "Aligning Teacher Compensation with Systemic School Reform" (see note 33).

37. See W. Bengt Holmstrom, "Managerial Incentive Problems—A Dynamic Perspective," republished in *Review of Economic Studies* 66 (1999): 169–82.

38. See C. Prendergast, "The Provision of Incentives in Firms," *Journal of Economic Literature* 37 (March 1999): 7–63.

39. See Eugene Kandel and Edward Lazear, "Peer Pressure and Partnerships," *Journal of Political Economy* 100, no. 4 (1992): 801–17.

40. D. Ballou and M. Podgursky, "Teacher Pay and Teacher Quality" (Michigan: W. E. Upjohn Institute for Employment Research, 1997).

41. Ibid.

42. Ibid.

43. Additional details and evidence on the effects of some of these programs, as well as of other performance-related pay programs, are presented in Peter Dolton, Steve McIntosh, and Arnaud Chevalier, *Pay and Performance*, Bedford Way Papers (University of London, Institute of Education, 2003).

44. Kelley, "The Motivational Impact of School-Based Performance Awards" (see note 6); H. G. Heneman and A. T. Milanowski, "Teachers' Attitudes about Teacher Bonuses under School-Based Performance Award

Programs," *Journal of Personnel Evaluation in Education* 12 (1999): 327–41; Kelley, Heneman, and Milanowski, "Teacher Motivation and School-Based Performance Awards" (see note 29).

45. S. Smith and R. Mickelson, "All That Glitters Is Not Gold: School Reform in Charlotte-Mecklenburg," *Educational Evaluation and Policy Analysis* 22, no. 2 (2000): 101–27, evaluated the Charlotte-Mecklenburg program outcomes by contrasting them to outcomes observed in nonparticipating North Carolina urban school districts. They compared progress on SAT scores and dropout rates for a range of age levels in program schools against statewide averages. However, they did not adequately control for potential differences between program schools and nonprogram schools. Further, Charlotte-Mecklenburg is a complex reform program that involves many policy developments in addition to performance-based rewards. This makes it difficult to identify the unique effect of the performance-related pay programs. More recently in North Carolina, another interesting incentive program was implemented for a three-year period beginning in 2001. The program awarded an annual bonus of $1,800 to certified math, science, and special education teachers working in high-poverty public secondary schools. Charles Clotfelter and others, "Compensating Salary Differentials for Teachers in High-Poverty Schools: Evidence from a Policy Intervention in North Carolina" (Sanford Institute of Public Policy, Duke University, 2006), suggest that this sum was sufficient to reduce mean turnover rates by 12 percent, and even more among experienced teachers.

46. H. Ladd, "The Dallas School Accountability and Incentive Program: An Evaluation of Its Impacts on Student Outcomes," *Economics of Education Review* 18, no. 1 (1999): 1–16.

47. C. Clotfelter and H. Ladd, "Recognizing and Rewarding Success in Public Schools," in *Holding Schools Accountable: Performance-Based Reform in Education,* edited by H. Ladd (Brookings, 1996).

48. S. T. Cooper and E. Cohn, "Estimation of a Frontier Production Function for the South Carolina Educational Process," *Economics of Education Review* 16 (1997): 313–27; M. Boozer, "The Design and Evaluation of Incentive Schemes for Schools: Evidence from South Carolina's Teacher Incentive Pay Project," paper prepared for the National Academy of Sciences Conference on Devising Incentives to Improve Human Capital, Irvine, Calif., December 17–18, 1999.

49. Details of this program are provided in a publication issued by the chief scientist of the Israeli Ministry of Education: *The Differential Compensation: Principles for Allocation* (Jerusalem, 1995; in Hebrew).

50. This program closely fits the framework of a rank order tournament as analyzed in E. Lazear and S. Rosen, "Rank-Order Tournaments as Optimum Labor Contracts," *Journal of Political Economy* 89 (1981): 841–64; and Jerry Green and Nancy L. Stokey, "A Comparison of Tournaments and Contracts," *Journal of Political Economy* 91 (1983): 349–64. In such schemes, prizes depend on the rank order of the winner of a contest or tournament.

51. See Victor Lavy, "Evaluating the Effect of Teachers' Performance Incentives on Pupils' Achievements," *Journal of Political Economy* 110 (December 2002): 1286–317.

52. Glewwe, Ilias, and Kremer, "Teacher Incentives" (see note 15).

53. R. Eberts, K. Hollenbeck, and J. Stone, "Teacher Performance Incentives and Student Outcomes," WP00-65 (Michigan: Upjohn Institute for Employment Research, 2000).

54. D. N. Figlio and L. W. Kenny, "Do Individual Teacher Incentives Boost Student Performance?" (University of Florida, 2003).

55. T. Dee and B. Keys, "Does Merit Pay Reward Good Teachers? Evidence from a Randomized Experiment," *Journal of Policy Analysis and Management* 23, no. 3 (2004): 471–88.

56. For more details, see Israel, Ministry of Education, High School Division, *Individual Teacher Bonuses Based on Student Performance: Pilot Program* (Jerusalem, December 2000; in Hebrew).

57. Victor Lavy, "Paying for Performance and Teachers' Effort, Productivity, and Grading Ethics," Working Paper 10622 (Cambridge, Mass.: National Bureau of Economic Research, 2004).

58. See Dolton, McIntosh, and Chevalier, "Pay and Performance" (see note 43), for an extensive survey and discussion of the performance-related pay program for teachers in the United Kingdom.

59. Adele Atkinson and others, "Evaluating the Impact of Performance-Related Pay for Teachers in England," CMPO Working Paper 04/113 (Bristol, 2004); and S. Burgess and others, "The Intricacies of the Relationship between Pay and Performance for Teachers: Do Teachers Respond to Performance Related Pay schemes?" CMPO Working Paper 01/35 (Bristol, 2001).

60. Dale Ballou, "Pay for Performance in Public and Private Schools," *Economics of Education Review* 20 (2001): 51–61.

Learning in the Teaching Workforce

Heather C. Hill

Summary

The U.S. educational system invests heavily, in both time and money, in continuing education for teachers. In this article Heather Hill examines the effectiveness of two forms of teacher learning—graduate coursework and professional development.

She focuses first on graduate education. Almost half of all teachers have a master's degree. Many states allow graduate coursework to count toward recertification requirements. Some districts require teachers to complete a master's degree within several years of hiring, and many others reward it with salary increases. Education reformers often recommend requiring master's degrees. But much graduate coursework appears to be of low intellectual quality and disconnected from classroom practice. Most research finds no link between teachers' graduate degrees and student learning unless the degree is in the teacher's primary teaching field.

Hill then examines professional development. Most workshops, institutes, and study groups appear to be brief, superficial, and of marginal use in improving teaching. But it does not have to be this way, says Hill. Professional development can enhance teaching and learning if it has three characteristics. It must last several days or longer; it must focus on subject-matter-specific instruction; and it must be aligned with the instructional goals and curriculum materials in teachers' schools. Such high-quality programs do exist. But they are a tiny fraction of the nation's offerings. One problem, says Hill, is that researchers rarely evaluate carefully either local professional development or its effect on student learning. Most evaluations simply ask participants to self-report. Lacking reliable evaluations, how are teachers and district officials to choose effective programs? Clearly, much more rigorous studies are needed.

To make continuing education effective, school districts should encourage teachers to take graduate coursework that is more tightly aligned with their primary teaching assignment. And districts should select professional development programs based on evidence of their effectiveness. Finally, central planners must ensure that items on the menu of offerings closely align with district standards, curriculum materials, and assessments.

www.futureofchildren.org

Heather C. Hill is an assistant professor and associate research scientist at the University of Michigan.

When teachers enter the workforce, their education is far from complete. The first years of teaching are themselves powerful instructors, as teachers gain familiarity with the students, materials, and content that they teach. Studies that link student achievement to teacher characteristics frequently identify an advantage, in terms of student gains, for teachers who are beyond the first several years of teaching. In addition, most states predicate the renewal of teaching certificates on continuing education in the form of additional university coursework and degrees, professional development, or both.[1] In national surveys, nearly every teacher reports participating yearly in one of these activities. Teachers' continuing education, then, might prove a key resource for improving workforce knowledge and skills. But is it?

In this article I review research on teachers' continuing education. I use the term *continuing education* to encompass two distinct categories of learning opportunities: those that yield graduate-level credit and degrees and those traditionally called "professional development," but now viewed by many scholars as inclusive of not only workshops and in-service programs but also school-based teacher study groups, mentoring relationships, and even experiences such as becoming certified by the National Board for Professional Teaching Standards (NBPTS). To assess teachers' continuing education and its effects, I address four sets of questions. First, what requirements and incentives exist for participation, and how do teachers respond? Second, what do teachers *do* in continuing education? What content is offered for teachers to learn? Third, do these learning opportunities improve teaching knowledge and

skill, and ultimately enhance student achievement? And finally, how effective is the *system* of continuing education in improving the knowledge and skills of the teaching force and in improving student achievement?

Throughout, I pay attention to the various incentives in the system—incentives for teachers, for professional development providers, and for district and state officials—that shape the availability and effectiveness of professional learning. I begin by reviewing the small research base on teachers' graduate education, then explore the larger body of research on teachers' learning in other formats.

Graduate Education

Like many other professionals, teachers pursue graduate degrees either to enable entry into the field or to continue formal training once in the workforce.

Incentives and Requirements for Graduate Education

According to government statistics, approximately 45 percent of teachers have a master's degree.[2] Two types of master's degree are typical. One is a Master of Arts in Teaching, usually earned in a one-year program by those seeking a career change through certification. The second is a more general degree, pursued by teachers already in the labor force. Although no firm data exist on the prevalence of either degree, government statistics show that the share of teachers holding master's degrees jumps from 16 percent among those with three or fewer years of experience to 62 percent among those with more than twenty years of experience.[3] A national survey found that roughly one-fifth of all mathematics and science teachers reported having taken a disciplinary or discipline-specific teaching methods course within the past three years.[4] Wide enrollment in graduate programs appears common in the teacher labor force. Why?

One reason is that incentives for pursuing such a degree are strong. More than thirty states allow graduate coursework to count toward recertification requirements. Some districts require teachers to complete a master's degree within several years of hiring. Many other districts provide salary increases for teachers who get a master's or specialist's degree. According to one report, the average salary increase is 11 percent for a master's degree and 17 percent for an education specialist's degree.[5]

What Do Teachers Do in Graduate Education?

Although participation in graduate education is common and although education reformers often recommend that master's degrees be required, little is known about the content of graduate coursework.[6] Existing studies tend to focus on the need for program redesign rather than on close examination of current offerings, but descriptions of these offerings suggest that many are of low intellectual quality, are disconnected from classroom practice, and are often fragmented, because teachers take courses to fulfill state requirements absent a coherent plan for learning.[7] Peggy Blackwell and Mary Diez quote from one teacher educator who decries the "drive-by" degree: "It's pre-service warmed over. If you apply, you get in; and if you get in, you get out."[8] More recently, incentives have shifted toward teachers' completing online master's programs in education, as these courses require no commuting or classroom time, and in some cases much less work than courses in bricks-and-mortar programs. The prevalence of poor-quality learning experiences has historical precedent: Blackwell and Diez note that until the mid-1800s, master's

degrees were "essentially . . . an unearned degree given for a fee."[9] Understanding more about the content, rigor, and effects of online and traditional master's degree programs is a key area for future study.

Can Graduate Education Improve Teaching and Learning?

A number of studies have addressed the link between teachers' graduate degrees and student learning. In most cases, they find that having a master's degree is unrelated to student achievement. The handful of studies that find significant links find both positive *and* negative effects.[10] Thus the overall effect of graduate education on teacher productivity is likely close to zero. Significantly, though, most studies fail to determine whether a teacher's advanced degree is related to the subject he or she teaches.[11] Several studies that specifically examine the effects of teacher characteristics on high school students' mathematics achievement find that having a master's degree in *mathematics* significantly predicts student gains.[12] This finding, however, has been replicated only with high school students and their teachers, and the significant effects may be an artifact of the statistical models used rather than an outcome of real teacher learning. More mathematically proficient teachers, in this scenario, would choose to complete a master's degree in mathematics, and these more proficient teachers might improve student achievement even absent their higher degree. More rigorous studies are needed, including studies at other grade levels and for other subject areas.

Does Graduate Education Improve Teaching and Learning?

Overall, little evidence suggests that the *system* of graduate education improves the knowledge and skills pertinent to producing student learning. Teachers, responding to state or district incentives, pursue advanced degrees and coursework. Higher education institutions—and increasingly, online "institutions"—respond to this market by providing easy-to-obtain degrees of varying, probably poor, quality. Without policy intervention, there are few incentives for change in this system.

Professional Development

More studies have examined the content and effectiveness of teacher learning in professional development settings—traditional workshops, institutes, and teacher study groups. In this section I discuss incentives for participation, the content of professional development, its effectiveness, and the effectiveness of the system in improving teaching and learning.

Incentives and Requirements for Professional Development

Nearly every state and school district provides inducements for teachers to participate in professional development. To start, most states give teachers the option of accumulating professional development hours or credits toward recertification; the modal state requirement is 120 hours over a five-year period.[13] A handful of states also require teachers to study specific topics or work with specific providers, and several require teachers to develop and follow professional development plans. School districts often add other requirements, including mandatory programs for all instructional staff or an investment of time beyond state requirements, or both.

The ubiquity of professional development is reflected in what teachers say they do. Data compiled by the National Center for Education Statistics (NCES) show that in 1999–2000, 99 percent of teachers surveyed

reported participating in professional development activities over the past year.[14] But the time invested was typically brief: just over half of respondents reported the equivalent of one day or less of professional development, and only a minority reported more than thirty hours of study within the past year.[15] Although short workshops might be effective in providing piecemeal instructional activities or very general ideas, many scholars believe that given the complexity of teachers' work, short workshops have little effect on teaching or learning. And indeed, recent research identifies program length as one key predictor of teacher learning in professional settings.[16] Longer programs simply give teachers more time to learn.

What Do Teachers Do in Professional Development?

By all accounts, professional development in the United States consists of a hodgepodge of providers, formats, philosophies, and content. Most providers are locally based, serving school districts within the immediate geographic range.[17] Providers include local teachers and district personnel, independent contractors, university faculty, and curriculum materials publishers and their representatives. The learning opportunities they offer range from "one-shot" day-long workshops to extended institutes (typically a week or more in the summer) to forms of professional development embedded in teachers' daily work, such as lesson study (see box 1), mentoring and coaching, grade-level team meetings, or even more informal in-school collaborations.[18] There is also a range of philosophies about teacher learning, from those that advocate the direct instruction of teachers in specific teaching techniques to those that see teacher development as organic, driven by teachers' own needs, ideas, and self-directed learning. Content varies widely, from

Box 1. Lesson Study

One form of professional development now popular in the United States is lesson study. In lesson study, teachers collaboratively create a detailed plan for one lesson; one member of the group then teaches this lesson, while others observe. After the lesson, the group debriefs and revises the lesson—at which point it may be taught again by another teacher. In this excerpt below, a lesson study facilitator discusses his experience working with the mathematics faculties of two high schools.

For us, the biggest hurdle was convincing teachers to allow others to watch them teach. Whenever you approach a faculty with lesson study, once you say "other people will be watching you teach," half the people leave the room. We had to convince the teachers that the observers were not there to watch the teacher, but instead to watch the students. The observers' goal is to see whether the lesson the group has produced is going to be effective in producing student learning.

This means that the group has to create a lesson so that observers have something to observe. The lesson must be more participatory and involve students' voices more than typical lessons do. Otherwise the observers can't do their job. This in itself was a major shift for both of the faculties I worked with.

In one school, teachers' eyes were really opened to the idea that if you want to understand what students are learning from a lesson, you have to get students talking more. These teachers had never thought to do that. But beyond that, I'm not sure how much impact lesson study had; many teachers were doing it simply because the district thought it was a good idea. This faculty also had a history of little collegiality and lots of conflict. So perhaps just getting teachers to work together and watch one another teach will lead to good things.

In the other school, teachers' eyes were opened to this idea about student talk and learning. And teachers became a much more cohesive group. Previously, I'd say they were collegial, in the sense that they discussed what they were teaching that day, but they had never discussed *how* to teach it. Through lesson study, they realized that the *how* is really important to talk about.

"generic" workshops that outline general principles, such as active learning or cooperative grouping for any subject area, to highly specific topics, such as the use of particular software or how to deliver early reading instruction from a particular set of curriculum materials. As one might predict, neither form nor content of most professional development is standardized nationally; both are likely to be influenced heavily by the knowledge and predisposition of the provider, and perhaps secondarily by the needs of the district and teachers served.

In recent years, scholars and policymakers have led a reform effort driven by research that suggests that content-focused professional development is effective in changing what teachers know and do. The research recommends a focus on specific subject matter, curriculum materials, and teaching methods linked to subject matter and materials. It also recommends that professional development cover student learning of specific content and take place in novel formats, such as extended workshops, lesson study, or in-school mentoring and collabora-

Figure 1. Percentage of Teachers Choosing Selected Topics of Teacher Professional Development, 2000

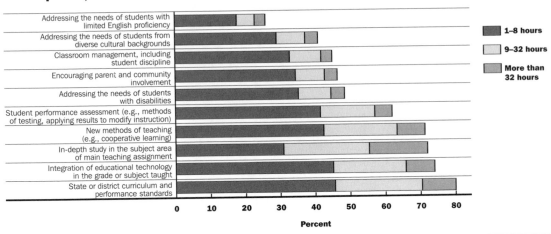

Source: National Center for Education Statistics, *Teacher Preparation and Professional Development: 2000*, NCES 2001-088 (U.S. Department of Education, 2001), table 2, p. 15.

tion. A key question is the extent to which professional development fulfills these recommendations.

Two sources of evidence bear on this question. The first is a national survey of K–12 teachers conducted by the National Center for Education Statistics in 2000. As figure 1 shows, "generic" professional development topics, such as student diversity, classroom management, and encouraging parental involvement, were relatively less popular than more subject-matter-specific topics, such as state or district instructional policy, in-depth study in content areas, and student performance assessments. Other NCES data from the same period show that 59 percent and 73 percent of teachers report focusing on subject matter content and methods, respectively, during their professional development experiences in the past year.[19] But figure 1 also reveals that most teachers report that such experiences last eight hours or less. The one exception is subject-matter-focused workshops, which most teachers report to last more than one day.

The second source of data is a survey of K–12 mathematics and science teachers in 2000, conducted by Horizon Research.[20] Teachers report both the format and the content of their professional development for these specific subjects. Figure 2 presents data on the format of professional development for teachers of mathematics. Traditional workshops, peer observations, and lesson study had the highest rates of teacher engagement in the three years before the study. Other activities, such as distance learning, serving as a mentor, attending state or national meetings, and applying for national board certification were less often reported. Data from other questions about the content of teachers' professional development show that popular topics in K–4 include deepening content knowledge, understanding student thinking, learning inquiry-oriented teaching methods, and assessing student learning; technology and special needs students were less frequent topics of study. Nevertheless, the share of teachers who reported that professional development focused on any of these topics "to a great extent" was quite small, ranging between 8 and

Figure 2. Percentage of Teachers Who Received Mathematics Professional Development in Selected Formats in the Past Three Years

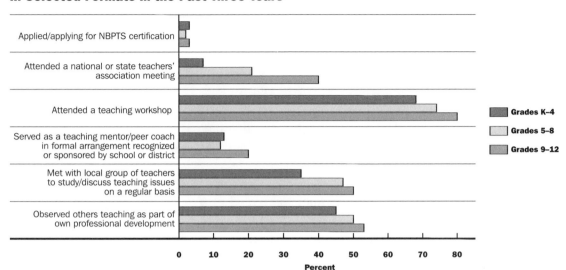

Source: Horizon Research, *The 2000 National Survey of Science and Mathematics Education: Compendium of Tables* (Chapel Hill, N.C., 2002), p. 3.12.
NBPTS = National Board of Professional Teaching Standards.

11 percent for the most popular activities. By contrast, between 35 and 50 percent of teachers reported that last year's professional development did not focus at all or focused only slightly on any of these topics.

Results from these surveys suggest that although subject-matter-specific professional development is perhaps more prevalent today than in the past, efforts to reform teachers' in-service learning opportunities have been only partially successful. Further, the short duration of most teachers' professional development opportunities suggests that their experiences may be superficial or fragmented. The much-derided "generic" professional development workshop may be disappearing; what has replaced it is less clear.

Moreover, while national surveys can measure the *content* of professional development, they cannot assess its *quality*. Even profes-

sional development that meets standards for best practices, that lasts several days or longer, and that focuses squarely on subject-matter content, teaching, and learning can falter if content is presented inaccurately or if information about student learning is flawed or superficial.[21] Few studies, however, have examined the quality of professional development available to teachers who have not been fortunate enough to find respected providers or exemplary programs. Those studies that do are not encouraging. One reported that even an innovative and highly respected professional development program in mathematics had little intensive focus on mathematical ideas and content.[22] Another found that during the late 1990s most mathematics professional development treated elementary school mathematics superficially, offering fragmented explanations and disconnected activities to cover important topics.[23] In some cases, the math was barely evident amidst the "hands-on" activities done by teachers.

There is a clear need for more study in this area. Little is understood, for instance, about the overall preparation and knowledge of the people delivering professional development; about how content and quality vary from place to place; and about how well opportunities for professional development align with curriculum, assessments, and standards in the typical school district. These issues will become even more pressing as professional development services become available on a wider scale through the Internet and standardized curricula for teachers, a major trend that I discuss below.

Can Professional Development Improve Teaching and Learning?

Professional development can, unequivocally, enhance teaching and learning. Many carefully designed studies over the past twenty-five years have shown that teacher learning can lead to improved student outcomes. Several representative studies offer insights about what the research, as a whole, indicates about effective professional development.

Tom Good, Douglas Grouws, and Howard Ebmeier were among the first to study how teachers' professional development relates to student achievement.[24] As reported in 1983, the authors designed an intervention aimed at fostering "active mathematics teaching," including daily review, extended development of new mathematical content, and student practice with new content. They assigned teachers randomly to either a treatment or a control group. Teachers in the treatment group were given a detailed teaching manual and introduced to the program during two ninety-minute workshops. After two months, students of treatment teachers had gained a full standard deviation more than the students of control teachers on tests given before and after the intervention. This

early experimental study suggests that professional development, in combination with a highly structured classroom intervention, can improve student achievement.

One of the best-designed and most widely cited studies focused on improving teachers' knowledge of children's problem-solving skills in addition and subtraction. As reported by Thomas Carpenter and colleagues in 1989, forty teachers were randomly assigned either to a month-long workshop on Cognitively Guided Instruction (CGI) or to four hours of more typical professional development.[25] In CGI, teachers studied research on children's thinking, discussed principles of instruction that might be derived from the research, and designed their own programs of instruction based on this research. The control group solved mathematics problems "of a more esoteric nature."[26] Students whose teachers attended CGI surpassed students in control classrooms in problem-solving skills; the two groups were roughly equivalent in solving simple addition and subtraction word problems. Classroom observations revealed that CGI teachers spent significantly more time on word problems than did control teachers and less time on number facts problems. CGI teachers also listened more frequently to students describing how they solved problems and were more supportive of students' use of different solution strategies.

More recently, in 2001, Geoffrey Saxe, Maryl Gearhardt, and Na'ilah Suad Nasir reported on a study examining how professional development focusing on fractions influenced teacher and student learning.[27] Teachers using new curriculum materials were randomly assigned to one of two groups. The first was an intensive program designed to build teachers' mathematical knowledge, to familiarize them with children's mathematical thinking about fractions, and to introduce new instructional methods. The other was a support group for using the new materials; it did not study content or student learning but instead met periodically to discuss "particular practices: instructional methods appropriate for specific lessons; the role of manipulatives; assessment methods . . . ; and homework." Researchers who administered before and after tests on fractions to the students of these two groups of teachers found that students of teachers in the intensive group gained over a standard deviation more than students of teachers in the support group. Despite a small sample size, this effect was highly statistically significant (that is, the data are sufficient to ensure the result did not occur by chance).

Also in 2001 Deborah McCutchen and several colleagues analyzed a similar professional development program in early reading.[28] They assigned teachers either to a comparison group or to a two-week instructional institute focused on letter-sound relationships (phonology), student learning of letter-sound relationships (phonological awareness), and explicit instruction in both phonology and comprehension. Teachers in the treatment group deepened their knowledge of phonology as assessed on a pencil-and-paper test and engaged in more classroom activities directed toward phonological awareness (in kindergarten) and featuring explicit comprehension instruction (in first grade). Students whose teachers implemented the practices advocated by the professional development learned more than students of those who did not. Further, differences between the treatment and comparison groups emerged in first grade, with students taught by treatment group teachers performing significantly better on tests of phonological awareness, reading comprehension, vocabulary, and spelling.

A different kind of teacher development program is available through the National Board of Professional Teaching Standards (NBPTS). The NBPTS offers experienced teachers an opportunity to apply for and receive additional certification, which is viewed by many as an indicator of excellence in teaching and which in some districts and states leads to a salary increase commensurate with that of re-

Students whose teachers implemented the practices advocated by the professional development learned more than students of those who did not.

ceiving a master's degree. Notably, many national board–certified teachers report that the process of becoming certified, which includes developing and submitting a portfolio recording their teaching practice, is a substantial professional learning opportunity in itself (see box 2). Peer-reviewed journal articles on the effects of NBPTS certification on teacher learning and student achievement are scarce. A variety of reports and unpublished research have offered mixed findings, although the most carefully crafted study, by Dan Goldhaber and Emily Anthony, finds a small positive effect of NBPTS certification.[29] Yet it might be that any positive effect resulted not from teacher learning during the certification process, but because more effective teachers tend to apply for and succeed in the certificate program.

Although the content of effective professional development has varied over time and

Box 2. The National Board for Professional Teaching Standards

The National Board for Professional Teaching Standards (NBPTS) offers certification to educators. Candidates are evaluated on their performance on assessment center exercises—open-ended problems featuring common teaching dilemmas—and four portfolio entries. Teachers who gain NBPTS certification are rewarded with higher salaries in some districts and states. Below, an NBPTS-certified teacher discusses his experience.

I wanted at the end of my career to be able to say that I knew something about teaching elementary school, beyond just saying I'd taught for twenty years. The NBPTS had articulated some core ideas about teaching and learning that aligned well with what I care about. If I were going to be measured by something, that seemed like a pretty good set of standards.

When I completed the process, in 1997, there were six components to the portfolio. Each asks you to document some aspect of your teaching—for instance, how you use writing to advance content knowledge in another discipline, how you integrate science and social studies, and how you establish a classroom community. The methods of documentation included student work, lesson plans, and videotape of my actual teaching.

I worked with another teacher also going through NBPTS certification, which was a big help. Over the course of the year we worked, she and I would visit the other's classrooms, look through the other's materials, and read the other's narratives. My principal and another teacher also read sections of my application. Getting other people's feedback on my teaching, or having them look at my teaching and notice certain things, was pivotal for my learning.

The certification process also helped me learn that instruction is purposeful and targeted at student learning. The portfolio was tightly constructed around key questions: What are your purposes in teaching? How does your instruction help you achieve those purposes? And what did students learn?

The most powerful part of this experience was that it was embedded in work I was supposed to do anyway, like analyzing my students' work and planning instruction. It had a real impact on my day-to-day teaching with my kids. Professional learning grounded in my own practice through careful documentation of that practice, and interaction with others about that practice, was very rich and satisfying. So much so that my school developed a professional development group that used this same set of ideas. We worked together for another five years. We wanted to keep learning.

---

across disciplines, some general principles can be gleaned from these and other studies.[30] First, increasing the time invested pays off in terms of effects on teaching and learning. The studies discussed above typically engaged teachers in all-day summer institutes for between two and four weeks. Research does not indicate precisely how much time is sufficient, but one-day workshops, in most cases, are unhelpful. The exception is the Good, Grouws, and Ebmeier study, which paired a short workshop with a highly structured instructional intervention.

Second, content matters. Content that focuses on subject-matter-specific instruction and student learning—and in the case of mathematics and early word reading, helping teachers learn the content itself—affects student achievement. In other words, teachers' learning opportunities should be grounded in the work they do in classrooms. When teachers study the content, curriculum materials, assessments, and instructional methods they will be using, student achievement improves. Using "classroom artifacts," such as student work or assessment results, is also a common feature of effective professional development. By contrast, several studies have suggested that professional development focused on more generic topics neither changes teaching nor improves student learning.

Third, teachers' professional development should be aligned with and support the instructional goals, school improvement efforts, and curriculum materials in teachers' schools. Learning about phonology, for instance, does little for teachers in schools where direct phonics instruction is not supported. And learning new ways to teach scientific inquiry does little for teachers who have no curriculum or lab materials to support such inquiry in class. Conversely, teachers will make better use of materials, assessments, and other classroom resources if their professional development is tied closely to those resources. At present, however, teachers are skeptical about the links between their professional development and school programs; only 18 percent report that their professional development is linked to a great extent to "other program improvement activities" at their school. Although another 38 percent report moderate links, 44 percent report few or no links between their professional development and school programs.[31]

Finally, there is a strong sense in the professional development scholarly community that collective participation of entire schools and "active" learning, such as reviewing student work, giving presentations, and planning lessons, lead to improved teaching and student outcomes. No rigorous studies, however, have investigated the effects of these aspects of professional development.

Does the Professional Development System Improve Teaching and Learning?

Despite positive news about the effects of specific professional development experiences, there is little evidence that the *system* of professional development, taken as a whole, improves teaching and learning in the United States. In fact, professional development is still widely believed, despite years of efforts at improvement, to be of marginal use. Even teachers are unenthusiastic about the quality of their own professional development; in Horizon's study, only one-fifth of science teachers and one-quarter of mathematics teachers reported that their professional development changed their teaching practices (figure 3). Very large shares reported that it only confirmed their existing practices. And self-reports are famously inflated.

One likely reason why professional development does not affect school outcomes is that only a tiny fraction of nationwide offerings are high-quality programs.[32] Although similar, locally grown programs likely exist, surveys by Michael Garet and others and by David Cohen and me suggest that quality programs reach relatively few teachers.[33]

Increasingly, however, nonprofits and commercial ventures have begun to publish or provide professional development materials that are intended for wide use. In mathematics, for instance, Developing Mathematical Ideas (DMI), a program from the Educational Development Center in Massachusetts, offers training and manuals for staff developers interested in using case-based professional

Figure 3. Percentage of Teachers Reporting That a Science Professional Development Topic "Caused Me to Change My Teaching Practices"

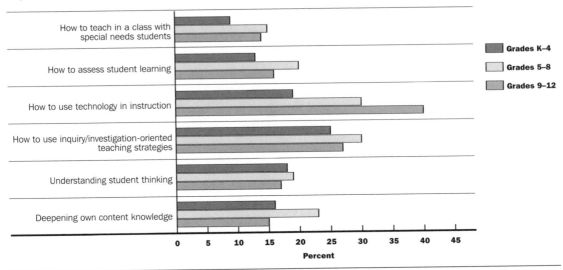

Source: Horizon Research, *The 2000 National Survey of Science and Mathematics Education: Compendium of Tables* (Chapel Hill, N.C., 2002), p. 2.16.

development. Cognitively Guided Instruction, discussed above, does much the same. Math Solutions, a two-decade-old firm in California, provides professional development widely through a combination of national and local staff (see box 3). Open Court, a curriculum materials publisher, offers summer institutes and video-based and online professional development in conjunction with its reading program. LessonLab offers teachers a combination of online and in-person study of mathematics and reading. Whether these efforts will improve teaching and learning on a large scale remains to be seen.

Another reason why there is little evidence that the system taken as a whole improves teaching and student learning is the sheer paucity of data about outcomes. Almost no local professional development—and even most efforts offered by respected university faculty, nonprofit, and commercial professional developers—is rigorously evaluated, in the sense of researchers looking for changes in teacher knowledge and instructional practice. Even more seldom do researchers investigate the effect on student learning. More often, evaluations simply ask participants to report whether and how the program affected their own teaching. One reason for the absence of rigorous evaluation is the complexity of mounting such a study: measuring teacher knowledge, skills, and practice is difficult; and measuring student achievement, even more so. Another reason, though speculative, is the lack of capacity in the local evaluation corps; anecdotal evidence suggests that most independent evaluators lack the research design or statistical skills necessary to conduct rigorous evaluations.

Lacking results from rigorous evaluations, teachers, district officials, and others are left without information as to which professional development opportunities enhance teacher performance and student learning. As any economist will quickly point out, consumer choice in an information-poor market does not generally lead to efficient outcomes; low-quality goods will persist, while high-quality

Box 3. Extended Professional Development in Mathematics
One increasingly common format for professional development is a summer institute followed by school-level collaboration and mentoring during the school year. One teacher reflects on her experiences with such a program, Math Solutions.

The two-week summer session was intense. There were long days, and then we had to go home and do mathematics homework. The math problems were very challenging and also very interesting. A friend of mine with a mathematics Ph.D. would often do the homework with me and comment on how interesting school mathematics could be.

Our whole school had a two-year contract to work with Math Solutions, which is very unusual in professional development. During the school year, Math Solutions program staff taught in my classroom. That by itself was an incredible help—even just watching them teach a single lesson with my students. Watching the questioning styles they used gave me a whole new toolkit. I had already been using novel math problems with my students, but this helped me to get those students to explain their answers more clearly, and to be less timid about rigorous mathematical work. I also came to understand how you can present algebraic ideas to second graders.

One benefit of the Math Solutions approach was that everyone in our school was in it together. It became a very collaborative effort—my grade-level team continued to work together on curriculum even after the formal professional development was over.

---

goods will go unnoticed. A district official, for instance, who wanted to compare the outcomes from professional development in mathematics offered by CGI, DMI, Math Solutions, and LessonLab could not do so, even though these are among the most widely used programs in the country. Even if all four programs had undergone rigorous before-and-after evaluations, there is no guarantee that the outcome measures would be similar, or even remotely comparable. Teachers and district officials thus lack the necessary resources to choose effective professional development.

A third reason for the lack of effects relates to the incentives in the system. Although teachers might be required to engage in professional development, they are not required to learn from it. For their part, providers' incentives are to sell more professional development—which means supplying programs that

teachers enjoy, not programs from which they can learn.

A fourth reason for the lack of effect of professional development, as a whole, on teaching and learning is the incoherence of the system itself. One finding from research on professional development is that teachers learn more, or at least report learning more, when their opportunities to learn are aligned with the curriculum materials, assessments, and standards they are asked to use every day in their classrooms.[34] Although there is reason to believe that this coherence is growing—several publishers now offer substantive professional development that aligns with their curriculum materials, for instance—it is still relatively rare. More often, teachers might choose professional development from a list of available options, regardless of the materials and assessments used in their district.

Despite these shortcomings, professional development that is aligned with policy, instruction, and assessment is often cited as a key component of reform efforts at the school and district levels. For instance, throughout the 1990s New York City's District 2 maintained a comprehensive effort to improve instruction in specific content areas and used professional development as a chief instrument toward that end.[35] The district used a variety of professional development providers and a range of formats, from formal workshops to extended mentoring and peer networks. It even allowed control over the process at the school level. But the professional development system was anchored in a shared vision of instructional improvement, was pervasive, and was, in literacy, focused on a specific instructional approach.[36] More generally, because teacher professional development is often embedded in wider reform efforts, such as new policies, forms of assessment, and curriculum materials, it is difficult to separate out the effect of the professional development itself. Further, few high-quality studies of broadly implemented professional development exist. As the field moves toward more centralized provision of professional development services, there is a critical need for such study.

Conclusion

Fostering continuing teacher education is a significant undertaking, and constitutes a significant expenditure, in the U.S. educational system. Nearly every teacher participates in some form of continuing education every year. Graduate degrees bump salaries 11–17 percent for the nearly half of teachers who hold them. Cost estimates for professional development range between 1 and 6 percent of district expenditures, with many hovering in the 3 percent range.[37] The bulk of the cost lies in teacher release time and in planning time for those providers who work within

school districts.[38] The vast majority of dollars and time, however, appears misspent.

Given this reality, the challenge is to design a system of continuing education that enhances teachers' ability to improve their own effectiveness and their students' achievement. The rudiments are in place, in that programs do exist that improve both. The challenge for policymakers is to motivate changes in the system of continuing education, and in particular to provide incentives for both higher-quality fare and more focused and deliberate teacher participation.

At the moment, there are many ideas, but there is little evidence, about how to proceed. Certainly, school districts should stop offering financial incentives for teachers to complete nonrelevant graduate degrees and start rewarding degrees that are more tightly aligned with teachers' primary teaching assignments. Districts should also select professional development programs and approaches based on evidence of their effectiveness. Programs lacking such evidence can be evaluated using teacher- and student-level outcome measures: change in teacher performance on pencil-and-paper assessments and classroom observation rubrics and change in basic measures of student achievement.[39] And central planners must ensure that items on the menu of offerings closely align with district standards, curriculum materials, and assessments. Whether choices about teacher learning are made at the teacher, school, or district level and regardless of who controls these choices, alignment must be tight. Finally, as more data from state, district, and formative assessments become available, continuing education can be crafted to fill gaps in teachers' knowledge and skills that can lead to poor student performance.

Notes

1. Lori Cavell and others, *Key State Education Policies on PK–12 Education: 2004* (Washington: Council of Chief State School Officers, 2004).

2. National Center for Education Statistics, *Teacher Preparation and Professional Development: 2000,* NCES 2001-088 (U.S. Department of Education, 2001).

3. National Center for Education Statistics, *Teacher Quality: A Report on the Preparation and Qualifications of Public School Teachers,* NCES 1999-080 (U.S. Department of Education/OERI, 1999).

4. Horizon Research, *The 2000 National Survey of Science and Mathematics Education: Compendium of Tables* (Chapel Hill, N.C., 2002).

5. Dan D. Goldhaber and Dominic J. Brewer, "When Should We Reward Degrees for Teachers?" *Phi Delta Kappan* 80 (1998): 134–38.

6. Karen Zumwalt and Elizabeth Craig, "Teachers Characteristics: Research on the Indicators of Quality," in *Studying Teacher Education: The Report of the AERA Panel on Research and Teacher Education*, edited by Marilyn Cochran-Smith and Kenneth Zeichner (Mahwah, N.J.: Lawrence Erlbaum Associates, 2005).

7. Peggy J. Blackwell and Mary Diez, "Toward a New Vision of Master's Education for Teachers" (Washington: National Council for Accreditation of Teacher Education, 1998); Alan R. Tom, "Reinventing Master's Degree Study for Experienced Teachers," *Journal of Teacher Education* 50, no. 4 (1999): 245–53.

8. Blackwell and Diez, "Toward a New Vision" (see note 7), p. 10.

9. Ibid., p. 6.

10. Rob Greenwald, Larry V. Hedges, and Richard Laine, "The Effect of School Resources on Student Achievement," *Review of Educational Research* 6 (1996): 361–96.

11. Andrew J. Wayne and Peter Youngs, "Teacher Characteristics and Student Achievement Gains: A Review," *Review of Educational Research* 73 (2003): 89–122.

12. Dan D. Goldhaber and Dominic J. Brewer, "Does Teacher Certification Matter? High School Certification Status and Student Achievement," *Educational Evaluation and Policy Analysis* 22 (2000): 129–46; Brian Rowan, Richard Correnti, and Robert J. Miller, "What Large-Scale Survey Research Tells Us about Teacher Effects on Student Achievement: Insights from the *Prospects* Study of Elementary Schools," *Teachers College Record* 104 (2002): 1525–67.

13. National Association of State Directors of Teacher Education and Certification, *Knowledgebase Table E1: Professional Development Description* (Whitinsville, Mass., 2004).

14. NCES, *Teacher Quality* (see note 3), p. 11.

15. National Center for Education Statistics, *Characteristics of Public School Teachers' Professional Development Activities: 1999–2000,* NCES 2005-030 (U.S. Department of Education, Institute of Educational Sciences, 2005). This statistic came from the School and Staffing Survey, which asks the duration of teacher participation "in any professional development activities specific to and concentrating on the content of the subject(s) you teach." Given this wording, it is difficult to know what was included (for example, graduate coursework) or excluded (for example, school-based teacher study groups).

16. David K. Cohen and Heather C. Hill, *Learning Policy: When State Education Reform Works* (Yale University Press, 2001); Michael S. Garet and others, "What Makes Professional Development Effective? Results from a National Sample of Teachers," *American Educational Research Journal* 38, no. 4 (2001): 915–45; Heather C. Hill and Deborah L. Ball, "Learning Mathematics for Teaching: Results from California's Mathematics Professional Development Institutes," *Journal of Research in Mathematics Education* 35 (2004): 330–51.

17. Results from our attempt to locate and survey midwestern providers of professional development in mathematics afford one window into how the system works. Our goal was to locate the *average* professional development provider working in local school districts. Using three midwestern states as our sampling frame, we called all districts located in cities with populations of 20,000 or more and asked them to name the individual(s) providing mathematics professional development to teachers. Of roughly fifty professional development providers named by school district staff, only four resided outside the state in which they provided their service. Only four of twenty-six respondents to our actual survey reported that offering professional development was a full-time job; other respondents were curriculum coordinators, teachers, and consultants.

18. The comments in this and other boxes in this article come from interviews by the author with individuals who wish to be anonymous.

19. NCES, *Characteristics of Public School Teachers' Professional Development Activities* (see note 15).

20. Horizon Research, *The 2000 National Survey* (see note 4).

21. National Staff Development Council, *NSDC Standards for Staff Development*, www.nsdc.org/standards/index.cfm (August 2006).

22. Suzanne M. Wilson, Sarah Theule-Lubienksi, and Steven Mattson, "Where's the Mathematics? The Competing Commitments of Professional Development," paper presented at the annual meeting of the American Educational Research Association, New York, April 1996.

23. Heather C. Hill, "Professional Development Standards and Practices in Elementary School Mathematics," *Elementary School Journal* 104 (2004): 215–31.

24. Tom Good, Douglas Grouws, and Howard Ebmeier, *Active Mathematics Teaching* (New York: Longman, 1983).

25. Thomas P. Carpenter and others, "Using Knowledge of Children's Mathematics Thinking in Classroom Teaching: An Experimental Study," *American Educational Research Journal* 26 (1989): 499–531.

26. Ibid., p. 507.

27. Geoffrey Saxe, Maryl Gearhardt, and Na'ilah Suad Nasir, "Enhancing Students' Understanding of Mathematics: A Study of Three Contrasting Approaches to Professional Support," *Journal of Mathematics Teacher Education* 4 (2001): 55–79.

28. Deborah McCutchen and others, "Beginning Literacy: Links among Teacher Knowledge, Teacher Practice, and Student Learning," *Journal of Learning Disabilities* 35, no. 1 (2001): 69–86.

29. For studies that find a positive effect of NBPTS certification, see Dan Goldhaber and Emily Anthony, "Can Teacher Quality Be Effectively Assessed? National Board Certification as a Signal of Effective Teaching" (Washington: Urban Institute, April 2005). For studies that find small or no effect on student achievement,

see Charles Clotfelter, Helen F. Ladd, and Jacob Vigdor, "Teacher Quality and Minority Achievement Gaps" (Durham, N.C.: Terry Sanford Institute of Public Policy, October, 2004); and William J. Sanders, James J. Ashton, and Paul S. Wright, "Comparison of the Effects of NBPTS-Certified Teachers with Other Teachers on the Rate of Student Academic Progress" (SAS Institute, March 2005).

30. See also Garet and others, "What Makes Professional Development Effective?" (see note 16); Cohen and Hill, "Learning Policy" (see note 16); Paul Cobb and others, "Assessment of a Problem-Centered Second-Grade Mathematics Project," *Journal for Research in Mathematics Education* 22 (1991): 13–29.

31. NCES, *Teacher Preparation* (see note 2), p. 19.

32. For an elaboration of this argument, see Cohen and Hill, "Learning Policy" (see note 16).

33. Garet and others, "What Makes Professional Development Effective?" (see note 16); Cohen and Hill, *Learning Policy* (see note 16).

34. Garet and others, "What Makes Professional Development Effective?" (see note 16); Cohen and Hill, *Learning Policy* (see note 16).

35. Richard F. Elmore and Deanna Burney, "Investing in Teacher Learning: Staff Development and Instructional Improvement in Community School District #2, New York City" (New York: National Commission on Teaching and America's Future, 1997).

36. Mary Kay Stein and Laura D'Amico. "Inquiry at the Crossroads of Policy and Learning: A Study of a District-Wide Literacy Initiative," *Teachers College Record* 104 (2002): 1313–44.

37. Linda Hertert, *Investing in Teacher Professional Development: A Look at 16 Districts* (Denver, Colo.: Education Commission of the States, 1997); Kieran M. Killeen, David H. Monk, and Margaret L. Plecki, "School District Spending on Professional Development: Insights from Available Data (1992–1998)," *Journal of Education Finance* 28 (2002): 25–50; Judith W. Little, "District Policy Choices and Teachers' Professional Development Opportunities," *Educational Evaluation and Policy Analysis* 11, no. 2 (1989): 165–79; Allan Odden and others, "A Cost Framework for Professional Development," *Journal of Education Finance* 28 (2002): 51–74; Karen Hawley Miles, "Rethinking District Professional Development Spending to Support School Improvement: Lessons from Comparative Spending Analysis," in *School Finance and Teacher Quality: Exploring the Connections*, edited by Margaret L. Plecki and David H. Monk (Larchmont, N.Y.: Eye on Education, 2003).

38. Little, "District Policy Choices" (see note 37).

39. A number of instruments can be used to evaluate teacher learning from professional development. In reading, see McCutchen and others, "Beginning Literacy" (see note 28); Geoffrey Phelps and Stephen G. Schilling, "Developing Measures of Content Knowledge for Teaching Reading," *Elementary School Journal* 105 (2004): 31–48. In science, see "Assessing Teacher Learning about Science Teaching," www.horizon-research.com/atlast/; and also other instruments at www.horizon-research.com/instruments/. In mathematics, see "Learning Mathematics for Teaching," www.sitemaker.umich.edu/lmt; "Knowledge for Algebra Teaching," www.msu.edu/~kat/; and also Heather C. Hill and others, "Assessing Teachers' Mathematical Knowledge: What Knowledge Matters and What Evidence Counts?" in *Handbook for Research on Mathematics Education*, 2nd ed., edited by Frank Lester (Charlotte, N.C.: Information Age Publishing, forthcoming).

The Challenges of Staffing Urban Schools with Effective Teachers

Brian A. Jacob

Summary

Brian Jacob examines challenges faced by urban districts in staffing their schools with effective teachers. He emphasizes that the problem is far from uniform. Teacher shortages are more severe in certain subjects and grades than others, and differ dramatically from one school to another. The Chicago public schools, for example, regularly receive roughly ten applicants for each teaching position. But many applicants are interested in specific schools, and district officials struggle to find candidates for highly impoverished schools.

Urban districts' difficulty in attracting and hiring teachers, says Jacob, means that urban teachers are less highly qualified than their suburban counterparts with respect to characteristics such as experience, educational background, and teaching certification. But they may not thus be less effective teachers. Jacob cites recent studies that have found that many teacher characteristics bear surprisingly little relationship to student outcomes. Policies to enhance teacher quality must thus be evaluated in terms of their effect on student achievement, not in terms of conventional teacher characteristics.

Jacob then discusses how supply and demand contribute to urban teacher shortages. Supply factors involve wages, working conditions, and geographic proximity between teacher candidates and schools. Urban districts have tried various strategies to increase the supply of teacher candidates (including salary increases and targeted bonuses) and to improve retention rates (including mentoring programs). But there is little rigorous research evidence on the effectiveness of these strategies.

Demand also has a role in urban teacher shortages. Administrators in urban schools may not recognize or value high-quality teachers. Human resource departments restrict district officials from making job offers until late in the hiring season, after many candidates have accepted positions elsewhere. Jacob argues that urban districts must improve hiring practices and also reevaluate policies for teacher tenure so that ineffective teachers can be dismissed.

www.futureofchildren.org

Brian A. Jacob is assistant professor of public policy at the John F. Kennedy School of Government, Harvard University. The author is grateful for excellent research assistance provided by J. D. LaRock and for many helpful suggestions from Robin Jacob, Susanna Loeb, Jonah Rockoff, Cecilia Rouse, and other participants at the Future of Children conference.

Schools serving inner-city students face the challenge of preparing children from disadvantaged neighborhoods to be productive citizens. The task, always difficult, is more daunting today than ever. Although the United States has made important economic progress over the past half century, many of the nation's children remain impoverished. In 2004, according to the Census Bureau, 13 million American children under age eighteen lived in poverty—an overall child poverty rate of 17.8 percent. Perhaps more important, structural changes in the economy have dramatically raised expectations for public schools over the past several decades. Although it was once possible for adults to earn a productive living with only rudimentary academic skills, recent technological advances have made it increasingly difficult for those with anything less than a college degree to find a job that offers a living wage.[1] Today even manufacturing and other blue-collar jobs require knowledge of algebra, as well as sophisticated reading comprehension and problem-solving skills. In this new environment, schools are being asked to provide all students an education once enjoyed by only a select few.

Teachers play a critical role in schooling, particularly in inner-city school districts where children often have less support at home. But central-city districts often have difficulty finding qualified teachers. According to federal statistics in the Schools and Staffing Survey (SASS), 34.7 percent of central city schools had difficulty hiring a math teacher, compared with only 25.1 percent of suburban schools.[2]

In this article I examine the challenges that urban districts face in staffing their schools with effective teachers. First, I provide a detailed look at urban schools and school districts, highlighting some of the important ways in which urban districts differ from both wealthier suburban districts and high-poverty rural districts. Next, I describe the staffing difficulties encountered by urban schools, noting in particular that teachers in urban districts are less highly qualified than their suburban counterparts with respect to criteria such as experience, educational background, and teaching certification. I then review evidence on teacher effectiveness, exploring whether highly qualified teachers are the most effective at promoting student learning. After examining why it is hard for urban districts to staff their schools, I discuss policy options for raising the quality of the teacher workforce in urban areas and assess the evidence on each option.

A Portrait of Urban Districts and Schools

What is an urban school? For many Americans, the term *urban school* evokes an image of a dilapidated school building in a poor inner-city neighborhood populated with African American or Hispanic children. How accurate is that image? By definition, of course, urban schools are located in large central cities. But although these communities are often characterized by high rates of poverty, poverty itself is not unique to urban areas and can be found, in particular, in many schools in the nation's rural areas. In this section I highlight key features of urban schools and school districts that distinguish them from both rural and suburban districts. I then show how those features contribute to the staffing challenges faced by these districts.

The statistics shown in table 1 present a detailed portrait of urban schools and communities. Unless otherwise noted, the data are drawn from the Schools and Staffing Survey

Table 1. Students and Schools in Urban and Suburban Districts and in All Public Schools

Percent unless otherwise specified

Characteristic	All public schools	Central city	Suburban
Students			
Share African American	16.8	28.4	12.3
Share Hispanic	17.7	28.9	14.6
Share minority	39.7	64.0	31.8
Share receiving Title I services	27.5	40.4	19.7
Share participating in free or reduced-price lunch program	41.6	56.4	32.1
Share special education	12.8	12.9	12.6
Share limited English proficient	10.8	17.3	8.2
Share of 4th graders scoring proficient or advanced on NAEP math	32	27	36
Share of 4th graders scoring proficient or advanced on NAEP reading	30	22	33
Share of schools where > 90 percent of 12th graders graduated	73.0	55.0	73.2
Community			
Poverty rate	9.2	13.6	6.0
Employment rate	5.8	7.5	4.6
Violent crime rate per 100,000 inhabitants	466	506	377
Property crime rate per 100,000 inhabitants	3,517	3,697	4,110
School and district			
Number of students enrolled in public schools	47,315,700	13,972,000	24,915,800
Average number of students per school	537	636	589
Average number of students per district	. . .	9,980	3,664
Share of all children attending private schools	9.7	13.0	9.2
Average number of teachers not renewed or dismissed	3.1	12.4	3.0
Average share of teachers dismissed	. . .	1.4	1.2
School resources			
Per pupil expenditures, 2000–01 (dollars)	7,268	7,812	7,542
Average number of students per teacher	14.6	15.0	14.6
Average regular, full-time teacher salary (dollars)	44,400	45,400	46,100
Share of schools with temporary buildings	31.7	37.7	34.4
Share of schools that routinely used common areas for instructional purposes	19.2	21.3	19.0
Share of schools in which some teachers did not have their own classrooms because of lack of space	26.7	27.9	29.1
Share of schools with a library media center	93.7	92.9	94.1
Share of media libraries with computer access	92.7	92.3	94.5
Average number of workstations with Internet access in media libraries	13.1	13	14.2

Notes: Unless noted below, all statistics come from the 2003–04 Schools and Staffing Survey and were drawn from National Center for Education Statistics, "Characteristics of Schools, Districts, Teachers, Principals, and School Libraries in the United States, 2003–04, Schools and Staffing Survey," Report 2006-313 (U.S. Department of Education, 2006). The data in column 1 include all public schools; columns 2 and 3 refer, respectively, to schools in central cities and schools on the urban fringes of central cities (including large towns). Blank cells indicate that the relevant statistic was not available.

Data from the National Assessment of Educational Progress (NAEP) are for 2003 and were obtained from the DataExplorer tool on the website of the National Center for Education Statistics, www.nces.ed.gov/nationsreportcard/nde/. Column 1 includes data for all public schools; columns 2 and 3 refer, respectively, to schools in central cities and schools in the urban fringe of central cities.

Crime rate data are for 2004 and were drawn from the Uniform Crime Reports produced by the Federal Bureau of Investigation, as contained in the table found at www.fbi.gov/ucr/cius_04/offenses_reported/offense_tabulations/table_02.html. The data in column 1 refer to the entire United States; columns 2 and 3 refer, respectively, to rates for metropolitan statistical areas (MSAs) and cities outside MSAs. Per pupil expenditure data come from the Condition of Education report published by the Department of Education, accessed at http://nces.ed.gov/programs/coe/2004/section4/table.asp?tableID=91 (August 22, 2006).

Poverty and employment rates come from the 2000 Census, accessed using the American FactFinder data tool on the U.S. Census Bureau website. The figures in column 1 refer to the entire United States; figures in columns 2 and 3 refer, respectively, to central city areas in MSAs and non-central-city areas in MSAs.

of 2003–04, a nationally representative survey administered by the Department of Education. The top panel confirms that urban districts do indeed have high shares of poor and minority students. Roughly 64 percent of students in central cities are minority, as against only 32 percent in areas on the urban fringe or large towns (hereafter I will refer to these areas as suburbs). Similarly, 56 percent of students in central cities participate in free

---

Urban and suburban schools also differ from each other in terms of the resources available to students and teachers, although the many compensatory state and federal programs reduce the size of the disparities.

---

lunch programs and 40 percent receive services under Title I of the Elementary and Secondary Education Act of 1965 (federal funds earmarked for poor children), compared with 32 and 20 percent, respectively, in suburbs. On average, urban students score lower on standardized achievement exams than their suburban counterparts. For example, only 17 percent of fourth graders in central cities scored at the proficient level on the National Assessment of Educational Progress (NAEP) math exam, compared with 27 percent in suburban schools.

Poverty, as noted, is a feature of rural districts as well as urban districts. So is low student achievement. And urban schools resemble rural schools—and differ from suburban

schools—in two other respects. First, like some of the nation's rural schools (see the article by David Monk in this volume), urban schools educate many of the nation's immigrant children, for whom English is a second language. The share of students classified as limited English proficient is twice as high in central cities as it is in suburbs (17.3 versus 8.2 percent). Indeed, many large U.S. cities educate children from dozens (or even hundreds) of different nations. In New York City schools, for example, students speak more than 120 languages.[3] This rich array of languages makes it harder for schools to communicate with parents and also limits districts' ability to offer any home language instruction (whether full-blown bilingual education or simply periodic assistance in the home language) to many of their students. Again like students in rural schools in some areas of the nation, students in urban schools tend to have extremely high rates of mobility.[4] And when teachers are forced to adjust to accommodate an ever-changing set of students, this high mobility becomes disruptive not only for the "movers" but also for stable students.

The portrait of central cities drawn by the table is rather bleak: rates of unemployment, poverty, and crime are all high. The jobless rate in urban areas, for example, averaged 7.5 percent, as against 4.6 percent in the suburbs. And the rate of violent crime per 100,000 inhabitants was 506 in urban areas, compared with 377 in the suburbs (and only 202 in non-metropolitan counties). Beyond tangible measures of disadvantage such as poverty or crime, some researchers have also argued that many inner-city neighborhoods suffer from poor "social capital"—the informal connections between people that help a community monitor its children, provide positive role models, and give support to those in need.[5]

Urban and suburban schools also differ from each other in terms of the resources available to students and teachers, although the many compensatory state and federal programs reduce the size of the disparities. Indeed, per pupil expenditures were higher in cities than in the suburbs—$7,812 compared with $7,542, according to the 2004 SASS data. Such aggregate statistics, however, likely mask the extent of the disparities because they do not account for regional differences in the cost of living. They also fail to distinguish between the most and least under-resourced urban schools.

Many urban districts must contend with an eroding tax base, which makes them unusually dependent on state and federal funding. That reliance on outside actors further constrains urban districts. With the cost of living often higher in urban than in suburban and rural areas, urban school districts may have a harder time attracting workers, whether teachers or maintenance workers, than would private sector employers, who may be better able to adjust wages accordingly.

Differences in other "tangible" resources are small. For example, roughly 38 percent of urban schools were using temporary buildings, compared with 34 percent of suburban schools, and fewer teachers in urban schools reported that they did not have their own classrooms because of lack of space. More than 90 percent of schools in both types of districts reported having a library media center and computer workstations with Internet access.

Finally, urban districts are much larger than their suburban or rural counterparts. In some respects, that large size may be an advantage. For example, large urban districts might be able to negotiate better rates with suppliers

(of computers or telephones, for example) and can mount large-scale recruiting efforts that would be impossible for districts that hire only a handful of teachers each year. Districts like New York City and Chicago, for example, recruit not only nationwide but from foreign countries as well. But the large size of many urban districts may also entail disadvantages. Large districts are more likely to have complicated bureaucratic systems that prevent them from acting quickly and decisively. They also tend to face strong and well-organized teacher unions, which limit the authority of district leaders.

The size difference also affects competition between schools. The economist Caroline Hoxby has argued that competition between school districts (generally suburban districts) leads schools in these districts to become more efficient, since they must satisfy demanding parents or risk falling enrollments.[6] As Hoxby sees it, the key to such competition is that families in many suburban areas can easily move from one suburban district to another. Although other researchers have criticized Hoxby's analysis, it is certainly true that, at least in theory, there may be important benefits of competition between schools.[7] Hence, it is important to understand the type and extent of competition that urban districts face. Urban districts do not face serious competition from each other (though they do face competition from suburban districts).[8] But urban school districts face considerably more competition from private schools than do suburban or rural districts. Statistics from the SASS indicate that roughly 13 percent of children in central cities attend private schools, compared with only 9 percent in suburbs. Of course, one reason for that discrepancy may be that parents are dissatisfied with urban school education. But the high population density in cities makes private schools more cost-effective to operate, thus increasing the potential supply of private schools.

The Nature and Extent of Staffing Difficulties in Urban Schools

The problem that urban districts face in staffing their schools is often couched in terms of a teacher "shortage." But exactly what kind of shortage is it when virtually all classes eventually end up with some sort of teacher? It is helpful to consider the problem in terms an economist would use: a shortage occurs when demand exceeds supply. In the case of an urban school district, a teacher shortage means that the number of effective teachers the district wants to employ is greater than the number of effective teachers who are willing and able to work at a given salary. Districts respond to such shortages in a variety of ways: by hiring teachers with no certification or experience, by using long-term substitutes, or by increasing class sizes.

In practice, therefore, a teacher shortage in urban districts makes it hard to hire qualified teachers—so that the teachers who are hired are often less qualified than teachers in suburban districts. Table 2 presents some statistics from the 2004 SASS that illustrate the particular kind of hiring difficulties faced by urban districts. Roughly the same share of urban and suburban schools had at least one teaching vacancy, but urban schools were much more likely to have vacancies in critical areas such as math and science. Moreover, urban schools were substantially more likely to fill these vacancies by hiring a substitute (42.4 percent versus 30.0 percent) or hiring a less than fully qualified teacher (19.2 percent versus 14.4 percent).[9]

Teacher shortages in urban districts, however, are not uniform in nature and extent.

Table 2. Staffing Difficulties in Urban and Suburban Districts

Percent

Difficulty	Urban	Suburban
Share of schools with teacher vacancy in any area	75.4	76.9
Of schools with vacancy in given area, share with difficulty hiring		
General elementary	5.7	2.9
Special education	31.0	26.6
Math	34.7	25.1
Biology or life sciences	27.2	17.4
ESL	27.9	30.0
Of schools with vacancy, share that filled position in different ways		
Short- or long-term substitute	42.4	30.0
Less than fully qualified teacher	19.2	14.4

Source: NCES, "Characteristics of Schools, Districts, Teachers, Principals, and School Libraries in the United States, 2003–04, Schools and Staffing Survey," Report 2006-313 (U.S. Department of Education, 2006), table 16.

For example, shortages are greater in certain subjects and grades—most notably, secondary math and science and bilingual and special education at all levels. And the supply of teacher applicants in urban districts often differs dramatically from one school to another. The Chicago public schools, for example, regularly receive roughly ten applicants for each teaching position.[10] But many of these applicants are interested in particular, highly desirable schools, and district officials must struggle to find good candidates for some highly impoverished or dysfunctional schools. Similarly, in 2004–05 the New York City Teaching Fellows Program, an alternative certification program that places mid-career professionals into teaching jobs, received more than 17,500 applicants for 2,000 positions.[11] And a case study of four urban districts by the New Teacher Project found bureaucratic hurdles to be at least as significant as a shortage of people who show initial interest in working there.[12]

Given urban districts' difficulty in hiring, it is not surprising that urban teachers tend to be less experienced and to have fewer of certain conventional credentials than those in suburban districts. According to the SASS, 20.3 percent of teachers in urban districts had three or fewer years of experience, compared with 17.6 percent in suburban districts. Urban teachers also are less likely to stay at the same school for an extended period, with 52.4 percent (compared with 57.1 percent of suburban teachers) reporting having taught at the same school for four or more years. In addition, the 2003–04 SASS reports that urban teachers are slightly less likely than suburban teachers to have an MA degree (40.3 percent, compared with 42.9 percent).[13]

Indeed, many studies have found that teachers in schools serving poor and minority children in large cities are more likely to be inexperienced, less likely to be certified, and less likely to have graduated from competitive colleges than are suburban teachers. They also score lower on standardized exams and are more likely to be teaching subjects for which they are not certified.[14] A recent study of schools in New York State using exceptionally rich data concludes that teacher qualifications vary considerably across schools and are strongly correlated with student race and income.[15] For example, in some schools more than 30 percent of teachers failed the certification exam, while at other schools no teachers failed.[16] Some 21 percent of nonwhite students' teachers failed the certification exam compared with 7 percent of white students' teachers.

The authors found similar patterns even within New York City public schools. Teachers of poor and minority children were more likely to be less experienced, less likely to have graduated from competitive colleges,

and more likely to have failed the certification exam than teachers in other public schools in the same district. Researchers analyzing a detailed administrative data set of teachers in North Carolina came to similar conclusions. One report found that African American students are more likely to be taught by novice teachers.[17] Another found that even *within* schools, more highly qualified teachers (as measured by the competitiveness of their undergraduate institution, by advanced degrees, by experience, and by scores on the state licensure test) tend to teach more advantaged children.[18] Within the same school, for example, *prior* achievement test scores of students whose teacher scored in the bottom third on the state licensure exam were roughly 0.1 standard deviation lower than those of students whose teachers scored in the top third of the exam.

Another useful metric of quality, particularly for secondary schools, is the share of teachers who are teaching subjects for which they are not certified, a practice known as "out-of-field" teaching. According to data from the SASS, roughly one-third of all seventh- to twelfth-grade teachers had neither a major nor a minor in the field in which they taught.[19] Shares were considerably larger for math, life sciences, and physical sciences, where 36, 43, and 59 percent of teachers, respectively, were teaching out of field. Patterns were even more pronounced in high-poverty schools, where the share teaching out of field was 51 percent in math and 64 percent in physical sciences.

Recruitment or Retention?

Clearly teachers in urban schools are less qualified than those in more affluent areas, at least along many easily observable dimensions. But is the lower quality of urban teachers primarily a result of problems in recruitment or in retention? It could be that highly qualified teachers are equally likely to start out at urban and suburban schools, but that high-quality urban teachers are more likely to change schools or leave the profession.

In fact, problems in both recruitment and retention contribute to disparities in teacher characteristics. Recent studies of teachers in

---

It could be that highly qualified teachers are equally likely to start out at urban and suburban schools, but that high-quality urban teachers are more likely to change schools or leave the profession.

New York State found that first-year teachers in suburban and more advantaged urban schools were more highly qualified (that is, from more competitive colleges and less likely to fail the certification exam) than those in urban schools more generally. At the same time, attrition was considerably higher in schools and districts with higher rates of poverty and shares of minority students. In 2000, for example, teacher turnover was 15 percent in all public schools, compared with 22 percent in high-poverty urban schools.[20] Moreover, the teachers who tended to leave urban schools were more highly qualified than those who remained. A study of New York State teachers that tracked for five years the cohort who began teaching in 1993 found that teachers who transferred from one district to another and teachers who left the pro-

fession were less likely to have failed the certification exam and more likely to have graduated from a competitive college than those who remained in the same school.[21]

But a recent study of a large Texas district found that teachers who changed schools or left the district, or both, did *not* have lower measures of "value added" (improvements in student test scores attributable to a particular teacher) than those who remained in their school, although the departing teachers were less qualified on some other dimensions.[22] Although no single study should be considered definitive, this finding reinforces the need for caution in relying on teacher characteristics as a proxy for teacher effectiveness. While teachers who themselves have stronger academic backgrounds are more likely to leave the lowest-performing schools, it is not clear that these are actually the better teachers. It is possible to say definitively only that teacher attrition rates are higher in these schools.

Teacher attrition imposes costs not only on the students of the novice teacher who replaces the outgoing teacher but also on the school as a whole. For example, administrators and perhaps even other teachers must take time to orient and train new teachers, particularly if the school uses a particular curriculum. To the extent that principals adjust class sizes or the student composition of classes to provide new teachers with a somewhat easier load, other teachers in the school will necessarily shoulder a heavier burden. More generally, a staff with high turnover loses the institutional memory that could help it avoid "reinventing the wheel" or making costly mistakes.

Has NCLB Changed Anything?

The federal No Child Left Behind (NCLB) Act of 2001 established a series of accountability measures for schools. One, aimed at improving teacher quality nationwide, required each school district to certify, by the 2005–06 school year, that all core subject matter teachers are highly qualified—that is, that they hold a BA degree, are certified or licensed by the state, and demonstrate subject matter competence. Has NCLB influenced teacher quality in urban school districts?

Although the final verdict is not yet in, the preliminary answer appears to be no. To demonstrate subject matter competence, for example, the law requires new teachers to pass a set of exams. But it allows states to create other means by which experienced teachers can demonstrate competence. And according to some observers, states have used these alternative pathways, referred to as high objective uniform state standards of evaluation (HOUSSE), largely to circumvent the intent of the law.[23] In many states the HOUSSE system allows experienced teachers to become highly qualified by taking short professional development courses or participating in other activities of questionable value. In Florida, for instance, veteran teachers can meet HOUSSE content requirements and become "highly qualified" merely by receiving a satisfactory rating on their annual performance evaluation. Under New Hampshire's HOUSSE rules, teachers can substitute a "self-evaluation" process for the required objective assessment of subject knowledge to be deemed "highly qualified."[24]

At the same time, the teacher quality provisions in NCLB may have led to the introduction or expansion of alternative certification routes in some states. It is likely that the expansion of alternative certification opportunities has brought some highly effective teachers into urban districts, although it is difficult to quantify the benefits of such changes.[25]

Are More Qualified Teachers More Effective Teachers?

It is clear that teachers in urban schools, particularly urban schools serving poor and minority children, are less qualified than their suburban colleagues in terms of such conventional measures as experience and educational background. But are they are less effective teachers; that is, are they less able to promote the learning and development of their students? As discussed in the article by Richard Murnane and Jennifer Steele in this volume, a growing body of research is linking individual teachers to student achievement scores to provide a direct measure of teacher effectiveness. These studies attempt to control for student background characteristics (including past achievement scores), as well as classroom and school characteristics that likely influence a student's performance but should not be "counted" for or against the particular teacher. These "value-added" studies thus try to isolate the learning that a teacher adds to his or her students. Because the most rigorous and convincing such studies have been conducted in large districts such as Los Angeles, New York, and Chicago, the findings are particularly informative for policymakers and practitioners concerned with urban schools.

Two main research findings stand out. First, teacher effectiveness varies substantially as measured by a teacher's value added. Simply put, not all teachers are the same.[26] For example, recent estimates suggest that moving a student from an average teacher to one at the 85th percentile would raise that student's achievement test scores as much as reducing his class size by 33 percent.[27] The cumulative effect of teachers is even more striking. Researchers using Tennessee data, for example, find that a student who has three consecutive very high-quality teachers will gain 50 percentile points more on an achievement test than a student who has three consecutive average teachers.[28]

Second, many teacher characteristics bear surprisingly little relationship to student outcomes.[29] For example, according to a substantial body of research, certified teachers

---

According to a substantial body of research, certified teachers are not consistently more effective than uncertified teachers, older teachers are not more effective than younger teachers, and teachers with advanced degrees are not more effective than those without such degrees.

---

are not consistently more effective than uncertified teachers, older teachers are not more effective than younger teachers, and teachers with advanced degrees are not more effective than those without such degrees. Two recent studies of teacher certification in New York City find that teachers with no certification or with alternative certification are slightly less effective than traditionally certified teachers in their first year, but that they catch up with their peers within one to three years.[30]

Two teacher characteristics appear to be exceptions to the rule. The first is having one to three years of experience. Students of first-

or second-year teachers, for example, consistently do worse than those of more experienced teachers.[31] But beyond the first few years, experience does not appear to be particularly important. The second characteristic is high cognitive ability.[32] For example, some teachers who score higher on certification exams and some who attend more competitive undergraduate institutions produce larger performance gains for their children.[33] The body of research that examines this issue is limited, so this finding should only be considered suggestive.[34]

Another finding of particular importance for urban districts involves the interaction between teacher and student race. Teachers appear to be more effective with students of their own race or ethnicity.[35] Exactly why this is so is unclear, but observers suggest that both passive teacher effects, such as the teacher's simply serving as a role model, and active teacher effects, such as communication styles, pedagogy, and curriculum design, may play a role.

A recent study examined this issue using data from the Tennessee class-size reduction experiment, which randomly assigned teachers and students to classrooms. (The random assignment eliminates the possibility that teachers and students are assigned in ways that would confound analysis—for example, if more motivated and supportive black parents sought out black teachers for their children or if an older white teacher were assigned to teach a higher-performing class with many white children because of a seniority transfer.) In this setting, an additional year with a teacher of the same race increased student performance by 2–4 percentile points.[36] Another recent study of teacher effectiveness in a large urban Texas district finds that black students gain roughly 0.1 standard deviation more when they have a black teacher than when they have a white teacher.[37]

However compelling these studies seem, they should not be considered definitive. Perhaps most important, insofar as teacher quality varies systematically with the student racial composition in the school, it is difficult to separate teacher quality from teacher race. Consider, for example, a scenario whereby the least competent white teachers end up in schools with a high share of black students because these schools are disproportionately poor, and the "best" white candidates are able to find jobs in more affluent schools. In this case, these studies may end up comparing the "average" black teacher with a set of "below-average" white teachers, leading one to overstate the benefit of having a same-race teacher.[38]

In fact, this situation illustrates a more general limitation of value-added measures. To control fully for unmeasured student characteristics that might influence teacher performance, value-added studies often compare teachers within the same school, thus limiting their ability to measure accurately the relative effectiveness of teachers in different schools. The difficulty is further increased in comparing teachers across districts.

What are the implications of value-added research for staffing urban schools? On one hand, the relative inexperience of urban teachers, as well as their often lower cognitive ability, suggests that they may be less effective at raising student achievement. (The benefits of experience found in research, however, are relatively small and exist only for teachers in their first few years.) On the other hand, urban teachers' relative lack of traditional certification probably does not make them less effective.

Hence, at the most general level, the value-added studies offer two insights. First, a qualified teacher is not necessarily an effective teacher. Second, policies to enhance teacher quality must be evaluated in terms of their effect on student achievement. Both insights have implications for designing and assessing strategies to enhance teacher quality in urban districts. For example, given the negative link between teacher race and certification test scores, schools that recruit teachers with higher certification scores might hire fewer African American and Hispanic teachers, which could be exactly the wrong policy if the evidence on same-race teachers holds true.

Why Is It Hard to Recruit and Retain Teachers in Urban Districts?

I draw once again on economics to provide a framework within which to consider the challenges of staffing urban schools. An urban district might experience a shortage of effective teachers for two reasons. One is supply; that is, schools are not able to attract enough high-quality teachers. The other is demand; that is, schools do not hire the right types of teachers. Several key supply and demand factors contribute to teacher shortages in urban districts.

Supply Factors

The most commonly discussed reasons for urban teacher shortages focus on supply—the number of teachers who are willing to work in an urban district at given salary levels at any given time. Not surprisingly, wages are important both in recruiting and in retaining qualified teachers. People are more likely to enter teaching when starting teacher salaries are high relative to salaries in other occupations. And they are more likely to leave teaching when outside wage options are higher.[39]

Working conditions appear to be even more important than wages, particularly for teachers in urban schools. Research in this area typically compares the salaries and student characteristics in the schools (or districts) that teachers leave with those in the schools (or districts) that teachers enter. A study of Texas, for example, found that mobility patterns among public school teachers were more strongly correlated with student characteristics than with salary levels.[40] Young teachers who switched districts gained only 0.4 percent in salary (about $100), but their new districts had student achievement levels roughly 0.07 standard deviations higher than those of the districts they left. And their new schools had substantially smaller shares of poor and minority children. Indeed, the study found that teachers prefer a school with higher achievement levels, above and beyond its racial composition. It also found that African American and Hispanic teachers are less sensitive to student racial composition than are white teachers. In fact, conditional on student achievement and poverty levels, black teachers were more likely to remain in their districts as the share of black children in their schools rose, whereas white teachers were significantly more likely to leave.[41]

A study of teachers in Georgia reached similar conclusions.[42] Elementary teachers left low-performing, high-minority schools, but black teachers responded less to the racial composition of the school than did white teachers. A recent study of New York City found that teachers with high scores on the state certification exam are much more likely to leave low-performing schools than their colleagues, even after controlling for factors such as student and teacher race.[43] This finding suggests that teacher and student ability—rather than race per se—may be responsible for the teacher mobility patterns observed in such studies.

Although these studies shed light on teacher mobility, they cannot distinguish between supply factors and demand factors, making it difficult to interpret some of the findings. For example, most teacher mobility studies cannot say whether black teachers are less likely to leave high-minority schools for reasons of supply—because they simply prefer to remain in these environments (perhaps because they are more effective than their white colleagues)—or for reasons of demand—because they do not have the other opportunities available to their white colleagues. Another limitation of these studies is that if they do not fully account for all the working conditions relevant to teachers, they may understate the importance of salary.[44]

A less commonly discussed reason for the limited supply of high-quality teachers in urban areas involves geography. Unlike many other professions, elementary and secondary education operates in a predominantly local labor market. Researchers from Stanford and the State University of New York conducting extensive studies in New York State find that teachers prefer to teach close to where they grew up and in areas demographically similar to their hometown.[45] The high turnover in low-achieving urban schools, particularly among more highly qualified teachers, may thus in part reflect a preference for living close to home rather than a desire to avoid low-achieving or minority children. To the extent that teacher qualification and effectiveness are correlated, this phenomenon will contribute to a damaging cycle, whereby poorly educated graduates from disadvantaged districts return to teach in those same districts.

Demand Factors

A growing body of evidence suggests that demand is also at work in urban teacher shortages. Specifically, principals and administrators in high-poverty urban schools may not recognize or value high-quality teachers either in hiring or in retention decisions. A study based on national data from the early 1990s finds that teacher candidates from the most selective colleges and universities (candidates who research suggests may be effective teachers) are not as likely to be hired as those from less selective institutions, even after taking into account the number and type of schools to which the applicants applied.[46]

Why might this be the case? One explanation is that principals simply have different objectives or opinions about what constitutes a "high-quality" teacher. For example, principals may be looking for a teacher who can provide students with a good role model or enforce strict discipline rather than one who can best teach math or reading. Or principals may believe that college selectivity is not a good indicator of teacher performance. Another explanation is that principals cannot accurately assess teacher quality in the hiring process, either because they lack information or because it is simply difficult to judge future performance.

In fact, principals seem to have some difficulty identifying the relative effectiveness even of their own teachers—those with whom they interact and whom they observe—and not just those whom they see briefly in a job interview. Principals do seem to be able to identify the best and worst teachers in their schools—but not to distinguish between teachers in the middle of the ability distribution, roughly between the 20th and 80th percentiles.[47] The most common mistakes that principals tend to make are to

give too much weight to the teacher's most recent experience and not to account properly for the ability level of incoming students in the teacher's class.[48]

Finally, dysfunctional bureaucracy can contribute to teacher shortages in urban districts. A case study of four urban districts by the New Teacher Project, for example, found that these districts lost good candidates because of late hiring.[49] Among the causes for late hiring were policies that allowed exiting teachers to provide late notification to the district, policies that allowed experienced teachers to transfer between schools at the last minute, late state budget deadlines, and antiquated and dysfunctional human resource departments. Together, such bureaucratic problems kept these districts from making many offers until July or August, months after surrounding districts had made offers and long after many highly qualified candidates had accepted other jobs. Another study argues that high levels of out-of-field teaching in urban schools can be explained in large part by the inefficient assignment of teachers rather than actual shortages.[50]

How Can Urban School Districts Improve the Quality of Their Teachers?

Urban districts have tried various initiatives, ranging from recruitment to retention to professional development, to improve the quality of their workforce. Some programs take a free-market approach to encourage more teachers to enter the profession; others rely on more prescriptive regulations or guidelines. Many policies target specific types of teacher candidates (for example, those from elite colleges, or with particular language skills, subjects, or grade levels), while others are broad in scope. Despite the many reform initiatives, however, researchers have gathered little evidence on the effectiveness of these programs.

Supply-Oriented Strategies

Many of the most common strategies focus on increasing the supply of teacher candidates. Examples of such policies include salary increases, improved working conditions, and alternative paths into teaching and mentoring.

Higher Salaries. One way to improve teaching quality is to increase salaries—either by uniform increases for all teachers or by targeted salary increases or bonuses. Although higher salaries do boost retention rates, uniform salary increases seem unlikely to pass a cost-benefit test. The difficulty of recruiting and retaining teachers varies dramatically across schools, education levels, and subject areas. Even in highly disadvantaged urban districts, for example, some elementary schools have little trouble hiring for general teacher positions. Uniform salary increases will inevitably provide additional compensation to many teachers who would have taught in the same position anyway.

A potentially more cost-effective approach is to offer targeted bonuses or higher salaries to attract and retain teachers in hard-to-staff schools and subject areas. Indeed, many states and districts have experimented with such programs. In 1998, for example, Massachusetts combined a national recruitment campaign, $20,000 signing bonuses, and a seven-week "fast track" certification process to attract highly qualified new teachers to high-need districts. But the program had limited success in placing bonus recipients in high-need schools (many ended up teaching in affluent, high-achieving districts), and many of the bonus teachers left teaching within several years.[51] In 2001 North Car-

olina began giving $1,800 annual bonuses to teachers of math, science, and special education in middle and high schools serving low-income or low-performing students. Despite some confusion regarding eligibility requirements, researchers have found that the introduction of this bonus payment reduced turnover of the targeted teachers by roughly 12 percent, relative to what it would have been in the absence of the program. Interestingly, the policy seemed to have the strongest effect for experienced teachers.[52] Although the evidence to date is limited, state and district officials might consider a targeted salary enhancement program with clear eligibility rules and substantial dollar amounts.

Improved Working Conditions. A second way to enhance the quality of the workforce is to improve working conditions. But research offers little practical guidance here. Most studies focus on student characteristics such as race, ability, and behavior, all of which are hard to change. Generally, studies suggest that most teachers are attracted to high-functioning schools with competent administrators, dedicated colleagues, and reasonably well-behaved children, who are "teachable" even if they may come from poor families and have low skills. These are schools where teachers feel they can make a difference. But from a policy perspective, the problem is that such a school is exactly what most school reform efforts are trying to create. Thus trying to improve working conditions in isolation involves a Catch-22: to improve working conditions to attract effective teachers, it is necessary to reform the whole school, but whole school reform will not work without effective teachers.

Yet another way to attract and, especially, to retain teachers is to change the structure of the teaching career. Much has been written about career ladders, which would allow teachers to pursue in-depth professional development and take on responsibilities outside the classroom, such as mentoring other teachers or developing curriculum. Indeed, international comparisons show that teaching and learning is organized quite differently in other countries. In Japan, for example, teachers spend only half their time in the classroom and the other half on extensive professional development activities.[53] Although 20 percent of teachers leaving high-poverty urban schools report that more opportunities for advancement might induce them to stay,[54] there is little systematic evidence on whether such programs increase teacher retention.[55] Hence, the career ladder strategy may be worth pursuing more carefully, combining well-designed policy changes with rigorous evaluation studies.

Alternative Paths into Teaching. In recent years, debate has been brewing within the academic and policy communities over the relative effectiveness of regularly certified versus alternatively certified or uncertified teachers. This issue, unlike some others, has generated relatively good research evidence. The most rigorous and well-designed evaluations to date indicate that, at least for elementary school math and reading teachers, teachers with traditional certification and those with alternative certification differ little in average effectiveness. With the exception of Teach for America (TFA), where attrition rates are high, the attrition rates of the two groups do not seem to differ substantially, either. And in the case of TFA, taking attrition and effectiveness together over the long run, there is still little advantage to hiring a traditionally certified teacher over a TFA candidate, or vice versa.

This finding suggests that urban districts should not require all candidates to obtain traditional certification, but should rather encourage the development of a variety of high-quality alternatives. More generally, research underscores the importance of identifying and encouraging effective teachers regardless of their certification status. Individual districts generally have some flexibility when it comes to hiring alternatively certified teach-

> *In Japan, for example, teachers spend only half their time in the classroom and the other half on extensive professional development activities.*

ers, although teacher certification policy is most often decided by the state.

Specific Recruitment Strategies. Districts have pursued various strategies to recruit people, particularly minorities, into teaching. Some have created partnerships between K–12 school districts and local colleges to encourage students to enter teaching. Others have offered scholarships or loan forgiveness for candidates who commit to teaching for a certain period. The Urban Teacher Academy Project (UTAP) in the Broward County Public Schools in Florida combines a high school program with college scholarships and a guaranteed teaching job.[56] The high school program includes mentoring and training, field trips, teaching and tutoring at local elementary schools, and other special programs. But evidence on how well such programs work is virtually nonexistent. A recent review of the research by analysts at RAND and the Education Commission of the States (ECS) concludes that "there were simply no adequate studies available on the great majority of the specific recruitment strategies that have been employed by states and districts."[57]

Teacher Mentoring Programs. Many districts have tried to reduce attrition through induction and mentoring programs for new teach-

---

Hiring practices have received relatively little attention from educators and policymakers, even though their improvement may offer districts considerable opportunities to improve the workforce.

---

ers. Induction programs typically involve meetings, informal classes for new teachers, and peer-support groups. Mentoring programs generally pair novice teachers with experienced teachers, although the type and extent of interaction between the teachers vary considerably. Educators claim that such programs are critical for retaining high-quality teachers, and surveys find that a lack of support is a key reason why teachers change schools or leave the profession. A recent review found 150 published empirical studies of mentoring and induction programs, but only twelve included a comparison group and were judged minimally rigorous, and only three met the highest research standards.[58] Of these three, only one examined teacher or student outcomes. It found that 141 teachers in New Mexico who participated in a mentor-

ing program had only a 4 percent annual attrition rate compared with the statewide average of 9 percent.[59] Mathematica Policy Research is now rigorously evaluating two high-intensity, well-respected induction programs—one designed by the New Teacher Center at the University of California–Santa Cruz and the other developed by the Educational Testing Service. Both rely heavily on mentor teachers who receive extensive training and are released from teaching for an entire year. Each mentor works with twelve teachers on a wide range of issues important to new teachers.[60]

Demand-Oriented Strategies

Likewise, urban schools have also tried various strategies to affect demand for teachers.

Improve Hiring Practices. Hiring practices have received relatively little attention from educators and policymakers, even though their improvement may offer districts considerable opportunities to improve the workforce. As noted, Chicago's public schools get roughly twenty certified applicants for every general education elementary teaching position. There are three ways in which hiring practices might be improved to enhance the quality of the teacher workforce in urban districts.

First, urban districts could streamline the administrative procedures associated with hiring so that they can make job offers more quickly. Although the ability to make timely offers depends in part on collective bargaining agreements and state budgeting issues, districts could make considerable improvements through mundane bureaucratic reforms.

Second, districts could improve their ability to identify effective teachers from the pool of candidates. Many districts do not hire the best available candidates, and principals even have trouble differentiating between teachers with whom they have worked for years. All districts and principals now use some type of screening in hiring—most commonly, interviews by district staff and school personnel. Many districts also use personnel assessments to identify effective teachers. One of the most frequently used assessments, the Gallup Teacher Insight Assessment, consists of multiple-choice items and open response questions that assess each candidate's pedagogical knowledge and personality traits.[61] But how districts use these assessments or whether they can identify effective teachers is not clear. Better screening of applicants could help them improve their workforce considerably.

A third, related issue is whether teachers are hired by the district or by the school. In large districts, teachers have traditionally been hired by the central office and then placed into schools with little careful consideration. To the extent that schools have unique needs, principals have specific preferences, and teachers have unique strengths and weaknesses, a more decentralized process would likely result in better matches between teachers and schools. Indeed, many large urban districts have recently switched to decentralized hiring. Chicago, for example, hosts several job fairs each year, where teacher candidates can interview school representatives, who can then make independent decisions about whom they would like to hire. But although decentralized hiring could improve the match between teachers and schools, it might also lead to more inequities if more effective schools are better at identifying effective teachers or if these schools are more attractive to effective teachers.

Selectively Dismiss Ineffective Teachers. One option that has received little attention in discussions of teacher quality is to dismiss underperforming teachers. Although most educators would agree that grossly incompetent teachers should be removed from the classroom, dismissals are rare. In urban districts in 2003–04, the share of teachers dismissed or not renewed was 1.4 percent—a figure that likely overstates the share of teachers dismissed for cause, since poor performance is only one of many factors that can lead to nonrenewal. Indeed, according to an informal survey of the human resource departments in several large urban districts, less than 1 percent of the teaching force is dismissed each year, with slightly more tenured than untenured teachers dismissed.

What might explain the apparent reluctance of administrators to dismiss teachers? One often-cited explanation is administrative hurdles involving firing outlined in collective bargaining agreements, including a documentation and appeal process that principals describe as extremely burdensome. Although this explanation certainly holds true for tenured teachers, dismissing untenured teachers is considerably less difficult. Yet dismissals of probationary teachers are still rare. One reason might be that dismissing a teacher imposes considerable costs on a principal or school, or both. Administrators must take the time and energy to hire a replacement and integrate the new teacher into the school. And because new teachers are less effective, on average, than experienced teachers, replacing an older teacher with a novice, all else equal, is likely to worsen student performance in the short run.

Thus it will make sense for a principal to dismiss a teacher only if she is certain that the teacher is less effective than the replacement will be and if the benefits associated with the new "more effective" teacher outweigh the costs associated with firing and hiring. In theory, it is not clear how often these conditions will be met.

In an intriguing new study, several researchers have tried to estimate the costs and benefits of the teacher dismissal decision using data from New York City. They show

---

A teacher whose students make larger than average gains in her first two years is likely to produce larger than average student gains thereafter.

---

that data on student achievement gains during a teacher's first two years in the classroom make it possible to predict reasonably well how effective that teacher will be later. In other words, a teacher whose students make larger than average gains in her first two years is likely to produce larger than average student gains thereafter. Conversely, a teacher who performs poorly in the first two years is unlikely to undergo a radical transformation in year three. Moreover, the researchers find extremely large differences between teachers during their first years of teaching in terms of raising student performance. That is, not all teachers are the same— or close to the same—even as they begin teaching. Then the researchers calculate how much teachers improve on average in the first few years of teaching. As do other studies, they find that second- and third-year teachers are more effective than first-year

teachers, but the difference is relatively modest. Putting all these pieces together, the authors are able to estimate the relative benefit of dismissing an ineffective (that is, below-average) untenured teacher, assuming that one would be able to replace the teacher with an average novice teacher.

Their findings are surprising. Using quite conservative assumptions about the costs of replacing teachers, they conclude that denying tenure to the bottom *quarter* of new teachers would substantially improve student achievement.[62] In comparison with the current dismissal rate of roughly 1 percent, a proposal that calls for denying tenure to 25 percent of new teachers seems shocking. Yet the intuition behind the conclusion is quite plausible. Given the tremendous variation in effectiveness documented even among first-year teachers, in conjunction with a relatively modest benefit to an additional year of experience, replacing an ineffective teacher with the "average" new teacher will almost certainly be a net gain for a school.

Does this mean that urban districts should start firing a quarter of their new teachers each year? At least two issues would have to be addressed before implementing such a policy. First, the system would have to be reasonably fair to individual teachers. Even if the system described above would improve student outcomes on average, it would certainly make "mistakes" in some cases. For example, a potentially effective teacher might produce very low student achievement gains during her first two years for idiosyncratic reasons. Conversely, a poor teacher might, by chance, have students during his first two years that make reasonable gains. Second, care would have to be taken about how such a policy would affect the supply of people who choose to enter teaching. A college student considering a teaching career who knows that she has a one-in-four chance of being dismissed within three years may be less willing to enter the profession. If the individuals who are discouraged from entering teaching by such a policy are indeed less competent than others, then this type of strategy might be helpful. But if the policy discouraged potentially effective teachers, it could be detrimental in the long run.

A final point is worth noting. Even if the preceding analysis were absolutely correct, and it were possible to address the cautions described above, this policy would apply only to the relatively limited set of teachers for whom it is possible to calculate value-added measures—namely, reading and math teachers in grades three to eight and a handful of high school teachers whose students take consistent standardized exams across grades.[63] Hence, even in an ideal setting, this type of dismissal policy would be only a partial solution to the issue of ineffective teachers. A comprehensive human resources approach will necessarily include other strategies, such as professional development, mentoring, and improved hiring practices.

Conclusions

Staffing urban schools with effective teachers poses a formidable challenge for superintendents and state officials. The response to the teacher quality provisions in NCLB illustrates that it can be much easier to relabel the problem rather than address it directly. Evidence on teacher recruitment and retention suggests several important lessons.

First, there is no silver bullet. The problem is too large and too complex to be solved easily. Policymakers and educators must resist falling into unproductive battles over issues, such as certification, that tend to pit the free-

market camp against the professionalism camp in the same way as the "reading wars" of the 1980s and 1990s pitted phonics advocates against whole-language advocates.

Second, local responses to this problem are limited in important ways. The importance of geography and working conditions in teacher decisions suggests that it may be difficult or extremely expensive to solve the problem through recruitment and retention alone. Professional development, performance incentives, or other policies to improve the effectiveness of the *existing* workforce are important complements to recruitment and retention policies.

Third, at least part of the problem may be operational. The inability of many urban districts to make offers to teacher candidates until July or August could be addressed, at least in part, by improving human resource systems and renegotiating certain contract provisions with local unions.

Finally, researchers and policymakers should focus more energy on demand-oriented strategies that would improve the ability of district administrators to identify and hire the most qualified applicants. The tremendous variation in teacher quality—even within schools and among teachers who have the same certification and experience—highlights the importance of understanding what makes an effective teacher and of helping administrators better predict who will be successful in the classroom. It is imperative that teacher screening tools such as the Gallup Insight Assessment or the Haberman Interview Protocol, which are used by hundreds of school districts nationwide, be rigorously validated.

Because even districts that are extremely efficient in hiring will invariably hire some teachers who do not perform well in the classroom, it is also important to consider teacher tenure policy. Although it is politically and financially costly to dismiss existing teachers, it is easier to distinguish between effective and ineffective teachers once they start teaching than to predict which teachers will be effective. The recent proposal to deny tenure to one-quarter of new teachers has met with some strong opposition. The lesson the proposal offers, however, is not that 25 percent, or any other specific share, of teachers is incompetent. Instead, it is that focusing on recruitment and retention alone may be a mistake. Although dismissal policies are complicated and controversial, it is imperative that researchers and policymakers begin to address this issue.

Notes

1. Richard J. Murnane and F. Levy, *Teaching the New Basic Skills: Principles for Educating Children to Thrive in a Changing Economy* (New York: Free Press, 1996).

2. These data come from the following report based on the 2003–04 School and Staffing Survey: National Center for Education Statistics (NCES), "Characteristics of Schools, Districts, Teachers, Principals, and School Libraries in the United States, 2003–04, Schools and Staffing Survey," Report 2006-313 (U.S. Department of Education, 2006), table 16.

3. http://usinfo.state.gov/scv/Archive/2005/Dec/29-304152.html (August 21, 2006).

4. D. Kerbow, "Patterns of Urban Student Mobility and Local School Reform," *Journal of Education of Students Placed at Risk* 1, no. 2 (1996): 147–69; K. L. Alexander, D. R. Entwisle, and S. L. Dauber, "Children in Motion: School Transfers and Elementary School Performance," *Journal of Educational Research* 90, no. 1 (1996): 3–12.

5. Robert D. Putnam, *Bowling Alone: The Collapse and Revival of American Community* (New York: Simon and Schuster, 2000); Robert J. Sampson, Stephen Raudenbush, and Felton Earls, "Neighborhoods and Violent Crime: A Multilevel Study of Collective Efficacy," *Science* 277 (1997): 918–24; Robert J. Sampson, Jeffrey Morenoff, and Felton Earls, "Beyond Social Capital: Spatial Dynamics of Collective Efficacy for Children," *American Sociological Review* 64 (1999): 633–60.

6. Caroline M. Hoxby, "Does Competition among Public Schools Benefit Students and Taxpayers?" *American Economic Review* 90, no. 5 (2000); Caroline M. Hoxby, "School Choice and School Productivity (Or, Could School Choice Be a Rising Tide That Lifts All Boats?)," in *The Economics of School Choice*, edited by C. Hoxby (University of Chicago Press, 2003).

7. For more details on the critique of Hoxby's original analysis, see Jesse Rothstein, "Does Competition among Public Schools Benefit Students and Taxpayers? A Comment on Hoxby (2000)," *American Economic Review* (forthcoming), and Hoxby's response, "Competition among Public Schools: A Reply to Rothstein," Working Paper 11216 (Cambridge, Mass.: National Bureau of Economic Research, 2004). For further evidence on the impact of competition among schools, see Victor Lavy, "From Forced Busing to Free Choice in Public Schools: Quasi-Experimental Evidence of Individual and General Effects," Working Paper 11969 (Cambridge, Mass.: National Bureau of Economic Research, January 2006).

8. Open enrollment programs, also known as intradistrict choice, may provide an analogous type of competition for public schools in large cities, although there is little evidence that such programs have a substantial impact on student outcomes. See, for example, J. Cullen, B. Jacob, and S. Levitt, "The Effect of School Choice on Student Outcomes: Evidence from Randomized Lotteries," *Econometrica* 74, no. 5 (2006): 1191–230; J. Cullen, B. Jacob, and S. Levitt, "The Impact of School Choice on Student Outcomes: An Analysis of the Chicago Public Schools," *Journal of Public Economics* 89, nos. 5–6 (2005): 729–60.

9. NCES, *2003–04 Schools and Staffing Survey*, http://nces.ed.gov/pubs2006/2006313.pdf (April 1, 2006).

10. Personal communication with Nancy Slavin, Director of Teacher Recruitment, Chicago Public Schools, March 2006.

11. E-mail communication with Andy Sokatch of the New Teacher Project, August 25, 2006.

12. Jessica Levin and Meredith Quinn, *Missed Opportunities: How We Keep High-Quality Teachers out of Urban Schools* (New York: New Teacher Project, 2003).

13. According to an analysis by Ingersoll, 91.6 percent of teachers in U.S. public schools are fully certified, with slightly lower shares in secondary schools compared with elementary schools. The certification rates are only slightly lower in high-poverty urban schools, suggesting that lack of certification might not be as prevalent as one might have suspected. Richard M. Ingersoll, "Out-of-Field Teaching and the Limits of Teacher Policy" (Center for the Study of Teaching and Policy and the Consortium for Policy Research in Education, 2003).

14. Charles T. Clotfelter, Helen F. Ladd, and Jacob L. Vigdor, "Who Teaches Whom? Race and the Distribution of Novice Teachers," *Economics of Education Review* (forthcoming); Hamilton Lankford, Susanna Loeb, and James Wyckoff, "Teacher Sorting and the Plight of Urban Schools," *Educational Evaluation and Policy Analysis* 24 (2002): 37–62.

15. Lankford, Loeb, and Wyckoff, "Teacher Sorting" (see note 14).

16. These figures are reported for the 10th and 90th percentiles of the New York State school distribution.

17. Clotfelter, Ladd, and Vigdor, "Who Teaches Whom?" (see note 14).

18. Charles T. Clotfelter, Helen F. Ladd and Jacob L. Vigdor, "Teacher-Student Matching and the Assessment of Teacher Effectiveness," Working Paper 11936 (Cambridge, Mass.: National Bureau of Economic Research, 2006).

19. Ingersoll, "Out-of-Field Teaching and the Limits of Teacher Policy" (see note 13).

20. Richard M. Ingersoll, "Why Do High-Poverty Schools Have Difficulty Staffing Their Classrooms with Qualified Teachers?" (Center for American Progress and Institute for America's Future, 2004).

21. Lankford, Loeb, and Wyckoff, "Teacher Sorting" (see note 14).

22. Eric A. Hanushek and others, "The Market for Teacher Quality," Working Paper 11252 (Cambridge, Mass.: National Bureau of Economic Research, 2005). Jonah E. Rockoff, Thomas J. Kane, and Douglas O. Staiger come to a similar conclusion, "What Does Certification Tell Us about Teacher Effectiveness? Evidence from New York City," Working Paper 12155 (Cambridge, Mass.: National Bureau of Economic Research, 2006).

23. Kate Walsh and Emma Snyder, "Searching the Attic: How States are Responding to the Nation's Goal of Placing a Highly Qualified Teacher in Every Classroom" (National Council on Teacher Quality, 2004).

24. Education Trust, "Telling the Whole Truth (or Not) about Highly Qualified Teachers" (2003).

25. I would like to thank Cecilia Rouse and Susanna Loeb for pointing out this potential effect.

26. For recent studies of teacher value added, see Jonah E. Rockoff, "The Impact of Individual Teachers on Student Achievement: Evidence from Panel Data," *American Economic Review* 94 (2004): 247–52; Hanushek and others, "The Market for Teacher Quality" (see note 22); Daniel Aaronson, Lisa Barrow, and William Sander, "Teachers and Student Achievement in the Chicago Public High Schools," *Journal of Labor Economics* (forthcoming); Kane, Rockoff, and Staiger, "What Does Certification Tell Us about Teacher Effectiveness? Evidence from New York City" (see note 22); and Donald Boyd and others, "Explaining the Short Careers of High-Achieving Teachers in Schools with Low-Performing Students," *American Economic Review, Papers and Proceedings* (May 2005).

27. Rockoff, "The Impact of Individual Teachers on Student Achievement" (see note 26); Hanushek and others, "The Market for Teacher Quality" (see note 22).

28. William L. Sanders and June C. Rivers, *Cumulative and Residual Effects of Teachers on Future Student Academic Achievement* (Knoxville: University of Tennessee Value-Added Research and Assessment Center, 1996).

29. For a review of the earlier literature relating student achievement to teacher characteristics, see Eric A. Hanushek, "The Economics of Schooling: Production and Efficiency in Public Schools," *Journal of Economic Literature* 24(1986): 1141–77; and Eric A. Hanushek, "Assessing the Effects of School Resources on Student Performance: An Update," *Educational Evaluation and Policy Analysis* 19 (1997): 141–64.

30. Kane, Rockoff, and Staiger, "What Does Certification Tell Us about Teacher Effectiveness?" (see note 22); Donald Boyd and others, "How Changes in Entry Requirements Alter the Teaching Workforce and Affect Student Achievement," Working Paper 11844 (Cambridge, Mass.: National Bureau of Economic Research, 2005).

31. Rockoff, "The Impact of Individual Teachers" (see note 26); Hanushek and others, "The Market for Teacher Quality" (see note 22).

32. Ronald E. Ferguson, "Paying for Public Education: New Evidence on How and Why Money Matters," *Harvard Journal on Legislation* 28 (1991): 465–98; Ronald G. Ehrenber and Dominic J. Brewer, "Do School and Teacher Characteristics Matter? Evidence from High School and Beyond," *Economics of Education Review* 13 (1994): 1–17.

33. For a recent example, see Clotfelter, Ladd, and Vigdor, "Teacher-Student Matching" (see note 18).

34. For example, an unpublished study on Florida teachers indicates that college entrance exam scores are not associated with student achievement gains. Douglass Harris and Timothy Sass, "The Effects of Teacher Training on Teacher Value-Added," Working Paper (Florida State University, March 2006).

35. Ronald F. Ferguson, "Teachers' Perceptions and Expectations and the Black-White Test Score Gap," in *The Black-White Test Score Gap,* edited by Christopher Jencks and Meredith Phillips (Brookings, 1998).

36. Thomas S. Dee, "Teachers, Race, and Student Achievement in a Randomized Experiment," *Review of Economics and Statistics* 86 (2004): 195–210.

37. Hanushek and others, "The Market for Teacher Quality" (see note 22).

38. Others have hypothesized that certain teachers may be more effective with low-achieving students, while others may be more effective with high-achieving students. There is little good evidence on this question, although some research suggests that a teacher's ability extends, at least to some extent, to students of all ability levels. That is, teachers who are particularly (in)effective with low-ability students also tend to be (in)effective with high-ability students. See, for example, Brian A. Jacob and Lars Lefgren, "Principals as Agents: Subjective Performance Measurement in Education," Working Paper 11463 (Cambridge, Mass.: National Bureau of Economic Research, 2005); Hanushek and others, "The Market for Teacher Quality" (see note 22).

39. Peter J. Dolton and Wilbert van der Klaaw, "The Turnover of Teachers: A Competing Risks Explanation," *Review of Economics and Statistics* 81 (1999): 543–52; Todd R. Stinebrickner, "An Empirical Investigation of Teacher Attrition," *Economics of Education Review* 17 (1998): 127–36; Todd R. Stinebrickner, "An

Analysis of Occupational Change and Departure from the Labor Force. Evidence of the Reasons That Teachers Leave," *Journal of Human Resources* 37 (2002): 192–216.

40. Eric A. Hanushek, John F. Kain, and Steven G. Rivkin, "Why Public Schools Lose Teachers," *Journal of Human Resources* 34 (2004): 326–54.

41. It is worth noting that factors such as neighborhood crime rates may be an important aspect of working conditions that act to disadvantage urban districts.

42. Benjamin Scafidi, Todd Stinebrickner, and David L. Sjoquist, "Race, Poverty, and Teacher Mobility," *Economics of Education Review* (forthcoming).

43. Boyd and others, "Explaining the Short Careers of High-Achieving Teachers in Schools with Low-Performing Students" (see note 26).

44. Susanna Loeb and Marianne Page, "Examining the Link between Teacher Wages and Student Outcomes: The Importance of Alternative Labor Market Opportunities and Non-Pecuniary Variation," *Review of Economics and Statistics* 82 (2000): 393–408.

45. Donald Boyd and others, "The Draw of Home: How Teachers' Preferences for Proximity Disadvantage Urban Schools," *Journal of Policy Analysis and Management* 24 (2005): 113–23.

46. Dale Ballou, "Do Public Schools Hire the Best Applicants?" *Quarterly Journal of Economics* (1996): 97–133. Interestingly, administrators do appear to value candidates with a higher grade point average.

47. Jacob and Lefgren, "Principals as Agents" (see note 38).

48. The study of the large Texas district described above provides some additional evidence on this. The researchers examine teachers who switch districts, and examine whether those teachers with higher quality end up in districts with better salaries or working conditions. They find that teachers with more advanced degrees and certification tend to go to districts with higher salaries and fewer black students, but that there is no relationship between teacher value added and the type of district where they end up. This suggests that districts may not be hiring teachers who are most effective in practice.

49. Levin and Quinn, *Missed Opportunities* (see note 12).

50. Ingersoll, "Out-of-Field Teaching and the Limits of Teacher Policy" (see note 13). Suppose, for example, that a school had to teach eight biology classes and seven chemistry classes, and that the standard work load is five classes per teacher. In this scenario, the school would have to hire three teachers total to cover the biology and chemistry classes. Assuming that teachers are only certified in one field (which is likely to be the case, since certification generally requires a college major in the field), it is not possible for the school to have every biology and chemistry class covered by a "certified" teacher unless it hires more than three teachers. If the school hires two biology teachers and one chemistry teacher, then the second biology teacher will likely be forced to teach two chemistry courses, which will be considered "out-of-field" teaching. Ingersoll argues that this phenomenon is, in part, a result of schools' trying to provide a broad array of services with limited resources. Of course, it is not clear what an individual principal could do in this case, given the array of courses that the school is required to offer.

51. R. Clarke Fowler, "The Massachusetts Signing Bonus Program for New Teachers. A Model of Teacher Preparation Worth Copying?" *Education Policy Analysis Archives* 11 (2003); Edward Liu, Susan M. John-

son, and Heather G. Peske, "New Teachers and the Massachusetts Signing Bonus: The Limits of Inducements," *Educational Analysis and Policy Evaluation* 26, no. 3 (2004).

52. Charles T. Clotfelter and others, "Teacher Bonuses and Teacher Retention in Low Performing Schools: Evidence from the North Carolina $1,800 Teacher Bonus Program," *Public Finance Review* (forthcoming); Charles T. Clotfelder and others, "Would Higher Salaries Keep Teachers in High-Poverty Schools? Evidence from a Policy Intervention in North Carolina," Working Paper 12285 (Cambridge, Mass.: National Bureau of Economic Research, 2006).

53. Harold W. Stevenson and James W. Stigler, *The Learning Gap: Why Our Schools Are Failing and What We Can Learn from Japanese and Chinese Education* (New York: Touchstone, 1992).

54. Ingersoll, "Why Do High-Poverty Schools Have Difficulty Staffing Their Classrooms with Qualified Teachers?" (see note 20).

55. Bruce W. Hall, L. Carolyn Pearson, and DeLos Carroll, "Teachers' Long-Range Teaching Plans: A Discriminant Analysis," *Journal of Educational Research* 85 (1992): 221–25; Susan M. Johnson and Sarah E. Birkeland, "Pursuing a 'Sense of Success': New Teachers Explain Their Career Decisions," *American Educational Research Journal* 40 (2003): 581–617.

56. Jacqui Goddard, "In Florida, a Bid to Expand the Teaching Pool," *Christian Science Monitor*, January 5, 2005.

57. Michael B. Allen, "Eight Questions on Teacher Recruitment and Retention: What Does the Research Say?" (Denver: Education Commission of the States, 2005).

58. Richard Ingersoll and Jeffrey M. Kralik, "The Impact of Mentoring on Teacher Retention: What the Research Says" (Denver: Education Commission of the States, 2004); Allen, "Eight Questions on Teacher Recruitment and Retention (see note 57).

59. S. J. Odell and D. P. Ferraro, "Teacher Mentoring and Teacher Retention." *Journal of Teacher Education* 43, no. 3 (1992): 200–04.

60. Steven Glazerman and others, "Design of an Impact Evaluation of Teacher Induction Programs: Final Report," Report 6137-070 (Mathematica Policy Research, January 11, 2006).

61. For more information on the Teacher Insight Assessment, see http://education.gallup.com/content/default.aspx?ci=868.

62. Robert Gordon, Thomas J. Kane, and Douglas O. Staiger, "Identifying Effective Teachers Using Performance on the Job," White Paper 2006-01 (The Hamilton Project, Brookings, April 2006); Kane, Rockoff, and Staiger, "What Does Certification Tell Us about Teacher Effectiveness?" (see note 22).

63. There are several additional complications and caveats associated with the analysis presented in Gordon, Kane, and Staiger, "Identifying Effective Teachers" (see note 62), and Kane, Rockoff, and Staiger, "What Does Certification Tell Us" (see note 22). First, the correlation between math and reading effectiveness is not perfect, so that one could potentially end up dismissing ineffective math (reading) teachers who were quite effective in the other subject. More generally, early measures of value added are less predictive of subsequent student achievement in reading relative to math and less predictive for teachers in the middle grades than for elementary grades teachers.

Recruiting and Retaining High-Quality Teachers in Rural Areas

David H. Monk

Summary

In examining recruitment and retention of teachers in rural areas, David Monk begins by noting the numerous possible characteristics of rural communities—small size, sparse settlement, distance from population concentrations, and an economic reliance on agricultural industries that are increasingly using seasonal and immigrant workers to minimize labor costs. Many, though not all, rural areas, he says, are seriously impoverished.

Classes in rural schools are relatively small, and teachers tend to report satisfaction with their work environments and relatively few problems with discipline. But teacher turnover is often high, and hiring can be difficult. Monk observes that rural schools have a below-average share of highly trained teachers. Compensation in rural schools tends to be low, perhaps because of a lower fiscal capacity in rural areas, thus complicating efforts to attract and retain teachers.

Several student characteristics, including relatively large shares of students with special needs and with limited English skills and lower shares of students attending college, can also make it difficult to recruit and retain high-quality teachers. Other challenges include meeting the needs of highly mobile children of low-income migrant farm workers.

With respect to public policy, Monk asserts a need to focus on a subcategory of what might be called hard-to-staff rural schools rather than to develop a blanket set of policies for all rural schools. In particular, he recommends a focus on such indicators as low teacher qualifications, teaching in fields far removed from the area of training, difficulty in hiring, high turnover, a lack of diversity among teachers in the school, and the presence of migrant farm workers' children. Successful efforts to stimulate economic growth in these areas would be highly beneficial. He also calls attention to the potential for modern telecommunication and computing technologies to offset some of the drawbacks associated with teaching in rural areas.

www.futureofchildren.org

David H. Monk is dean of the College of Education at Pennsylvania State University. The author gratefully acknowledges assistance received from Pedro Villarreal III in gathering research, from Sharon Patrick in preparing the manuscript, and from insightful comments offered by Kai Schafft and William Duncombe as well as by the editors of this volume.

In many discussions of rural schools and school districts, *rural* is simply a catchword denoting everything that is not urban or metropolitan. Such usage overlooks the complexity of rural communities and school districts, as well as the considerable variation within them. In examining recruitment and retention of teachers in rural areas, I begin with the premise that *rural* is an important analytic category. I examine rural communities in detail and then survey the organizational structure of their schools and the demographics and educational needs of their students to see how each affects the ability of rural schools to attract and retain high-quality teachers. I conclude with an assessment of implications for policy.

Attributes of Rural Communities

As the noted rural sociologist Daryl Hobbs has observed, one of the problems with past generalizations about rural America is that rural America defies generalization.[1] But it is possible to describe in some detail the features of a rural community. Some of these features can be considered fundamental to or inherent in a rural community; others are simply associated with such a community.

Among the inherent characteristics are small size, sparse settlement, narrowness of choice (with regard, for example, to shopping, schools, and medical services), distance from population concentrations, and an economic reliance on agricultural industries, sometimes in tandem with tourism. In keeping with Hobbs's assertion, not all of these essential characteristics necessarily apply to each rural community. For example, a community might be small but densely settled. The term *rural*, then, might imply small, but small need not imply rural. Even assuming uncritically that rural implies small can be problem-

atic: sometimes large-enrollment centralized school districts serve geographically large rural settings. Likewise, certain regions, such as the newly coined "micropolitan statistical area," can be simultaneously urban and rural. As defined by the U.S. Census Bureau, each of these relatively sparsely settled regions must have at least one urban cluster with a population of at least 10,000 but less than 50,000.[2]

The economic base of rural communities tends to be place-bound. Enterprises like agriculture engage seasonal workers, and other place-bound industries like meatpacking are increasingly using immigrant workers to minimize labor costs.[3] Indeed, the rural economic base may be shifting to include more industries that are place-bound and that can make use of low-skill workers. Such shifting has far-reaching effects for the schools in general, and for their ability to recruit and retain high-quality teachers in particular.

Other attributes are not inherent in rural communities but nevertheless tend to be closely associated with them. For example, many rural areas are seriously impoverished.[4] Indeed, the incidence of poverty in conventionally defined nonmetropolitan areas is higher (14.6 percent) than it is in metropolitan areas (11.4 percent), although poverty rates are highest (16.6 percent) in metropolitan central cities.[5] Among the 250 poorest counties in the United States, 244 are rural, and out of the more than 8 million children attending public schools in rural areas, 2.5 million live in poverty.[6]

Rural communities are also associated with aging populations and with population and job loss. For example, populations have dropped in rural areas in response to declines in traditional rural industries like wood products, textiles, apparel, and leather, coupled with agribusiness consolidations and the decline of family farms.[7] These trends have created one of the most pressing challenges facing many rural communities—namely, retaining younger populations.[8]

But rural communities are also associated with positive attributes, such as beauty and serenity. And economies in rural areas grew briskly after the 1990–91 recession and grew more rapidly than those in urban areas in the first part of the 1990s.[9] One study attributes the more rapid growth to technological innovations of the information age, new forms of work organization that permit workers to reside away from population centers, and the expansion of jobs that do not require college degrees. The study sees the largest share of jobs in the near-term rural economy as requiring more than a high school degree, but not as much as a college degree.[10]

Finally, rural communities vary widely both within themselves and across regions of the nation. Some rural areas, particularly resorts, for example, feature extremely valuable real estate, whose high property taxes have implications for funding rural schools. Yet poverty can exist in these same resort settings. Highly valued properties are typically held by part-time residents who engage permanent residents in low-wage service jobs like waiting on tables and caretaking. Real estate prices can become so high that permanent residents are forced to live elsewhere and to commute into the resort communities. In states where property owners vote on school budget referenda, it can be hard to secure the support of the absentee landowners for maintaining the schools even if the property wealth base is high.

Rural school districts in the western United States also differ from those in the east,

partly because of geography and partly because of history. In years past, many small country schoolhouses dotted the nation's eastern, particularly northeastern, states. As school district consolidation has proceeded over the years, the number of districts has declined substantially, but many small districts continue to exist, particularly in New York and Pennsylvania. Elsewhere, particu-

---

Rural school districts in the western United States also differ from those in the east, partly because of geography and partly because of history.

---

larly in the south, county-level districts are more common, and consolidation efforts are more typically focused on individual schools.

A legacy of consolidation can have important internal implications for schooling.[11] Consolidation can join separately organized communities that vary widely in terms of their culture, values, and worldview. Teachers and other school officials in consolidated districts must then find ways to bring together the differing perspectives into a common and coherent schooling endeavor. When consolidations are contentious, teachers and administrators must do what they can to forge a new community identity. As the prevalence of hyphenated school district names in the aftermath of school consolidations suggests, the task is not easy. The presence of multiple community identities within a school district is a common hallmark of a rural school setting.

Table 1. Number of Students, Teachers, and Schools, by School Type and Student Enrollment, Public Schools, 2003–04

School type and enrollment	Students	Teachers	Schools
All public schools	47,315,700	3,250,600	88,113
Rural/small town	8,427,900	617,000	23,802
Student enrollment			
Fewer than 100	320,900	48,700	6,895
100–199	1,182,300	118,800	7,922
200–499	12,543,200	978,900	35,685
500–749	12,290,800	850,300	20,156
750–999	7,229,600	466,300	8,396
1,000 or more	13,748,800	787,700	9,059

Source: National Center for Education Statistics, *School and Staffing Survey, 2003–04* (U.S. Department of Education, 2006).

One final twist is that sometimes rural attributes can be taken on voluntarily. Some schools and school districts, for example, are small out of choice rather than out of necessity. To the degree that added costs are associated with small scales of operation, policymakers have been more sympathetic to providing relief for places that have no choice but to be small. Of course, in practice, the choice-necessity distinction can be a vexing one to draw.

Assessing the Scope of the Rural Sector

Estimates of the number of rural districts and schools in the United States vary according to how they are defined. According to the Common Core of Data collected by the National Center for Education Statistics (NCES), 7,824 school districts were classified as rural in 2002–03—close to half (49 percent) of the school districts in the nation.[12] These rural districts operated 24,350 schools, served more than 7.6 million students, and employed more than 523,000 full-time equivalent (FTE) teachers.[13] And these estimates may be undercounts because many rural areas are embedded within school districts in other categories, including urban districts.

Table 1 reports data collected as part of the NCES's 2003–04 School and Staffing Survey (SASS). The table acknowledges the complexity of the definition question by providing separate breakdowns according to the characteristics of the community served and the size of the school. Clearly, rural schools, which are defined in different ways in the table, represent a significant share of schools in the nation.

Organizational Features of Rural Schools

Several organizational features of rural schools directly affect teacher recruitment and retention. Among the most important are demographic characteristics of the teachers, teachers' workloads, and teachers' salaries.

Characteristics of Teachers in Rural Schools

Table 2 shows how several key teacher attributes—experience, advanced schooling, and race—are distributed among schools of different types and sizes. It suggests, in particular, a discrepancy between rural and small schools in the average level of teacher experience. The share of inexperienced teachers, though relatively low in rural areas, is high in the smallest

Table 2. Share of Teachers with Selected Attributes, by School Type and Student Enrollment, 2003–04

Percent

School type and enrollment	Share with three or fewer years of full-time experience	Share with master's degree or higher	Share white, non-Hispanic
All public schools	17.8	48.1	83.1
Rural/small town	14.6	41.9	90.2
Student enrollment			
Fewer than 100	21.0	37.6	81.3
100–199	17.9	40.7	88.4
200–499	16.6	47.8	86.8
500–749	17.7	46.9	82.3
750–999	18.3	47.4	79.8
1,000 or more	18.9	51.9	80.7

Source: See table 1.

schools, perhaps suggesting the smallest schools face the greatest hiring and retention challenges. These data are consistent with the findings of a study using a sophisticated research methodology that controlled for the influence of other background characteristics.[14] The table shows that both rural schools and the smallest schools have a below-average share of more highly trained teachers, and that rural schools have an above-average share of non-Hispanic white teachers.

The data in table 2 are consistent with Robert Gibbs's findings in 2000 that teachers in rural areas are only about half as likely to have graduated from top-ranked colleges or universities as their peers in urban areas (7 percent for rural teachers and 15 percent for urban teachers).[15] Researchers also consistently find that teachers in rural areas have comparatively low educational attainment, which suggests one reason why rural areas may be less likely to offer college-preparation programs. Elizabeth Greenberg and Ruy Teixeira report, for example, that 93 percent of twelfth graders in urban areas were enrolled in schools that offered calculus, as

against 64 percent of rural twelfth graders. They found similar gaps in other content areas.[16] William Carlsen and I also found that rural science teachers were less likely to have graduate degrees and more likely to have majored in education with less course work in science and mathematics than their urban counterparts.[17]

Table 3 provides insights into the hiring practices of small and rural districts. For example, it shows that the share of rural districts requiring full standard state certification for the field to be taught is larger than the share of all public school districts with that requirement. Here again, rural districts and small districts differ, with a somewhat smaller share of the very smallest districts—those with fewer than 250 students—requiring full certification. The share is even lower for the largest districts. The table also shows that rural and small districts are less likely to require passing scores on state tests as well as standardized tests such as the Praxis examinations required by some states for certification (though passing scores on the Praxis examination vary from state to state).

Table 3. Share of Districts Requiring Selected Hiring Criteria, by School Type and District Student Enrollment, 2003–04

Percent

School type and enrollment	Full standard state certification for field taught	Passing score on state test of basic skills	Passing score on Praxis core professional practice	Passing score on Praxis II content area
All public school districts	77.4	64.1	29.1	26.9
Rural/small town	79.2	59.7	26.7	25.2
Student enrollment				
Fewer than 250	73.8	53.2	11.8	9.4
250–999	77.3	64.3	25.3	21.5
1,000–1,999	79.8	68.3	36.3	33.8
2,000–4,999	80.5	69.1	40.2	38.9
5,000–9,999	77.3	68.9	42.3	44.5
10,000 or more	72.1	66.8	38.3	39.4

Source: NCES, *Schools and Staffing Survey, 2003–04*, District Data File (U.S. Department of Education, 2006), table 38.

Table 4 makes clear the difficulty that schools of different types and sizes encounter in filling various teaching positions. Relatively small shares of schools report difficulty hiring general elementary teachers, although the smallest schools have more difficulty than most. In classic shortage areas like special education, mathematics, and the sciences, however, the share tends to be higher in the rural and the smallest schools, again suggesting that these schools face special challenges in recruiting teachers.

Working Conditions for Teachers in Rural Areas

Studies comparing working conditions for teachers in rural and other kinds of school settings have found differences in average class size and in the mix of courses taught, particularly at the secondary level.

Pupil-teacher ratios are relatively low in both elementary and secondary schools that enroll few students. According to the NCES, elementary schools with fewer than 300 students report pupil-teacher ratios of 13.3, compared with 20.3 for schools with more

than 1,500 students. Figures for secondary schools are comparable, although they tend to be lower.[18] The lower pupil-teacher ratios in smaller schools affect different aspects of teacher workloads. On the positive side, smaller schools tend to have smaller class sizes, although cost sensitivities can prompt measures like combining grade levels. Smaller class sizes, all else equal, are an attractive feature of working in small or rural schools.

Other advantages can stem from a small school or small classroom environment. Rural teachers, for example, report more satisfaction with their work environments and feel they have greater autonomy and more direct influence over school policy.[19] Evidence also suggests fewer problems with discipline in rural areas.[20]

On the negative side, smaller numbers of students limit the ability of teachers to specialize and may require them to deal with wider ranges of pupil needs. This drawback is perhaps most obvious at the secondary level, where a single high school science teacher

Table 4. Share of Schools with Teaching Vacancies in Selected Subject Areas Having Difficulty Filling These Vacancies, by Type of School and Student Enrollment, 2003–04

Percent

School type and enrollment	General elementary	Special education	English language arts	Social studies	Mathematics	Biology	Physics
All public schools	3.9	29.2	8.1	4.0	28.8	20.9	27.7
Rural/small town	3.9	33.1	11.4	6.3	29.6	20.9	29.7
Student enrollment							
Fewer than 100	6.3	37.5	10.6	7.9	24.6	17.0	23.2
100–199	2.9	29.2	19.6	8.1	34.7	29.6	40.6
200–499	4.3	26.8	12.5	3.8	29.1	17.4	25.4
500–749	3.9	27.5	4.4	2.8	27.0	21.3	27.0
750–999	2.5	31.9	2.2	5.0	25.3	20.9	25.7
1,000 or more	1.9	32.7	7.8	3.2	31.0	21.9	28.9

Source: NCES, *Schools and Staffing Survey, 2003–04*, Public School, BIA School Data Files (U.S. Department of Education, 2006), table 15.

may teach all the science subfields, but even in elementary schools teachers can find themselves dealing with a wider age span than is customary elsewhere because grade levels have been combined.

Smaller student enrollment can also make it hard for schools to offer more specialized courses. In earlier research using data from New York, I found that increasing enrollment up to 100 in a grade level in secondary schools predictably broadened the curriculum. Increasing enrollment beyond 100, however, often resulted in increased sections of existing courses rather than in more varied courses.[21]

The smaller numbers of students in rural schools can also affect school stability from one year to the next. Schools with larger numbers of students tend to enjoy a cushion against change. But when students are few, the school or district can change substantially from one year to the next in ways that affect the work of teachers. Recent federal legisla-

tion, most particularly the No Child Left Behind (NCLB) law, raises the stakes for fluctuations from one year to the next, notably in calculating the adequate yearly progress (AYP) accountability yardsticks. Failures to meet AYP standards because of fluctuations stemming from small numbers make small schools vulnerable to sanctions even when teaching performance is exemplary. The small number problem is exacerbated when the performance levels of subpopulations are assessed, making the already small numbers even smaller. The Bush administration has begun to provide increased flexibility to small and rural districts as part of its refinement of NCLB, but making accountability measures sensitive to the realities of small and rural schools and districts remains a challenge.

Salaries of Teachers in Rural Schools

Table 5, which compares average salaries across school and district types and sizes for 2003-04, shows that compensation tends to be low in both rural and small school settings. Salaries for teachers in the smallest schools are

Table 5. Average Base Salary for Regular Full-Time Teachers and Share of Teachers with Supplemental Income, by School Type and Student Enrollment, 2003–04

School type and enrollment	Average base salary (dollars)	Share of teachers (percent)		
		With extracurricular compensation	With compensation from other school sources	With an outside job
All public schools	44,400	40.2	13.6	15.9
Rural/small town	38,000	42.5	14.1	15.7
Student enrollment				
Fewer than 100	38,100	32.5	11.8	19.5
100–199	38,200	38.4	12.3	17.6
200–499	43,200	36.5	11.8	15.3
500–749	44,100	36.7	13.1	13.5
750–999	45,000	42.1	17.0	15.2
1,000 or more	46,700	47.7	14.6	19.0

Source: See table 1.

16.5 percent lower than the national average. The share of teachers in the smallest schools who report having an extra job is higher than the national average (19.5 percent compared with 15.9 percent for the sample as a whole). Teachers in the smallest settings are less likely than those in public schools nationwide to be receiving supplemental compensation for extracurricular work or from other school sources, though no such difference appears to exist for teachers in rural districts.

In a separate study Gibbs found that urban salaries are approximately 21 percent higher than rural salaries for starting teachers and 35 percent higher for teachers with master's degrees and twenty or more years of experience.[22]

Why Are Rural Teachers' Salaries Lower?
Researchers have offered various reasons to explain why teacher salaries are lower on average in rural and small school districts than in other areas.

Neoclassical economic theory holds that people's willingness to accept a particular wage is related in part to the attractiveness of the location where the work will be done. In highly attractive places, workers will be willing to accept a lower wage, so perhaps wages are low in rural areas because the attractiveness of the areas to teachers, on average, induces them to accept lower wages. The opposite, however, might be true if teachers, on average, are not receptive to rural living. In such a case, rural school districts would have to offer higher wages to attract a comparable pool of applicants. In such a case, again, the lower prevailing wages in rural areas could suggest that rural school districts make do with less qualified pools of candidates and are more likely to face retention problems.

Closely related to the mix of attractive and unattractive features in the locale is the mix of features of the job itself. On the one hand, the smaller pupil-teacher ratios and the relative absence of disciplinary problems and greater social cohesion (to the extent that it exists) could prompt teacher candidates to accept lower wages, all else equal. On the other hand, the inability to specialize and the need to teach wide ranges of students could be dispiriting to teachers and mean that higher wages would be necessary to attract and retain comparable candidates.

One aspect of teachers' work in rural areas that has not received much attention is the availability of services for students with special needs. Rural schools are likely to have to struggle to provide these specialized services because of combinations of poverty and higher costs owing to small scales of operation, and shortages of such services will tend to make teaching less attractive.

Differences in the underlying costs of living also explain some of the nominal differences in teacher wages. Housing costs, for example, tend to be higher in urban areas. But people in rural areas may depend more on automobiles than their counterparts in urban settings, a difference that has a bearing on the cost of living.

The lower wages in rural schools may also simply reflect a lower fiscal capacity in rural areas, coupled with only limited efforts by states to offset the effects of poverty through equalizing grant-in-aid programs.

Rural schools arguably face higher costs of operation because of their smaller size and sparsely settled locations. More concretely, small schools may have to hire and pay for more teachers on a per pupil basis because certain courses must be offered, if only to a few students. One way to absorb these extra costs is to pay lower salaries. As noted, schools are sometimes small by necessity; when school officials and voters choose to have small schools, it complicates the policy implications of size-related costs.

Such rural attributes as sparse settlement or geographic isolation can also raise transporta-tion costs and draw resources away from the core instructional program in general, and teacher salaries in particular.

Rural districts in micropolitan areas will be under pressure to offer wages and working conditions comparable to those of nearby ur-banized areas.[23] An inability or unwillingness to compete will lead to applicant pools with

---

The lower wages in rural schools may also simply reflect a lower fiscal capacity in rural areas, coupled with only limited efforts by states to offset the effects of poverty through equalizing grant-in-aid programs.

---

lower qualifications, all else equal. Districts in more isolated rural areas will feel less pressure to compete with neighboring districts, though isolation itself may adversely affect the available pool of candidates for teaching positions.

Teacher labor markets, in general, tend to be highly localized. A study by Donald Boyd and several colleagues shows that teachers want to teach in schools near where they grew up and prefer areas like their hometowns. For example, 61 percent of teachers entering public school teaching in New York State from 1999 to 2002 started teaching within fif-teen miles of their hometown; 85 percent began teaching within forty miles of their hometown.[24] Several studies stress the hard-ship the localized teacher market poses for urban areas, which tend to produce lower shares of college graduates than do suburban areas.[25] And similar challenges exist for rural areas, which also produce relatively low shares of college graduates. Indeed, one study finds that the share of rural youth getting some college education is lower than that of urban youth, so teacher supply problems are even more serious in rural areas.[26] It

---

It is hard to escape the conclusion that the real beneficiaries of the localized teacher market are the wealthy suburban districts that turn out high shares of college graduates and have attractive working conditions.

---

is hard to escape the conclusion that the real beneficiaries of the localized teacher market are the wealthy suburban districts that turn out high shares of college graduates and have attractive working conditions.

In a study of hiring in Pennsylvania, Robert Strauss found a dysfunctional penchant for hiring candidates with local ties, which he traced in part to the minimal limits in the school code on indirect conflicts of interest in hiring relatives or friends. Strauss faulted the willingness of school authorities to sacrifice academic credentials in favor of ties to the local area and even called into question the nation's commitment to local school board authority for school governance.[27] More recently, a study of hiring in a large Florida school district suggests that school principals

factor academic credentials into a broader array of considerations in what appears to be a rational assessment of the prospective teacher's fit with the organizational context of the school.[28] For example, if teachers with better academic credentials leave a rural school after very short periods of employment, it could be rational for the hiring authorities at that school to prefer other candidates whom they believe will stay in place longer. This could then translate into a preference for candidates who grew up in the vicinity of the school, even at the risk of introducing elements of provincialism into school operations.

Retention rates also influence teacher salaries. High turnover and an inclination to hire inexperienced people will lower average salaries. The data in table 2 suggesting that rural areas have lower shares of inexperienced teachers, while the smallest schools have a relatively high share of such teachers, are confirmed in work of Richard Ingersoll that finds teacher retention to be greater in rural than in other schools. He also finds that teachers leave smaller schools at higher rates.[29]

Anecdotal evidence suggests a sharp split in district experiences with respect to teacher retention. On the one hand, some teachers settle into small and rural districts and stay for extraordinarily long periods. Indeed, some teachers who grew up in or near a rural community spend their entire career in the same school—a boon or a horror, depending on your perspective. On the other hand, some teachers in these schools leave shortly after arriving in the classroom. Among the possible reasons for this revolving-door phenomenon are the disadvantages associated with rural living, the low salaries, and a tendency to assign greater weight to the drawbacks of rural school teaching (that is, seeing the wider range of students and subjects being taught as undesirable and more important than positive features such as smaller class sizes and fewer discipline problems). Teachers remaining in rural settings do so either by choice or because they cannot get work elsewhere. Presumably school authorities in rural areas seek teachers who are highly talented and genuinely interested in teaching in rural schools. It remains unclear how many teachers and prospective teachers fall into this category.

Features of Rural Student Populations

Several characteristics of students in rural schools, especially the share with special needs, the share with limited English skills, the share of highly mobile students, and the share of students who do not go to college, may impair the ability of rural schools to recruit and retain teachers.

One measure of the prevalence of students with specialized needs by school size and type is the share of students with Individualized Educational Programs (IEPs), which are required by federal law to establish eligibility for federally funded special education services. The share of students with IEPs is at best a crude measure of the incidence of needs because not all students with disabilities are recognized as such. Concerns also exist about the "overidentification" of students having special needs and receiving IEPs, perhaps as a regrettable way of removing them from regular instructional settings or of qualifying a district for additional federal and state financial aid, which may or may not reach the intended students. Another consideration, in small and rural settings, is that parents (particularly well-to-do parents) can respond to deficiencies in services by

moving to more highly populated areas with better services, thus reducing pressure on the rural districts to provide services.

A further possible difficulty with an IEP indicator is that IEPs themselves vary enormously in how demanding they are regarding the treatments and services identified. An IEP in a small, rural school could look quite different from one for a similar student in a large, urban school, though no relevant evidence seems to exist.

According to the NCES, rural schools look quite similar to the national average with respect to both the share of schools enrolling students with IEPs (on average, about 98 percent) and the share of enrolled students who received an IEP (on average, about 13 percent).[30] A lower share of the smallest schools has any students with IEPs (perhaps reflecting the tendency for parents to leave to find better offerings), but those with IEP students have a higher share of such students.

Other students with unusual needs are also putting pressures on rural schools. Efforts by meatpacking and other place-bound industries to cut costs by hiring recent immigrants are forcing schools to teach more students with limited English language skills. A study by Mark Grey finds enrollments of non-English-speaking students climbing in rural schools with little experience with such students. Grey also calls attention to the consequences for schools of high employee turnover in meatpacking.[31] Other researchers also cite the disruptive effects of high student turnover on schools.[32] Such problems run counter to the image of bucolic and tranquil rural schools and may over time affect the satisfaction that teachers in rural areas report with their working conditions.[33]

Rural districts in agricultural regions work with children of very low-income migrant farm workers, whose frequent comings and goings pose challenges for schools. Paul Green's review of research on migrant workers' living conditions uncovered crushing poverty and some of the harshest housing and labor conditions the United States has ever known. Edward R. Murrow's documentary, *Harvest of Shame,* broadcast on Thanks-

---

Rural districts in agricultural regions work with children of very low-income migrant farm workers, whose frequent comings and goings pose challenges for schools.

---

giving Day in 1960, called the nation's attention to the plight of farm workers. In 1971 Robert Coles's *Children of Crisis* also provided a detailed look at the conditions of migrant farm workers. A more recent assessment suggests that these conditions have remained disturbingly unchanged.[34]

Green points out that life expectancy in migratory farm families is quite low, about forty-nine years, and that infant mortality rates are quite high. He reports that stresses on migrant families are enormous and also cites maltreatment, malnutrition, and intermittent school attendance among their children.[35]

Reports that native children as well as teachers refuse to accept migrant children into the school culture do not reflect well on the schools that serve these students. One cannot help but wonder what the increased account-

ability provisions for schools in No Child Left Behind could inadvertently do to the willingness of schools to accept and provide appropriate education for these children. They could become marginalized and invisible, passed on from one set of largely indifferent institutional caregivers to the next with little sense of collective responsibility.

Instability in the student population of rural areas, however, is not limited to the comings and goings of migrant farm workers. It can also stem from poverty and the tendency of impoverished families to move from community to community to escape creditors and abusive spouses and to try to find work in economies where jobs are not stable.[36] Indeed, parallels exist with inner-city schools, where the comings and goings of students also pose significant educational challenges. As accountability measures are strengthened in response to NCLB and related state efforts, decisions need to be made and clarified about how to account for the progress of such highly mobile students. There is some risk that districts will be increasingly reluctant to incorporate mobile students into their programs out of a fear of being held accountable for what will presumably be low test scores.

One final characteristic of students in rural schools that may complicate teacher hiring and retention involves the likelihood of college attendance. As Gibbs argues, rural families have lower incomes and less wealth than urban families and are therefore less able to afford to send their children to college.[37] Moreover, rural students who do go to college are more likely to attend less expensive and less prestigious public colleges. The parents of children in rural areas are themselves less likely to have a college education, one of the well-established predictors of college attendance in the next generation.[38] As a consequence, college preparation courses are less well established in rural high schools than in others, thereby setting up something of a vicious cycle: college preparation programs are less prevalent in rural areas because demand is less well developed, and demand for such programs is less well developed because the programs do not exist.[39] The educational aspirations of rural youngsters will almost surely be low compared with those in other areas of the nation.

Implications for Policy

Some rural schools succeed admirably at attracting and retaining teachers whose qualifications are comparable to those of teachers at other kinds of schools. But for many rural schools, the quality of life in the community is lacking, working conditions are problematic, student needs are great, support services are limited, and professional support networks are inadequate. Salaries are lower for teachers in rural schools for many interconnected reasons, and certain types of rural schools struggle to appoint qualified teachers or make do with teachers who have fewer qualifications and face higher turnover rates. Moreover, teacher experience is also more limited in the smallest schools—a disturbing finding, given that teacher experience is emerging as one of the most important predictors of teaching effectiveness in the research literature.[40] And there is some reason to fear that inequalities in rural schools are becoming larger, particularly in light of the changing demographics of rural areas and the increases in the prevalence of bilingual students from impoverished backgrounds.

When it comes to public policy, this record suggests the need for a strategy focusing on a subcategory of what might be called hard-to-staff rural schools, rather than a blanket set of policies for all rural schools. In particular, the focus should be directly on such indicators as low teacher qualifications, teaching in fields far removed from the area of training, difficulty in hiring, high turnover, and a lack of diversity among teachers in the school, to name just a few. Efforts to identify hard-to-staff rural schools could parallel a similar effort focused on urban and suburban schools.

Assuming it is possible to identify hard-to-staff rural schools, what steps might be taken? Several interconnected approaches warrant further attention.

General Policy Options

One option would be to offer higher wages and benefits to teachers who are willing to work in hard-to-staff schools. The drawbacks associated with rural school teaching could, in theory, be offset by higher wages or improved benefits, or both, thereby improving the ability of officials in these areas to recruit and retain teachers comparable to their peers in other schools. For example, Mississippi offers an Employer-Assisted Housing Teacher Program that provides interest-free loans to licensed teachers in areas of critical shortage, along with a loan repayment program for student teachers who teach in rural areas of the state.[41]

The drawbacks to this approach are many. First, it could be prohibitively expensive to try to "buy your way around" a deeply problematic feature of rural life or schools. To the degree people dislike being isolated, for example, paying them to put up with isolation could be expensive. Moreover, no one knows how large the offsets would need to be or who should bear the burden of the cost. Perhaps the biggest problem of all is that a willingness to work in a hard-to-staff school for an agreed-upon bonus is no guarantee of effectiveness.

More promising, perhaps, are efforts to remove or modify the underlying conditions that are making the school difficult to staff. For example, policies in other government sectors affect the growth of bilingual populations in certain areas, and changes in these policies could have implications for schools. Presumably, steps can be taken to avoid sudden influxes of impoverished students with

In the case of immigration policies and migrant farm worker policies, the federal government would seem to be the logical party to bear the cost, given how many states are affected.

little English in certain schools. Or, if such population changes do take place, steps can be taken to better meet the needs of these students.

With respect to migrant farm workers, some progress has been made toward developing effective programs and building national databases that help affected schools track the progress of students.[42] The goal is to address the root cause of the difficulty and provide the needed relief. In the case of immigration policies and migrant farm worker policies, the federal government would seem to be the logical party to bear the cost, given how many states are affected.

To the degree that problems are rooted in differences in the economic capabilities of different regions, economic policies could help spur prosperity in regions where hard-

to-staff schools are located. Developing such policies would appear to be state and federal responsibilities.

Within the schools themselves, steps could be taken to offset some of the currently discouraging conditions. For example, modern telecommunications and computing technologies can reduce schools' need to rely on teachers in the classroom. A landmark NCES study of distance education technologies in the K–12 sector found that 36 percent of all school districts have students enrolled in distance education courses. Moreover, half the districts with students taking such courses reported that their students are in advanced placement or college courses, suggesting that districts are using these emerging technologies to enhance course offerings.[43]

The NCES study also found that rural districts were expanding their use of computing and telecommunication technologies, particularly in areas like advanced placement and college course offerings. Technology has long been seen as a way to overcome some of the drawbacks to rural settings, and districts are embracing these new opportunities at an accelerating pace. Steps that allow professional school personnel on site to tap into content knowledge will help solve a thorny and long-standing problem for schools in rural settings.

School and district reorganization could also help remove the root causes of distress. The reorganization logic on its face is compelling. If the difficulties can be traced to small scales of operation, why not remove the problem by reorganizing schools (and districts) into larger units? Quite a rich history surrounds reorganization, and efforts continue to this day.[44] Most if not all of the easily accomplished reorganizations, however, have already taken place; the remaining small units fall into the category of hard cases. It also seems a bit incongruous to be advocating re-organization in the face of prevailing thinking about the value of small high schools as a learning environment.[45]

In a number of areas, relatively simple improvements in basic human resource processes could yield improvements. For example, Dana Balter and William Duncombe, finding that districts in New York State make only limited use of the Internet to attract applicants, recommended significantly expanding use of the web.[46] Alaska has created statewide clearinghouses to help teachers find positions in rural areas. Timely posting and personalized follow-ups to inquiries can foster positive feelings about opportunities in rural areas. Parallel efforts to provide better support for those who accept job offers can have similarly positive effects on retention. Effective mentoring can break the tendency of new teachers to quickly leave rural settings.[47] Modern technology is also being used to build more effective professional communities of practice for teachers far from population centers. Carla McClure and Cynthia Reeves describe an array of initiatives, including online professional development, e-mentoring networks, and provision of student services such as speech therapy, psychological testing, and assessment using two-way, interactive telecommunications technology.[48]

When a school or district is small by choice rather than by necessity, and to the degree that its difficulties can be traced to the small size, the cost is logically borne by those electing to remain small, not passed along to others such as the taxpayers of an entire state. This reasonable position has, however, proven hard to put into place, and the failure of the political system to impose costs properly has complicated states' efforts to provide financial relief to schools and districts that face extra costs because of unavoidable small size.

Accountability issues also arise in the context of mobile student populations. Mark Grey notes the potential for windfalls to districts that lose students—and for corresponding burdens on districts that receive students at times when those students are not counted for aid purposes.[49] NCLB has significantly raised the accountability stakes for schools and districts and poses numerous questions about tracking and counting pupils, particularly mobile pupils.

One way to help solve the "problem" of the localized teacher market is a grow-your-own strategy. The idea is to take advantage of aspiring teachers' tendency to prefer to return "home" to teach, by working harder to cultivate interest and skill in teaching in areas with hard-to-staff schools. There are urban as well as rural variants of this strategy, and various writers have discussed the possibilities, although more typically from an urban perspective.[50]

Many states are pursuing grow-your-own strategies with a rural focus.[51] One promising approach involves working with paraprofessional aides already employed in rural schools to develop the requisite teaching skills. States are also finding that partnerships with colleges and universities that place aspiring teachers in rural areas can help break down negative stereotypes about teaching in rural schools.

Finally, a better understanding of the causes of staffing difficulties—in rural, urban, or suburban schools and districts—will allow policymakers to develop more effective and presumably less costly policy interventions. The United States invests phenomenal resources in developing and maintaining teachers, and research to improve the quality of teaching in hard-to-staff schools, regardless of where they may be located, can be expected to pay handsome dividends.

The No Child Left Behind Policy Context

Many analysts have examined the effects of NCLB on small and rural schools.[52] One interesting feature of this legislation is the Rural Education Achievement Program (REAP). The program is modest in size, with some 6,000 schools meeting the eligibility requirements and awards averaging about $20,000.[53]

But compliance issues abound with respect to how the law applies to rural settings. For example, the federal government's definition of a highly qualified teacher, including a requirement for full certification, a bachelor's degree, and demonstrated competence in all subject areas being taught, can create substantial problems for small rural schools, where teachers must teach in many different subject areas. Similarly, measures of student performance, particularly when the focus is on subgroup performance, create special challenges when there are few students in each of the various categories. As noted, small student numbers can cause volatile changes from year to year, and the challenge is to hold rural schools accountable to the spirit of the law even in the face of structural and measurement problems that can be quite troubling.

The U.S. Department of Education has made many modifications of NCLB to address the concerns coming from rural states, and former Secretary Rodney Paige created a special task force to help the department be responsive to its rural constituencies.[54] It is too soon to know whether the adjustments have been appropriate.

The attention NCLB is drawing to the importance of having highly qualified teachers in every classroom could help to move forward a serious policy agenda to improve the ability of rural schools to attract and retain teachers who function effectively.

Notes

1. Daryl Hobbs, "Foreword," in *Rural Education and Training in the New Economy*, edited by Robert M. Gibbs, Paul L. Swaim, and Ruy Teixeira (Iowa State University Press, 1998), p. viii.

2. See www.census.gov/population/www/estimates/aboutmetro.html.

3. Mark A. Grey, "Secondary Labor in the Meatpacking Industry: Demographic Change and Student Mobility in Rural Iowa Schools," *Journal of Research in Rural Education* 13, no. 3 (1997): 153–64.

4. David L. Brown and Thomas A. Hirschl, "Household Poverty in Rural and Metropolitan-Core Areas of the United States," *Rural Sociology* 60, no. 1 (1995): 61; Don E. Albrecht, Carol Mulford Albrecht, and Stan Albrecht, "Poverty in Nonmetropolitan America: Impacts of Industrial, Employment, and Family Structure Variables," *Rural Sociology* 65, no. 1 (2000): 87–103; Leif Jensen, Diane K. McLaughlin, and Tim Slack, "Rural Poverty," in *Challenges for Rural America in the Twenty-First Century*, edited by David L. Brown and Louis E. Swanson (Penn State Press, 2003), pp. 118–31.

5. Jensen, McLaughlin, and Slack, "Rural Poverty" (see note 4), table 9-1, p. 122.

6. Gregory C. Malhoit, "Providing Rural Students with a High-Quality Education: The Rural Perspective on the Concept of Educational Adequacy" (Washington: Rural School and Community Trust, 2005), p. 11; Lorna Jimerson, *The Competitive Disadvantage: Teacher Compensation in Rural America* (Washington: Rural School and Community Trust, 2003).

7. See, for example, Jane L. Collins and Amy Quark, "Globalizing Firms and Small Communities: The Apparel Industry's Changing Connection to Rural Labor Markets," *Rural Sociology* 71 (2006): 281–310; Thomas A. Lyson and Amy Guptill, "Commodity Agriculture, Civic Agriculture and the Future of U.S. Farming," *Rural Sociology* 69, no. 3 (2004): 370–85.

8. Kai A. Schafft and others, "The Community Context for Rural Youth Educational and Residential Aspirations," paper prepared for the annual meeting of the Rural Sociological Society, 2006. See also Georgeanne Artz, "Rural Brain Drain: Is It a Reality?" *Choices* 4 (2003): 11–15; and Bradford Mills and Gautam Hazarika, "The Migration of Young Adults from Non-Metropolitan Counties," *American Journal of Agricultural Economics* 83 (2001): 329–40.

9. Robert M. Gibbs, Paul L. Swaim, and Ruy Teixeira, eds., *Rural Education and Training in the New Economy: The Myth of the Rural Skills Gap* (Iowa State University Press, 1998).

10. Ibid.

11. I shall use the term *consolidate* broadly to include various types of centralization, annexation, and related phenomena. For an overview of this important historical feature of school districts, see David H. Monk and Emil J. Haller, *Organizational Alternatives for Small Rural Schools* (1986) (ERIC Document 281 694).

12. The NCES classified districts as rural if they were in local code 7 (rural, outside a metropolitan statistical area) or local code 8 (rural, inside a metropolitan statistical area). The NCES has revised these codes and has developed a more refined set of categories. For more information, see http://nces.ed.gov/ccd/rural_locales.asp.

13. Carla McClure and Cynthia Reeves, "Rural Teacher Recruitment and Retention: Review of the Research and Practice Literature," Appalachia Educational Laboratory (November 2004).

14. Richard M. Ingersoll, "Teacher Turnover and Teacher Shortages," *American Educational Research Journal* 38, no. 3 (2001): 499–534.

15. Robert M. Gibbs, "The Challenge Ahead for Rural Schools," *Forum for Applied Research and Public Policy* 15, no. 1 (2000): 82–87.

16. Elizabeth J. Greenberg and Ruy Teixeira, "Educational Achievement in Rural Schools," in *Rural Education and Training in the New Economy*, edited by Gibbs, Swaim, and Teixeira (see note 9), table 2.6, page 32.

17. William S. Carlsen and David H. Monk, "Differences between Rural and Nonrural Secondary Science Teachers: Evidence from the Longitudinal Study of American Youth," *Journal of Research in Rural Education* 8, no. 2 (1992): 1-10.

18. National Center for Education Statistics (NCES), *Digest of Education Statistics, 2004,* table 63.

19. Gibbs, "The Challenge Ahead for Rural Schools" (see note 15); Dale Ballou and Michael Podgursky, "Rural Teachers and Schools," in *Rural Education and Training in the New Economy,* edited by Gibbs, Swaim, and Teixeira (see note 9), 3–21.

20. Emil J. Haller, "High School Size and Student Indiscipline: Another Aspect of the School Consolidation Issue?" *Educational Evaluation and Policy Analysis* 14 (1992): 145–56.

21. David H. Monk, "Secondary School Size and Curriculum Comprehensiveness," *Economics of Education Review* 6, no. 2 (1987): 137–50.

22. Gibbs, "The Challenge Ahead for Rural Schools" (see note 15).

23. According to Jimerson, rural districts that lie in between the boundaries of urban and rural areas can face the greatest pressures to compete in recruiting and retaining teachers. Jimerson, *The Competitive Disadvantage* (see note 6).

24. Boyd and others, "The Draw of Home: How Teachers' Preferences for Proximity Disadvantage Urban Schools," Working Paper 9953 (Cambridge: National Bureau of Economic Research, March 2003).

25. Ibid.; Susanna Loeb and Michelle Reininger, "Public Policy and Teacher Labor Markets: What We Know and Why It Matters" (Michigan State University, Education Policy Center, April 2004).

26. Gibbs, "The Challenge Ahead for Rural Schools" (see note 15).

27. Robert Strauss, "Who Gets Hired to Teach? The Case of Pennsylvania," in *Better Teachers, Better Schools,* edited by M. Kanstroom (New York: Fordham Foundation, 1999), pp. 117–19.

28. Douglas N. Harris and colleagues, "When Supply Meets Demand: Principal Preferences and Teacher Hiring" (Florida State University), paper presented at the annual meeting of the American Educational Research Association, San Francisco, 2006.

29. Ingersoll, "Teacher Turnover and Teacher Shortages" (see note 14).

30. NCES, *Schools and Staffing Survey, 2003–04*, Public School, BIA School Data Files, tables 2 and 3.

31. Grey, "Secondary Labor in the Meatpacking Industry" (see note 3).

32. For a compelling example, see Michael Brunn, "The Social Organization of Diversity: The Changing Faces in Rural America," paper presented at the annual meeting of the Northern Rocky Mountain Educational Research Association, October 2002 (ERIC Document 469 367).

33. Recall the findings of Gibbs, "The Challenge Ahead for Rural Schools" (see note 15); and Ballou and Podgursky, "Rural Teachers and Schools" (see note 19).

34. Robert Coles, *Children of Crisis: vol. 2, Migrants, Sharecroppers, Mountaineers* (Boston: Little, Brown, 1971), and J. Moon, executive producer, *New Harvest, Old Shame* (Los Angeles: Corporation for Public Broadcasting, 1990), as cited in Paul E. Green, "The Undocumented: Educating the Children of Migrant Workers in America," *Bilingual Research Journal* 27, no. 1 (2003): 51–71.

35. Green, "The Undocumented" (see note 34).

36. Kai A. Schafft, "Poverty, Residential Mobility and Student Transience within a Rural New York School District," *Rural Sociology* 71, no. 2 (forthcoming).

37. Gibbs, "The Challenge Ahead for Rural Schools" (see note 15).

38. Ibid.

39. Ibid.

40. Jonah E. Rockoff, "The Impact of Individual Teachers on Student Achievement: Evidence from Panel Data," *American Economic Review* 94, no. 2 (2004): 247–52; and Douglas N. Harris and Tim R. Saas, "The Effects of Teacher Training on Teacher Value-Added" (Florida State University), paper presented at the annual meeting of the American Education Finance Association (2006).

41. McClure and Reeves, "Rural Teacher Recruitment and Retention" (see note 13), p. 10.

42. Angela Maria Branz-Spall and Roger Rosenthal, with Al Wright, "Children of the Road: Migrant Students, Our Nation's Most Mobile Population," *Journal of Negro Education* 72, no. 1 (2003): 55-62.

43. NCES, "Distance Education Courses for Public Elementary and Secondary School Students: 2002–2003," available at http://nces.ed.gov/pubsearch/pubsinfo.asp?pubid=2005010 (September 18, 2006).

44. See Monk and Haller, *Organizational Alternatives for Rural Schools* (note 11), for an overview of New York State's history. For a critical assessment of recent reorganization efforts in West Virginia, see Cynthia Reeves, "A Decade of Consolidation: Where Are the $avings?" (2004), a Challenge West Virginia document available at www.challengewv.org/resources.html.

45. Private foundation support, in particular from the Bill and Melinda Gates Foundation, has spurred interest in and creation of small high schools in recent years. For additional information, see Anne C. Lewis, "Washington Commentary: High Schools and Reform," *Phi Delta Kappan* 85, no. 8 (2004): 563; and Tom Vander Ark, "The Case for Small High Schools," *Educational Leadership* 59, no. 5 (2002): 55–59.

46. Dana Balter and William Duncombe, "Teacher Hiring Practices in New York State School Districts" (Maxwell School, Syracuse University, January 2005), available at www-cpr.maxwell.syr.edu/faculty/duncombe/.

47. Richard Ingersoll and J. Kralik, "The Impact of Mentoring on Teacher Retention" (Denver: Education Commission of the States, 2004).

48. McClure and Reeves, "Rural Teacher Recruitment and Retention (see note 13), p. 12.

49. Grey, "Secondary Labor in the Meatpacking Industry" (see note 3).

50. Boyd and others, "The Draw of Home" (see note 24); Loeb and Reininger, "Public Policy and Teacher Labor Markets" (see note 25).

51. McClure and Reeves, "Rural Teacher Recruitment and Retention" (see note 13), p. 9.

52. Rhonda Barton, "Challenges and Opportunities of NCLB for Small, Rural, and Isolated Schools" (Portland, Ore.: Northwest Regional Lab, 2003) (ERIC Document 482 267); Cynthia Reeves, "Implementing the No Child Left Behind Act: Implications for Rural Schools and Districts" (Northcentral Regional Lab, 2003) (ERIC Document 475 037); and Lorna Jimerson, "The Devil Is in the Details: Rural-Sensitive Best Practices for Accountability under No Child Left Behind," Rural Trust Policy Brief Series on Rural Education (Washington: Rural School and Community Trust, 2004).

53. Reeves, "Implementing the No Child Left Behind Act" (see note 52).

54. For more on the secretary's task force and the virtual town hall meeting that it sponsored, see http://www.ed.gov/about/offices/ods/ruraled/index.html.

Teachers Unions and Student Performance: Help or Hindrance?

Randall W. Eberts

Summary

Randall Eberts explores the role of teachers unions in public education. He focuses particularly on how collective bargaining agreements shape the delivery of educational services, how unions affect both student achievement and the cost of providing quality education, and how they support educational reform efforts.

Eberts's synthesis of the empirical research concludes that union bargaining raises teachers' compensation, improves their working conditions, and enhances their employment security—while also raising the cost of providing public education by upwards of 15 percent. The effect of unions on student performance is mixed. Students of average ability who attend school in union districts perform better on standardized tests, whereas low-achieving and high-achieving students perform worse. However, the overall gain in achievement does not make up for the higher cost.

Of late, unions have begun to be more supportive of school reform, moving from an adversarial bargaining model to a more collaborative one in which teachers and administrators share common goals and hold joint responsibility. Yet unions' desire to participate in reform does not match their fervor to organize in the 1960s and 1970s. While national union leadership has talked about reform, local affiliates have initiated most of the reform efforts, pioneering reforms such as accountability and incentive pay. In Eberts's view, one reason that unions have been slow to embrace reform efforts is the lack of consensus on their effectiveness. He argues that many reforms have been too narrowly focused; rather, effective schools result from well-designed systems and processes. In principle, adopting standards that help teachers focus on lessons they want students to learn, aligning their teaching to the lessons, and devising measurements that demonstrate that students are responding to these lessons can improve teaching as long as the public, policymakers, and school administrators acknowledge the complexity of the learning process and the broad outcomes that society desires.

www.futureofchildren.org

Randall W. Eberts is executive director of the W. E. Upjohn Institute for Employment Research. He gratefully acknowledges his colleagues Joe Stone and Kevin Hollenbeck for their collaboration on work referenced and used in this chapter. He thanks Allan Hunt for helpful comments on earlier drafts and Phyllis Molhoek for her assistance in preparing the manuscript. The views and observations expressed in the chapter are the sole responsibility of the author and do not necessarily represent positions of the W. E. Upjohn Institute for Employment Research.

America's need to provide high-quality education to its children has never been greater. In today's knowledge-based economy, education—and public education in particular—is at the center of U.S. efforts to maintain a competitive international edge. But many observers fear that those efforts are failing. In international tests, U.S. students rank only in the mid-range of nations in the critical areas of math and science. Public surveys reveal grave concern about the quality of public education—and also about efforts to improve it. Over the past several decades federal, state, and local policymakers have adopted one education reform after another, with little systemwide success. Some reforms focus on improving the existing system—for example, by adopting incentive pay and encouraging accountability. Others aim to create new systems—for example, by promoting vouchers and charter schools. So far, the public appears to prefer reforming the current system, not abandoning it.[1]

Some observers blame specific groups linked with public education for the slow pace of improvement. Some of the strongest attacks have been reserved for teachers unions, which are said to have captured schools to advance their own interests, not those of the students. Many critics of unions believe that collective bargaining has created a tangled web of rules that keep public schools from being able to respond to the changing needs of students and that the bargaining process has influenced public education more than any other factor.[2] As a result, they say, public education is both more costly and less effective than it should be. Such criticisms are not new. In 1983 the landmark study *A Nation at Risk*, by the congressionally mandated National Commission on Excellence in Education, alerted Americans to a crisis in educa-

tion.[3] The study, which challenged educators, policymakers, and parents to rethink the way students are educated, set in motion a wave of educational reform that continues to this day. Teachers, who had hitherto attracted little public notice, suddenly found themselves at center stage in the controversy over school quality. The nation's immediate response to the report was to set up systems to improve teacher and school accountability. Because the new focus—on monitoring and assessing teacher practices and on tying compensation to teachers' performance—was antithetical to two decades of work by teachers unions to decouple salaries from performance and to increase the autonomy of teachers in the classroom, teachers came to be perceived as reluctant participants in reform. Meanwhile, reform efforts gained little traction and yielded few, if any, sustained attempts at merit pay or systems of accountability. Today these same reforms remain under discussion and teachers unions continue to find themselves in the fray.

Aware of charges that they are resistant to change, teachers unions have voiced concern about school quality and urged the need for reform. Robert Chase, past president of the National Education Association (NEA), the nation's largest teachers union, called for a new unionism based on collaborative bargaining with school districts to help improve school performance. In an address at the National Press Club in 1997, he reminded his nearly 2.7 million members of the need for unions to take an active role in planning and implementing educational reforms.[4]

In this article I explore both the extent to which teachers' collective bargaining affects the quality of education and the role of bargaining in the educational reform movement. Beyond the rhetoric of union advocates and opponents, what do researchers know about how unions affect student achievement and the cost of providing quality education? Are unions a help or a hindrance? To what extent are they promoting constructive change to improve public education and to what extent are they thwarting such efforts?

Collective Bargaining by Teachers

Collective bargaining is the process by which teachers and administrators agree on a set of regulations that govern working conditions and determine compensation and fringe benefits. Dubbed a "web of rules," it can affect every dimension of the workplace and can subsequently influence educational outcomes.[5] It defines the rights and duties of teachers to particular assignments, guarantees teachers' participation in school governance and educational policymaking, establishes grievance procedures, and at times creates disciplinary sanctions for teachers' failure to achieve certain standards. It also provides for teacher participation in restructuring the workplace. More specifically, the far-reaching web of rules may include working conditions, such as the length of the school day, hours of instruction and preparation time, and interaction time with parents; class size; the number and responsibility of supplemental classroom personnel, such as aides; employment protection; assignment to schools and grade levels; criteria for promotion; reductions in force; professional services; in-service and professional development; instructional policy committees; student grading and promotion; teacher evaluation; performance indicators; grievance procedures; student discipline and teacher safety; and the exclusion of pupils from the classroom. The list goes on. Suffice it to say that collective bargaining agreements, through negotiated rules and regulations, establish school policy and govern how teach-

ers, administrators, parents, and students interact in the delivery of educational services. As the *Wall Street Journal* noted nearly three decades ago, "Teachers' unions have become crucial forces in deciding how public education should be run in the U.S."[6]

Laws governing public sector collective bargaining have come almost exclusively from

---

Suffice it to say that collective bargaining agreements, through negotiated rules and regulations, establish school policy and govern how teachers, administrators, parents, and students interact in the delivery of educational services.

---

state governments. Although the National Labor Relations Act (NLRA) of 1935, as amended in 1947, required employers to meet and confer in good faith with respect to wages, hours, and other terms and conditions of employment, it did not include public sector employers. Congress has considered legislation to govern negotiations of public employees, but states have assumed leadership.

Meaningful state legislation giving public employees a voice in determining the conditions of their employment was first enacted in the 1960s. Before then, two states, Alaska and New Hampshire, had allowed local governments to negotiate with groups representing public employees, but neither state extended to public employees the same rights as granted to private employees. Alaska's law (in 1935) and New Hampshire's law (in 1955) did not require or ensure bargaining; they only allowed local governments to negotiate under specified conditions. Permitting public employees to bargain, nonetheless, was a big step in treating private and public employees equally in the bargaining arena. Before passage of the two state collective bargaining

---

Today unions represent 67 percent of the nation's 3 million active public elementary and secondary school teachers.

---

laws, contracts between school boards and teachers unions were seen as an illegal delegation to school boards of local citizens' sovereign constitutional powers. Granting teachers and other public employees the power to bargain collectively was believed to give them clout over and above their private sector counterparts because they were already able, through the political process, to elect the public officials who would govern and manage the workplace.[7]

In 1962 Wisconsin became the first state to pass legislation governing public employee bargaining that resembled the language found in the NLRA. The Wisconsin statute required local governments to bargain in good faith with employee groups and also created administrative enforcement measures. It charged the Wisconsin Public Employee Relations Board with determining appropriate bargaining units, enforcing the prevention of prohibited practices, fact finding, and mediating disputes. The law also marked the beginning of widespread recognition of the rights of public employees to bargain collectively. Within the next five years, New York and Michigan passed similar laws, and by 1974 thirty-seven states had passed legislation permitting public employee bargaining—a number that remains unchanged to this day.

After public sector collective bargaining was legally recognized, teacher representation grew significantly. In 1974 roughly 22 percent of public school teachers were covered by collective bargaining. That share doubled in six years and grew to more than 60 percent by the mid-1980s. Today unions represent 67 percent of the nation's 3 million active public elementary and secondary school teachers.[8] The coverage rate for teachers is much higher than the average of 40 percent for all public sector employees. Representation varies geographically, with some teachers in all regions and all states reporting that they belong to a labor union or a similar association or else are nevertheless covered under a collective bargaining contract. The highest proportion of representation is in the Middle Atlantic region (88 percent), with the New England (82 percent), East North Central (81 percent), and Pacific (82 percent) regions close behind. Coverage is lowest in the West South Central region, at 40 percent, and slightly higher in the South Atlantic (47 percent) and East South Central (52 percent) regions.

Teachers were not always anxious to be a part of organized labor. In the early years of the NEA, members saw its role as promoting the professional side of teaching. Although NEA members were sensitive to their financial needs, the union's official posture was one of discourse, not collective action.[9] The American Federation of Teachers (AFT), by contrast, tried from its inception to bring teachers into the mainstream of organized labor. Unlike the larger and more powerful NEA, the AFT advocated collective action as the best way to promote the interest of teachers.

Researchers generally cite four reasons for the growth of collective bargaining for teachers.[10] The first, as noted, was the passage of state laws protecting teachers' rights to seek bargaining recognition. Second, declining enrollment and skyrocketing inflation in the 1970s eroded teachers' financial well-being, and general discontent with access to and influence over educational decisionmaking diminished teachers' sense of professionalism. Third, changing social conditions and workforce demographics and an increasing militancy and social awareness provided fertile ground for the union movement. Finally, as unionism in the private sector continually declined, union organizers came to see teachers and the public sector as ripe for organizing. And rivalry between the AFT and the NEA increased their fervor.[11]

During their formative years of collective bargaining, teachers unions patterned themselves after their private sector counterparts, which followed what has been called an industrial bargaining model.[12] According to the NEA's Chase, "When we reinvented our association in the 1960s, we modeled it after traditional, industrial unions. Likewise, we accepted the industrial premise: Namely, that labor and management have distinct, conflicting roles and interests . . . that we are destined to clash . . . that the union-management relationship is inherently adversarial."[13] The industrial model is based on an adversarial, not collaborative role, with management controlling the workplace and workers filling narrowly defined tasks. Such a model values standardized practice and views similarly

skilled workers as interchangeable, each to be treated alike. From the viewpoint of teachers in the classroom, administrators unilaterally set educational policy and teachers comply. Instruction is delivered uniformly to large groups of students, and the teaching force is undifferentiated. The primary role of unions is to protect workers from unrealistic demands of management, ensure a safe working environment, and extract the maximum compensation possible. Bargaining focuses more on teachers' interests and less on their performance and how that performance affects student outcomes. While perhaps more applicable to private sector production workers, such a stance places teachers at odds with their desire to be treated as professionals as they bargain in their self-interest.

The extent to which teachers unions affect school quality and ultimately student achievement depends on many factors. First, how successful are unions in negotiating higher salaries and fringe benefits? Second, how successful are they in negotiating provisions that affect workplace conditions, such as class size and transfers, which in turn may affect students' school-based learning environment? Third, how successful are unions in negotiating rules that govern teachers' interaction with students, parents, and other teachers? Fourth, how successful are they in shielding teachers from accountability for their own performance? All these factors and others must be considered to determine the bottom line of collective bargaining: what effect, if any, it has on student achievement.

Outcomes of Collective Bargaining Negotiations

I begin by examining the ability of teachers unions to affect their compensation, working conditions, employment security, and workplace governance through collective bargaining and then look at the evidence of the overall effect of union bargaining on student achievement.[14] I note at the outset that researchers at times draw a distinction between unionization and collective bargaining. Unionization is seen as the influence teachers exert on their school district through the bargaining power of their membership; collective bargaining, by contrast, has more to do with the establishment of rules governing the workplace and compensation through negotiated collective bargaining agreements. It is a subtle distinction, because the effects of bargaining power are seen in the ability of unions to negotiate higher compensation and to include key provisions in their contracts. Furthermore, bargaining power determines the strength with which contract provisions influence administrative decisions.[15]

A necessary foundation for bargaining power is the extent to which state laws permit and require collective bargaining. A recent review of state collective bargaining laws for the public sector found that the presence or absence of state laws governing union security and laws defining collective bargaining rights affects the wages of public sector employees.[16] For example, earnings of union workers are between 4 and 11 percent higher where an agency or union shop is either compulsory or negotiable than where it is not. Consequently, given the legal right to bargain collectively, public sector unions are able to increase the wages of their members, which in turn affects the allocation of resources in the public sector.

Teachers unions may wield power at the polls and through the political process, as well as around the bargaining table. As noted, one argument against allowing public sector bargaining was that public employees have the ability to elect the government officials who would govern and manage the workplace and allocate resources that directly affect the teachers' working conditions and compensation.[17] In addition to their individual votes, in many local jurisdictions, teachers and other public employees have the opportunity to form a strong voting bloc that can disproportionately affect the outcomes of school board elections, school bond elections, and other referendum ballots directly affecting public schools. Teachers unions can, and have, come out strongly against state referenda to allow charter schools and voucher systems, which they believe could divert students away from traditional public schools and thus reduce public school resources, their union ranks, and their bargaining and political power.[18] A state teachers union typically has a strong lobbying arm that finances media campaigns, supports political action committees, and contributes to specific campaigns through voluntary contributions from its members.[19]

Contract Provisions

Bargaining power may be reflected simply in the number of significant provisions found in contracts. One study of the collective bargaining contracts of New York State school districts, which are represented by either the NEA or AFT, found that these agreements are hierarchical, in that some provisions are more easily negotiated, while others, presumably more restrictive to management, are harder to include.[20] Thus contracts with more restrictive provisions, such as no reduction in the teacher workforce during the length of the contract, would seem to indicate greater bargaining power on the part of teachers unions. In fact, the study finds that the sheer number of contract provisions positively affects the negotiation of teacher salaries. Teachers in districts with fifty contract provisions (of a possible fifty-three predetermined categories) received $1,900 more, on average, than those in districts with the minimum number of items. Budget allocations are also affected by the inclusion or removal of specific contract provisions through the negotiating process, providing further evidence of the link between bargaining power and contract provisions.

Teacher Pay and Benefits

Two detailed studies, one by William Baugh and Joe Stone and the other by Caroline Hoxby, using different techniques and data samples, find that teachers covered by collective bargaining tend to earn 5 to 12 percent more than those who are not covered.[21] This is consistent with the typical range found for union pay premiums in other sectors.[22] Evidence on the fringe benefit premium is not as extensive. One study, based on contracts for New York State public schools, finds that bargaining has a larger effect on fringe benefits than it does on pay.[23] This finding corresponds to evidence from other sectors, where the effect of bargaining on fringe benefits is typically larger than the effect on pay. As noted, higher pay and fringe benefits, although they increase educational costs, may also increase the quality of education if they attract better teachers.

Working Conditions

The working conditions about which teachers appear to be most concerned are class size, time for preparation and other activities away from students, and autonomy in the classroom.[24] Three studies, each relying on different data sets, find that student-teacher ratios are 7–12 percent lower for union teachers than for nonunion teachers.[25] Teachers have also successfully negotiated provisions that regulate instructional and preparation time and limit the time they must devote to administrative duties and meeting with parents. A study by Eberts and

Joe Stone found that elementary teachers in union districts spend 4 percent more time in class preparation and administrative duties but 3 percent less time in instruction than their nonunion counterparts.

Another aspect of working conditions is teachers' mode of instruction. The Eberts and Stone study finds that teachers unions tend to "standardize" the workplace, by relying more on traditional classroom organization than on other instructional methods. In national data for fourth-grade students, it also finds that union schools are less likely to rely on specialized, less standard instructional methods in mathematics. Students in union schools spend 42 percent less time with a specialist, 62 percent less time with a specialized aide, 26 percent less time with a tutor, and 68 percent less time in independent, programmed study.[26] Such standardization, common to unionized workplaces, may affect average and atypical students in different ways.

Employment Security

Unions and their members also seek job protection from temporary downturns in enrollment and from reductions in employment as the costs of union pay and fringe benefits rise. Many public school teachers, both union and nonunion, are granted tenure after a few years of regular employment, which protects them from dismissal except for specific causes, few of which are related to performance. But in addition, unions protect employment by negotiating lower class size and reduction-in-force provisions. As noted, student-teacher ratios tend to be lower in union schools, even in the face of higher pay and fringe benefits. Reduction-in-force provisions are also prevalent in many district contracts. Their effectiveness in protecting employment can be seen in their positive effects on wages and their mitigating effects on terminations in districts with declining enrollments.[27]

Cost of Instruction

In other unionized sectors, the increased pay, better fringe benefits, improved working conditions, more standardized and regulated workplace, and protections against job loss common in union contracts typically come at the expense of a higher cost of production.[28] The same is true for public education. Although a few early studies found little or no difference in the costs of operating unionized schools, the two most detailed studies provide consistent evidence of higher operating costs.[29] One finds that the operating cost of unionized elementary schools is about 15 percent higher; of unionized high schools, about 8 percent higher.[30] The other, relying on different, more recent data, finds that the costs of operating unionized high schools are about 12 percent higher.[31]

By negotiating higher salaries and smaller class size, teachers unions may influence the way schools allocate their resources. It is possible that higher payroll costs could be covered by raising taxes, leaving the same money available for other educational spending unrelated to teacher compensation. But studies show that teachers unions distort the way educational spending is allocated because the higher compensation typically reduces funds available for other instructional purposes.

Administrative Flexibility

By their very nature, contracts restrict the discretion of administrators. They can dictate class size and teacher assignments, impose restrictions on teacher dismissal and reduction in force, and determine the extent to which teachers participate in key decisions. Codifying strict rules into a contract, which

may be in place for up to three years, could be problematic for administrators seeking to adapt to change. But although these provisions reduce the discretion of administrators, they need not completely impede their effectiveness. As one study reports, "truly effective principals usually accept collective bargaining and use the contract both to manage their building more systematically and to increase teacher participation in school decisionmaking. Less effective principals may view the contract as an obstacle to a well-run school and then use it as an excuse for poor management."[32] Superintendents may use union rules to strengthen their control over principals and centralize decisionmaking within the district. Such efforts may lead to more effective schools if they are aligned with the desired outcomes and if teachers and principals share similar views. Whether this takes place is an empirical issue that few analysts have examined with any rigor. The Eberts and Stone study finds from a national survey that the gap in perceptions between elementary school teachers and principals about a principal's active leadership is larger in union than in nonunion schools. The same is true for perceptions about teachers and principals working well together. By contrast, it finds no difference in perceptions regarding staff being well informed or identifying conflict. It also finds that time spent by principals in instructional leadership leads to higher test scores in union districts but lower scores in nonunion districts. These findings are only suggestive of the differences in attitudes and their effect on student achievement that stem from the greater structure introduced by collective bargaining contracts.[33]

Student Achievement

The question that causes the most public concern, of course, is whether teachers unions affect student achievement. Evidence on "productivity" from other (nonteacher) unionized sectors is mixed. In some sectors, union workers appear to be more productive; in others, less. In most cases, though, the differences are small, especially in the most rigorous studies.[34] For teachers the critical finding seems to be not whether teachers unions raise or lower student achievement, but how they influence the effectiveness of schools.

What is the evidence on student achievement? The evidence that is available is not ideal. One would like to assign students randomly to schools that are also randomly assigned to union or nonunion status and then observe student achievement over time. The best approximations to this ideal experiment use extensive statistical controls for both student and school attributes, as well as for the nonrandom assignment of students and schools. But even good approximations to the ideal have been difficult to achieve. Another approach has been to look at the effects of unions on schools' ability to attract and retain more qualified teachers, through higher pay and fringe benefits, better working conditions, and a greater voice in decisionmaking and teacher transfers. One study, by Susanna Loeb and Marianne Page, finds that higher wages attract a better pool of teacher applicants.[35] But another, by Susan Moore Johnson and Morgaen Donaldson, finds no consistent evidence that the quality of teachers has increased or decreased as a result of collective bargaining.[36] Although other studies have shown that teachers contribute to student achievement, they have difficulty identifying which teacher attributes are responsible.[37] Therefore, I review studies that link collective bargaining directly to student achievement, instead of trying to piece together the effect of unions on the various factors affecting student achievement.

Often, the most widely reported evidence is based on state data for SAT or ACT scores. Three prominent state studies find roughly similar positive effects for teachers unions on average scores on either the SAT or the ACT—between 4.5 and 8 percent.[38] One of these also finds a similar positive effect (4.4 percent) on high school graduation rates.[39] These studies are problematic, however, be-

For teachers the critical finding seems to be not whether teachers unions raise or lower student achievement, but how they influence the effectiveness of schools.

cause they have few controls for student and district effects and aggregate the student outcomes of vastly different school districts into one measure of student outcomes for each state.

A few studies have looked at student achievement using individual student data with relatively detailed controls for both student and school attributes.[40] Across four different samples of students (the Sustaining Effects Survey, High School and Beyond, the National Assessment of Economic Education, and the National Educational Longitudinal Survey) and three different grade levels (fourth, tenth, and twelfth), these studies yield remarkably consistent results. Collectively, they find that teachers unions raise average student scores on various standardized exams between 1 and 2 percent. Some also estimate the effect of unions on gains in test scores from the beginning to the end of the school

Randall W. Eberts

year. Eberts and Stone, for example, find that students in union districts have a 5 percent higher gain in before and after testing than students in nonunion schools. Given the differences among samples, grade levels, test measures, and empirical methodologies, the similarity of these findings cannot be ignored. Yet the effects are relatively small. Furthermore, they are positive only for aver-

---

Disparities in the way unions affect students of varying ability can be explained in part by the standardizing effect of unions on schools.

---

age-achieving students. Low- and high-performing students fare worse in union schools.[41]

Caroline Hoxby uses a different measure of student outcomes: high school dropout rates. Using district-level data, she finds that teachers unions are associated with a 2.3 percent increase in dropout rates and infers that unionization reduces student achievement.[42] Hoxby also finds that union effects on dropout rates are larger in areas with little interdistrict competition.

Hoxby's findings raise the question of how teachers unions can raise average student achievement on standardized exams (based on the four studies mentioned), yet also increase high school dropout rates. Given that her analysis is based on district data, one answer might be that low-scoring students are more likely to drop out, so that relatively higher-scoring students remain in the district to take the tests. But that does not explain the

positive achievement found in early grades (in the case of Eberts and Stone, fourth grade), where the dropout rates are much lower and the achievement results are still similar to those for high school.

Another explanation may lie in the methodologies used and the ability to control for factors affecting student achievement that are unrelated to unionization, as well as unobservable variables that may have caused teachers to unionize. A closer look at the two groups of studies—those based on individual student data and Hoxby's, based on district data—shows more similarities than differences in their methodologies.[43] Without considering the problems inherent in using student dropout rates to proxy student achievement, it is not apparent that one methodology is superior to another, because each has its advantage in controlling for important factors related to student achievement.[44]

A more satisfactory answer may lie in the evidence on the effect of unions on the distribution of student achievement, rather than on average student achievement. The finding by Eberts and Stone and others of an inverted-U-shaped effect of teachers unions on student achievement may help to reconcile the evidence of positive effects on achievement for average students with negative effects on high school dropout rates. Dropout rates are highly correlated with student success in schools, and low-performing students are much more likely to drop out. If teachers unions tend to reduce the academic success of weak students, one would tend to expect the dropout rate to increase, because it is the weakest students who are the most likely to drop out.

Disparities in the way unions affect students of varying ability can be explained in part by the standardizing effect of unions on schools. As noted, unionized schools rely to a greater extent on traditional classroom instruction and less on specialized modes of instruction. Because standard methods are likely to work best for the average student and specialized modes to work best for atypical students, one might expect the effects to differ by student ability.[45] This explanation is reinforced by Argys and Rees, who find that effects no longer differ after they take into account the type and size of the instructional setting and other related classroom factors.[46]

The evidence on how unions affect student achievement leads to the general conclusion that there is no simple answer and that generalization is difficult. The average-achieving student does not appear to be harmed by attending union schools and may even fare slightly better, whereas low-achieving, at-risk students and high-achieving students tend to do better in nonunion schools. Even though some threads of evidence are promising, researchers have much to learn about how unions affect student outcomes. What is known with some certainty is that the productivity gains of unionization, if any, do not match the increase in cost, upward of 15 percent, that unions place on education through higher compensation and their influence on resource allocation within schools.

Reform Initiatives

In recent years, both the NEA and the AFT have advocated a new model for collective bargaining known as reform bargaining. Reform bargaining recognizes that management and labor are not adversaries but share common interests, are jointly responsible for the outcomes of their organization, and should find it useful to collaborate to pursue those common goals. Instead of a standardized workplace in which duties are rigidly defined and compart-

mentalized, both management and labor strive for flexibility, and workers participate in site-based decisionmaking. For teacher collective bargaining, the new model calls for teachers and administrators to hold joint responsibility for schooling, share common goals, and collaborate in determining governance, instructional, and personnel issues.[47]

The first waves of reform initiatives, prompted in 1983 by *A Nation at Risk*, were not widely embraced by teachers unions. In many respects, the reform movement collided head-on with the union movement, which by the early 1980s included nearly two-thirds of the nation's public school teachers. As described by Lorraine McDonnell and Anthony Pascal in their study of the role of unions in implementing reform, the bargaining process continued to place material gain, such as higher salaries and benefits and better working conditions, over efforts to increase teacher professionalism and accountability.[48] Johnson and Kardos also conclude that many unions tried to stall reform in the belief that the public would soon lose interest. But they discovered that far from losing interest, the public instead began to call for sweeping changes, such as vouchers and charter schools, which could threaten the very existence of public schools and of the unions themselves.[49]

As in the race to organize teachers, the NEA and AFT have continued to jockey for position in leading the reform effort. Sensing the nation's concern about teacher complacency during the 1980s, the AFT began to soften its strong activist and militant stand in bargaining. Instead of pushing for hard-line positions on wage demands and bargaining provisions, the AFT has urged its affiliates to establish higher standards—to police its ranks, hold teachers accountable to union standards, and bargain cooperatively rather than contentiously with management.[50] The NEA, most recently with the public proclamations of President Chase, has echoed these sentiments while insisting on the urgent need for action.

Charles Kerchner and Julia Koppich note that union-sponsored reform does not have the momentum that collective bargaining had during the 1960s and 1970s.[51] They see three

---

While national union organizations have talked about reform, much of the effort has been initiated by local affiliates, sometimes with resistance from their parent organizations.

---

internal challenges to union reform. The first is a lack of clarity about goals. While union leaders do not lack vision, say the authors, the complexity of the task of improving school quality makes it hard for them to discuss the issue without raising teachers' fears of how reform will affect their work life and compensation. The second challenge is organizational undercapacity, because union leaders and members have not embraced the urgency of reform. Many teachers do not believe that public schools need to be reformed. Third, without the vision and commitment of teachers and leaders, it is difficult to build a strong political coalition that would legitimate reform roles. Furthermore, the lack of agreement about the effectiveness of many reform initiatives makes it difficult to convince teachers to implement the changes.

While national union organizations have talked about reform, much of the effort has been initiated by local affiliates, sometimes with resistance from their parent organizations. In 1996, a group of reform-minded NEA and AFT local affiliates formed the Teachers Union Reform Network (TURN). The brainchild of two local union presidents, TURN is funded primarily by grants from private foundations, not from the parent organizations. Its twenty-plus members meet regularly to exchange ideas and promote reform initiatives. Its goals include "improving the quality of teaching" and "seeking to expand the scope of collective bargaining to include instructional and professional issues."[52] Kerchner and Koppich have analyzed the collective bargaining contracts of twenty-one TURN members to see which types of provisions they find important for reform.[53] The provisions include (with the number of contracts in parentheses): shared decisionmaking and budgeting (21), uses of time (19), professional development (15), peer assistance and review (14), school-based staff and budget (14), intervention strategy for low-performing schools (10), alternative compensation, such as pay-for-performance (8), parent engagement (4), charter and pilot schools (4), and learning standards (2).

In many cases, success in including these provisions in collective bargaining agreements came about not from a broad acceptance of the new unionism at the national level, but from stances taken by local union leaders and school administrators. Several local unions and their districts stand out for pioneering initiatives addressing accountability and incentive pay. Both initiatives have gained considerable support among policymakers and have been implemented to varying degrees across the country; performance standards were most recently embodied in the No Child Left Behind Act (NCLB) of 2001. After briefly describing these initiatives, I will focus on evidence of their effectiveness in improving student outcomes, in particular, test scores.

Accountability

Reforms to improve the accountability of schools have sought either to improve or replace the existing public education system. Improvements within the system involve changes that directly affect the internal operations of schools. Chief among these are standards for student performance, measurement tools to track student progress, and prescribed consequences for students, teachers, and schools if standards are not met. Reforms that go outside the system put competitive pressure on schools to improve, by enhancing parental choice. This latter wave of reform has created a number of different voucher programs that enable parents to use public dollars to send their children to private schools. It has also created publicly supported "charter" schools, outside the direct control of local school boards, as alternatives to conventional public schools.

Both types of reforms were proposed and adopted by local teachers unions before they were instituted as state or national policy. Toledo, Ohio, is generally credited with paving the way among teachers unions in holding its members more accountable for performance. Throughout the 1970s, the union pressed to expand its role in evaluating teachers. It finally codified a plan in its collective bargaining agreement in 1981. Known as the Toledo Plan, it included two separate programs—an intern program for first-year teachers and an intervention program for experienced teachers who need substantial remediation. Both use consulting teachers, who take a three-year leave from the classroom to

serve as both mentor and evaluator. A nine-member Intern Board of Review, including five teachers, makes the final decision to renew or dismiss an intern. The board also determines whether a tenured teacher who is seen by the principal or the union's building committee as underperforming needs to undergo a performance review and get assistance. If performance does not improve sufficiently, the teacher may be let go.[54]

Incentive Pay

Other school districts adopted the peer evaluation system initiated by Toledo and expanded it to link pay to performance. For example, the Columbus, Ohio, Education Association adopted a peer evaluation system in 1986 but later agreed to school-based salary incentives and limits on the impact of seniority.[55] The Cincinnati Federation of Teachers recently expanded its peer review process and professional development academy by implementing a compensation system based on professional development instead of seniority. Teachers are assessed on predetermined quality standards and paid accordingly when they have achieved them. Seattle has taken pay for performance one step further by including student achievement as a quality standard.

Denver, probably more than any other school district to date, has pursued an ambitious pay-for-performance experiment. Ironically, in 1921 Denver became the first school district to replace a merit pay approach with a single salary schedule based on seniority. Seventy-eight years later the district administration and teachers association agreed on a two-year pilot that would base teachers' pay in part directly on the achievement of their students. As described by Donald Gratz, who was in charge of evaluating the Denver Incentive Program, the pilot provided small bonuses for teachers who met either one or two student achievement objectives that they themselves chose.[56] These objectives had to be approved by their principals. For each objective met, teachers received $750. For a school to join the pilot, 85 percent of its faculty had to vote for participation. Thirteen schools signed up.

The Denver Teachers Association had opposed the new compensation system as initially proposed but, wishing to avoid continued confrontation with the administration, agreed after winning three important concessions. One was that teachers' performance would be based on objectives of their own choice, with approval of their principals. Another was that an outside, objective party would evaluate the effectiveness of the pilot. The third was that the final plan would be subject to a general vote of the association's members. By the time the system was brought to a vote and approved in 2004, it had been modified extensively. The approved system included four components. Compensation was based on student growth objectives; on earned professional development units, including advanced degrees; and on two bonuses, one for serving in hard-to-staff assignments and the other for serving in hard-to-serve schools.

At first blush, it would seem that teachers unions should find standards-based systems attractive, because they promote standardization of the workplace. With clearly defined goals and objectives and mandates to adhere to these standards, teachers understand what is expected of them, are protected from capricious directives from administrators that may distract them from these goals, and can relate negotiated contract provisions, such as class size reduction, to the achievement of these standards. But teachers believe that standards-based accountability intrudes into their autonomy in the classroom. It dictates curriculum and the tests that the teacher should administer, and it establishes the outcomes that are expected. The first two items—curriculum and testing—have normally been outside the immediate discretion of teachers, although teachers do participate in their design and implementation. The third—being held accountable for student outcomes—is the major point of contention. Teachers believe that such accountability can expose them to arbitrary treatment by administrators and make them responsible for things outside their immediate control. They also believe it can base compensation on ambiguous criteria.[57] The few teachers associations that have adopted accountability systems linked to pay have opted to maintain some control over determining objectives and how outcomes are measured.

The Effectiveness of Accountability and Incentive Pay

Between the mid-1990s, when Denver first pursued a performance-based compensation system, and 2004, when it approved it, nearly every state implemented a school accountability program with the help and encouragement of the federal government, although most have not been linked directly to teachers' pay. For the most part, then, the question of whether teachers unions will agree to such accountability systems is moot, because they are imposed by state and federal laws. The question is how effective these programs are, particularly when they are imposed and not necessarily agreed to by teachers.

According to a recent study by Julian Betts and Anne Danenberg, these programs are based on three elements: content standards that mandate what students should know and when they should know it; an assessment system that tracks the progress of students in meeting the state standards; and a set of responses by the state that may include financial incentives, penalties, sanctions, or additional resources.[58] As the authors point out, supporters of such a system argue that making school performance more transparent to the public, including parents, can put needed pressure on schools to perform better. Proponents claim that schools will be forced to improve their operations and that teachers will be more productive when presented with well-defined goals and held accountable through close scrutiny of their adherence to these goals and a carefully designed system of consequences.

But critics point out that state standards may be unfair both to affluent districts with high expectations for their students and to low-income districts that lack adequate school- and home-based resources to meet student needs. For instance, they argue that imposing one standard on all students and penalizing districts that do not meet the standard while rewarding districts that do may divert resources from poor districts, which need the additional resources, to affluent districts, which do not. A related concern is that the state will be slow in adjusting these standards in response to changing times or the specific needs of selected school districts.

Critics are also concerned about the assessment system. Measuring a teacher's contribution to a student's progress is difficult because classrooms are not, as Gratz puts it, "scientifically controlled environments," but are subject to outside influences beyond the control of teachers.[59] Furthermore, critics worry about adverse incentives such as teaching to the test and focusing instruction on the narrower content covered by tests, rather than offering broader topics and more in-depth treatment of the material.

States have established standards-based accountability systems more on principle and their promise than on any evidence of their effectiveness. Evidence of the success of earlier accountability and incentive systems—those implemented before the recent adoption of high-stakes testing and accompanying incentive systems by states and the federal government—does not offer strong support. Even though most observers agree that it is

---

States have established standards-based accountability systems more on principle and their promise than on any evidence of their effectiveness.

---

human nature to respond to incentives, there may be several other factors that work against the effectiveness of performance measures in individual incentive-based compensation schemes—just as they often do in the private sector.

Four characteristics of teaching and learning in schools may reduce the effectiveness of incentive-based compensation: the reliance on subjectively measured outcomes; the need to perform multiple tasks during the day; the use of team teaching, where more than one teacher is responsible for the outcome of the student or the classroom; and the existence of multiple stakeholders with diverse objectives.[60] In addition, most school districts have little control over their revenue streams and cannot offer the sizable increases in compensation necessary to entice teachers to put forth the extra effort and to

Randall W. Eberts

assume the added risk inherent in a merit pay system.

The net result of all these forces remains an empirical issue. Yet little empirical evidence has been collected on the effects of merit pay on student achievement. Most of the early experiences with merit pay systems in school districts were rather short-lived and usually negative. For example, one major study found that 75 percent of merit pay programs that had been in existence in 1983 were no longer operational in 1993. An interesting self-described limitation of this study is that it did not examine student achievement. Its authors note: "We would especially have liked to have performed an in-depth analysis of the impact of incentive programs on student achievement. However, very few of the participating districts had attempted any systematic evaluation of the effects of their incentive plans on student achievement, even though a basic assumption behind incentive plans is that teachers can indeed significantly affect learning."[61]

A study of a Pennsylvania district found no gains in student achievement from a bonus system.[62] An analysis of Dallas's performance-based system found an increase of 10 to 12 percent in the pass rate on selected statewide tests.[63]

A recent evaluation of California's school accountability program, carried out by Betts and Danenberg, offers a more positive assessment of the effects of incentives.[64] The program, enacted in 1999, was based on highly specific and comprehensive standards, a new norm-referenced statewide test and high school exit exam, and a complex series of rewards and punishments for school staff and students. Betts and Danenberg analyze recent trends in test scores and school resources and find two particularly important trends: test scores have risen significantly since implementation of the accountability program, whereas instructional resources have declined. Both trends are particularly evident for the lowest-performing schools. In their view, the accountability reforms and public scrutiny have spurred genuine growth in achievement. They recognize that the patterns are consistent with teaching to the test or a growing familiarity with the tests and testing process, possibilities that detract from the success of the program. Nonetheless, they find that testing and related aspects of accountability have neither diluted the high school curriculum nor widened inequality between top- and bottom-performing schools.

Donald Gratz, the evaluator of the Denver Incentive Program, concludes that a "system that attempts to closely measure and regulate instruction provides negative, rather than positive incentives," and that a complex system that tries to capture results in a single test score fails to meet its objective of improving education.[65] Gratz does not dismiss standards. On the contrary, he contends that clearly identified goals with which all parties are familiar and lessons and assessments designed to achieve these goals are a major advance over previous methods used by the district. Adopting standards that help teachers focus on lessons they want students to learn, aligning their teaching to these lessons, and devising measurements that demonstrate that students are responding to them can improve teaching. The message of the Denver experiment, as echoed in the private sector, is that a system of accountability needs to capture the contribution of employees to the entire bottom line. For schools, such a system must acknowledge the complexity of the learning process and the broad outcomes that society desires.

Katharine Boudett, Elizabeth City, and Richard Murnane set out similar standards for effective schools. Effective schools have "a coherent instructional program well-aligned with strong standards," and in these schools "a community of adults committed to working together to develop the skills and knowledge of all students . . . have figured out how to find time to do this work and are acquiring the skills to do it well."[66]

There is a clear consensus that public education must be reformed. What is less clear is how to reform it. Evaluations of two reform efforts—accountability and incentive pay— show some signs of promise, but do not provide sufficiently convincing evidence of their effectiveness to elicit a groundswell of support from either union or nonunion school districts. In many instances, school reform initiatives have merely nibbled at the edges of the broader issues confronting improvements in school quality. The lessons learned from several attempts at accountability warn against adopting the narrow approach of linking teacher incentive pay directly to student test scores. They point instead to the ability to define and articulate the goals of education and align resources to accomplish those goals. Under current collective bargaining laws, for teachers and administrators to move toward more comprehensive reform, negotiations must allow for more shared responsibilities and greater flexibility in trying new approaches and responding to the students' needs. Restrictive provisions, such as class assignment based on a teacher's seniority and the rigid allocation of time among daily activities, must be replaced with provisions that allow for shared decisionmaking and budgeting between teachers and administrators, flexibility in the use of time, professional development, and peer assistance and review. Some teachers unions—but only a few—have

negotiated these items into their contracts. Some states, however, do not allow certain items, such as class size restrictions or class assignment based on seniority, to go unmentioned in the contract, and some do not allow teachers to evaluate their own peers and share in decisions reserved for management. Therefore, state laws may also need to be changed before teachers unions and administrators can negotiate more reform-minded contracts.[67]

The Future of the New Unionism and School Reform

Returning to the question posed in the title—have unions been a help or a hindrance to student achievement?—average students appear not to have been harmed by attending union schools. If anything, the performance of average students on standardized tests is slightly higher, but below- and above-average students fare worse. Still, the overall increase in productivity does not offset the higher costs of unionized districts. Furthermore, teachers unions reduce the discretion of administrators, impose rigid standards, and reallocate school expenditures toward higher compensation and greater employment and away from resources for specialized and enhanced instruction.

A broader question is whether unions will help or hinder school reform. And to that question, the answer remains unclear and speculative. Ask the public, and the response is divided evenly. The last time the Phi Delta Kappa/Gallup poll posed that question, 27 percent responded that unions helped, 26 percent said that they hurt, and 37 percent said they made no difference.[68] Ask the experts, and one receives strong arguments on either side. Proponents argue that only by bringing teachers fully into the process can reform succeed; opponents claim that once shared decisionmaking makes its way into collective bargaining contracts, flexibility is lost, reform initiatives are stifled, and attention soon shifts from what is right for the students to whether school administrators have adhered to the contract.[69]

Yet ask the teachers and administrators of school districts—union or not—who have pursued reform to improve the quality of ed-

---

Effective schools are not honeycombs of individual autonomous classrooms, but rather well-designed and well-executed systems and processes.

---

ucation, and one finds stakeholders who understand the complexity of the educational process and recognize the need to build an organization that can deliver high-quality education. Too often school reform takes a simple and naïve approach—if only teachers were held accountable, if only teachers were paid for their performance, if only students and parents were given a choice in schools, if only unions were disbanded, then the quality of the educational system would vastly improve. Obviously, there are teachers who are not accountable, not working to their full potential, and hiding behind the protection of unions. There are unions that put teachers before students and stand in the way of improving the quality of education. The truth is that we know little about what works and what does not in the current reform movement. What we do know, however, is that education is a complex process that defies sim-

ple approaches. Effective schools are not honeycombs of individual autonomous classrooms, but rather well-designed and well-executed systems and processes.

Can unions fit into that type of environment? Can administrations and school boards? To both questions, the answer is that some can and have but many have not. The problem lies in the inability of many to identify their purpose, set goals and objectives, align resources and policies with them, and find the expertise and leadership to carry them out. Attempts at reform have come and gone with little progress in school improvement. In recent years, the leadership of both major teachers unions has shared the concern about the deteriorating quality of education and has called for more teacher participation and collaboration. But only a few local teachers unions have initiated true reforms—at times in the face of resistance from their national parent organizations. Policymakers have called for more accountability from teachers and administrators but have enacted an accountability system that makes little, if any, connection between the actions of teachers and the outcomes of their students.

While there are no quick fixes for improving school quality, with respect to unions and collective bargaining a few steps could be taken that focus on building a high-performance organization. First, school districts need organizational role models, leadership, and resources. Second, union leadership and the teacher membership need to realign their focus and attitudes by assuming more responsibility for the outcomes of their students. Third, administrators and school boards must affirm the importance of teachers as stakeholders in the educational process and recognize, as high-performance school districts have, that a high-performing workforce requires a culture of teamwork and an understanding of what it takes to retain quality teachers. Fourth, teachers and administrators must work together to determine goals and objectives, and once established, align resources and activities to achieve them. Fifth, once resources and activities are aligned, a set of measures must be devised and used by the management team (which would include teachers and union leaders) to measure the performance of students and the level of satisfaction and professional growth of teachers and other staff. If properly implemented and followed, the goals and objectives and the monitoring system could serve teachers much as collective bargaining provisions do now.

Finally, teachers unions must embrace the tenets of the new unionism and actively pursue them in their collaboration with districts. This means that teachers must be willing to move away from the security of their contracts and assume, with the administration, a joint responsibility for schooling. With empowerment must come responsibility, and only through systems of accountability in which risk is recognized and accepted can real progress be made in improving the education of the nation's children.

Notes

1. According to a Phi Delta Kappa/Gallup Poll (September 2003), 75 percent of respondents favored reforming the existing system, whereas 23 percent favored promoting alternative systems.

2. Helen Raham, "Teacher Bargaining Today and Tomorrow," *School Business Affairs* 65, no. 4 (1999): 24–27.

3. National Commission on Excellence in Education, *A Nation at Risk: The Imperative for Educational Reform*, A Report to the Nation and the Secretary of Education (U.S. Department of Education, 1983).

4. Robert Chase, "The New NEA: Reinventing Teachers Unions for a New Era," remarks before the National Press Club, Washington, February 5, 1997, www.nea.org/nr/sp970205.html (March 11, 2002).

5. John Dunlop, *Industrial Relations System* (New York: Holt, 1958).

6. Sewall Gilbert, "Teachers' Unions and the Issue of Academic Standards," *Wall Street Journal*, January 6, 1983.

7. Harry H. Wellington and Ralph K. Winter, "The Limits of Collective Bargaining in Public Employment," *Yale Law Journal* 77, no. 7 (1969).

8. To estimate union representation, I used the Outgoing Rotation Group of the Current Population Survey (CPS) for the years 1996–2005. I included a decade of data to ensure a large enough sample. Teachers were defined as local government employees who had occupation codes 155–59 for the period 1996–2002 and occupation codes 2300–40 in 2003–05. Following Barry T. Hirsch and David A. Macpherson, "Union Membership and Coverage Files from the Current Population Surveys: Note," *Industrial and Labor Relations Review* 46, no. 3 (April 1993): 574–78, I consider two questions from the CPS. One question relates to membership: "On this job are you a member of a labor union or of an employee association similar to a union?" Those who answered no to this question were asked: "On this job, are you covered by a union or employees association contract?" Therefore, the inference from the first question is that those answering yes are members of a union or employee association that negotiates a contract and are covered under that collective bargaining contract. Nationally, 61 percent report that they are members of a union and another 6 percent report that they are not members but are covered under a collective bargaining agreement. Interestingly, the two regions with the lowest percentage of membership and coverage—East South Central and West South Central—have the highest percentage of teachers who are covered but not members (11 percent and 10 percent, respectively). Of course, since this is self-reporting, there may be biases in the responses, as discussed by Edward C. Kokkelenberg and Donna R. Sockell, "Union Membership in the United States, 1973–81," *Industrial and Labor Relations Review* 38, no. 4 (July 1985): 497–543.

9. Bruce S. Cooper, "Collective Bargaining, Strikes, and Financial Costs in Public Education: A Comparative Review" (Clearinghouse on Educational Management, University of Oregon, 1982).

10. Ibid.; and Steve M. Goldschmidt, "An Overview of the Evolution of Collective Bargaining and Its Impact on Education," *Proceedings of a Conference on the Effects of Collective Bargaining on School Administrative Leadership* (University of Oregon, Center for Educational Policy and Management, 1982).

11. The turning point may have been AFT's major victory in organizing New York City teachers in 1961. M.O. Donley Jr., *Power to the Teacher: How America's Educators Became Militant* (Indiana University Press, 1976), describes it as probably the biggest single success in the history of teacher organizing in the United States.

12. Susan Moore Johnson and Susan M. Kardos, "Reform Bargaining and Its Promise for School Improvement," in *Conflicting Missions? Teachers Unions and Educational Reform*, edited by Tom Loveless (Brookings, 2000), pp. 7–46.

13. Chase, "The New NEA" (see note 4).

14. This section relies heavily on Randall W. Eberts and Joe A. Stone, *Unions and Public Schools: The Effect of Collective Bargaining on American Education* (Lexington, Mass.: Lexington Books, 1984). While this research examines the effects of teacher collective bargaining during the late 1970s, its relevance to more current times is supported by more recent research that follows similar methodology and finds similar results. Dan Goldhaber, "Are Teachers Unions Good for Students?" in *Collective Bargaining in Education: Negotiating Change in Today's Schools,* edited by Joan Hannaway and Andrew Rotherham (Cambridge, Mass.: Harvard Education Press, 2006), pp. 141–57, in a recent review of the literature of the effects of teacher collective bargaining on student achievement, states that "there is relatively little research that directly links unionization and student achievement" (p.142). Furthermore, there is even less research that attempts to provide a comprehensive analysis of the various aspects of teachers unions and the multiple ways in which collective bargaining may affect student achievement. A reasonable benchmark to determine teachers' success at the bargaining table is the private sector. Richard B. Freeman and James L. Medoff, *What Do Unions Do?* (New York: Basic Books, 1984), offer a useful perspective from the effects of unions in the private sector on pay and benefits, working conditions, cost of instruction, and productivity.

15. For instance, a provision on class size is found in many contracts and allowed by state laws. However, whether class size is a district average or a cap on any specific class, and the action taken after the class size limit has been exceeded, depends on the strength of the local union in negotiating those provisions. The enforcement of class size restrictions varies across bargaining units. For example, Susan Moore Johnson and Morgaen Donaldson, "The Effects of Collective Bargaining on Teacher Quality," in *Collective Bargaining in Education: Negotiating Change in Today's Schools,* edited by Hannaway and Rotherham (see note 14), pp. 111–40, report that the collective bargaining agreement in Branford, Connecticut, requires a new class after class size is exceeded by more than two students, whereas the teacher contract in Lowell, Massachusetts, states that the administration will work in good faith to reduce class size when contracts become available.

16. Henry Farber, "Union Membership in the United States: The Divergence between the Public and Private Sectors," in *Collective Bargaining in Education: Negotiating Change in Today's Schools*, edited by Hannaway and Rotherham (see note 14), pp. 27–51.

17. Heather Rose and Jon Sonstelie, "School Board Politics, School District Size, and the Bargaining Power of Teachers Unions," Working Paper (San Francisco: Public Policy Institute of California, May 2006), hypothesize that teachers unions will be more powerful in large districts than in small ones. Their analysis of California school districts shows that the salaries of teachers, as a measure of a union's success in collective bargaining, are positively related to the number of eligible voters in the jurisdiction.

18. Paul Courant and others, "Public Employee Market Power and the Level of Government Spending," *American Economic Review* 69, no. 5 (1979): 806–17, show that in states where local school districts may raise their own tax revenues by raising local taxes, teachers unions may also use their political power to encourage local voters to support tax increases. On the other hand, Daniel Hoskins and David Margolis, "The Efficiency of Collective Bargaining in Public Schools," Working Paper (U.S. Federal Trade Commission, December 1997), find that teachers unions operating in areas where school boards must have their budget

approved by popular referendum tend to have significantly lower bargaining power than their counterparts in which the budget is implemented without being subject to public approval.

19. As a labor organization, a teachers union is not permitted to use member dues for political actions. However, members can voluntarily contribute to a political action committee, which is typically set up by the state affiliate of the local bargaining units for the purpose of political activism and fundraising to elect candidates who share the same goals as the teachers union. For example, the political action committee of the Michigan Education Association, the NEA-affiliated teachers union in Michigan, collected $1 million from 25,000 of its 160,000 members during the first half of 2006, an election year.

20. Eberts and Stone, *Unions and Public Schools* (see note 14).

21. William H. Baugh and Joe A. Stone, "Teachers, Unions, and Wages in the 1970s: Unionism Now Pays," *Industrial and Labor Relations Review* 35 (1982): 368–6; and Caroline M. Hoxby, "How Teachers Unions Affect Education Production," *Quarterly Journal of Economics* 111 (1996): 671–718. Morris Kleiner and D. L. Petree, "Unionism and Licensing of Public School Teachers: Impact on Wages and Educational Output," in *When Public Sector Workers Unionize*, edited by Richard B. Freeman and Casey Ichniowski (University of Chicago Press, 1988), pp. 305–19, find only a small differential, but rely on aggregate data with few controls.

22. Evidence in sectors other than education suggests that pay and fringe benefits for union workers typically exceed those of nonunion workers. While the magnitude of the differential can vary from one sector to another, Freeman and Medoff, *What Do Unions Do?* (see note 14), pp. 47, 67–68, find that the union pay differential is typically 8 to 10 percent higher for "identical" workers and the differential for fringe benefits is even higher.

23. Eberts and Stone, *Unions and Public Schools* (see note 14).

24. Ibid.

25. Ibid. Eberts and Stone, relying on national data from the Sustaining Effects Survey of elementary schools, find that the student-teacher ratio is nearly 12 percent lower for union teachers. Kleiner and Petree, "Unionism and Licensing of Public School Teachers" (see note 21), p. 316, using state-level data, also find lower (7 percent) student-teacher ratios for union teachers. Similarly, Hoxby, "How Teachers Unions Affect Education Production" (see note 21), p. 695, uses district-level data and finds a decline of about 9 percent in her preferred specification.

26. Eberts and Stone, *Unions and Public Schools* (see note 14), p. 156.

27. Ibid., pp. 119–20, 143–44.

28. In some exceptional cases, total costs of unionized production are lower at very large scales of integrated operations, as found, for example, by Steven G. Allen, "Unionization and Productivity in Office Building and School Construction," *Industrial and Labor Relations Review* 39 (1986): 187–201, in construction; and Wesley W. Wilson, Joe A. Stone, and M. C. Mitchell, "Product Selection and Costs in a Partially Unionized Industry," *Journal of Labor Research* 16 (1995): 81–95, in sawmills.

29. Jay G. Chambers, "The Impact of Collective Bargaining for Teachers on Resource Allocation in Public School Districts," *Journal of Urban Economics* 4 (1977): 324–39; and W. C. Hall and N. Carroll, "The Ef-

fect of Teachers' Organizations on Salaries and Class Size," *Industrial and Labor Relations Review* 28 (1975): 834–41.

30. Randall W. Eberts and Joe A. Stone, "Teachers Unions and the Cost of Public Education," *Economic Inquiry* 24 (1986): 631–44.

31. Hoxby, "How Teachers Unions Affect Education Production" (see note 21).

32. Lorraine M. McDonnell and Anthony Pascal, *Organized Teachers in American Schools* (Santa Monica, Calif.: RAND, 1979), p. 83.

33. Eberts and Stone, *Unions and Public Schools* (see note 14).

34. Studies of unions and productivity include John H. Pencavel, "The Distribution and Efficiency Effects of Trade Unions in Britain," *British Journal of Industrial Relations* 40 (1977): 137–56, for British coal fields; Kim B. Clark, "Unionization and Productivity: Micro-Econometric Evidence," *Quarterly Journal of Economics* 95 (1980): 613–39, for cement producers; and Ronald G. Ehrenberg and others, "Unions and Productivity in the Public Sector: A Study of Municipal Libraries," *Industrial and Labor Relations Review* 36 (1983): 199–213.

35. Susanna Loeb and Marianne Page, "Examining the Link between Teacher Wages and Student Outcomes: The Importance of Alternative Labor Market Opportunities and Non-Pecuniary Variation," *Review of Economics and Statistics* 82, no. 3 (2000): 393–408.

36. Johnson and Donaldson, "The Effects of Collective Bargaining" (see note 15).

37. See Daniel Aaronson, Lisa Barrow, and William Sander, "Teachers and Student Achievement in the Chicago Public High Schools," paper presented at the Labor Market Policy/Princeton Industrial Relations Section Tenth Annual Policy Conference sponsored by the University of Chicago, DePaul University, the University of Illinois, and the Federal Reserve Bank of Chicago, 2003; and Steven Rivkin, Eric Hanushek, and John Kain, "Teachers, Schools, and Academic Achievement," *Econometrica* 73, no. 2 (2005): 417–58.

38. Kleiner and Petree, "Unionism and Licensing of Public School Teachers" (see note 21); F. H. Nelson and M. Rosen, "Are Teachers Unions Hurting American Education? A State-by-State Analysis of the Impact of Collective Bargaining among Teachers on Student Performance," Technical Report (Milwaukee: Institute for Wisconsin's Future, 1996); Lala C. Steelman, Brian Powell, and Robert M. Carini, "Do Teachers Unions Hinder Educational Performance?" *Harvard Educational Review* 70, no. 4 (2000): 437–66.

39. Kleiner and Petree, "Unionism and Licensing of Public School Teachers" (see note 21).

40. These studies include Randall W. Eberts and Joe A. Stone, "Teachers Unions and the Productivity of Public Schools," *Industrial and Labor Relations Review* 40 (1987): 354–63; Martin I. Milkman, "Teachers Unions, Productivity, and Minority Student Achievement," *Journal of Labor Research* 18 (1997): 247–50; P. W. Grimes and C. A. Register, "Teachers Unions and Student Achievement in High School Economics," *Journal of Economic Education* 21 (1990): 297–308; and L. M. Argys and D. I. Rees, "Unionization and School Productivity: A Re-examination," *Research in Labor Economics* 14, edited by S. Polachek (Greenwich, Conn.: JAI Press, 1995): 49–68.

41. Sam Peltzman, "Political Economy of Public Education: Non-College-Bound Students," *Journal of Law and Economics* 39 (1996): 73–120, also found negative effects of unions on low-achieving students. He

used state-level data over several years, and his analysis may therefore be subject to the same estimation biases found in Kleiner and Petree and others using highly disaggregated data. It should also be mentioned that the effects of unions on these students varied over the period.

42. Hoxby, "How Teachers Unions Affect Education Production" (see note 21). H. L. Zwerling and T. Thomason, "The Effects of Teachers Unions on the Probability of Dropping Out of High School," *Journal of Collective Negotiations* 23 (1994): 239–50, also examined the effect of unions on dropout rates but found mixed results. Male students in union districts had lower dropout rates than those in nonunion districts, but female students did not. However, their controls for factors that could bias the estimates were not as extensive as Hoxby's.

43. Both groups use difference-in-differences techniques to control for unobservable time-invariant factors. The student-level studies, such as Eberts and Stone and Milkman, use pre- and post-test score data, which in essence controls for student, class, parental, and district factors that may affect student achievement but do not vary over time. They also include a long list of explicit factors that affect student achievement. Hoxby does not control for student characteristics through differencing, but does include an abbreviated list of factors in her estimation. She uses a difference-in-differences and instrumental variables approach to control for unobservable and steadily trending school and state characteristics that may affect both educational outcomes and the decision to unionize. Eberts and Stone also use instrumental variables to control for underlying factors that may cause teachers to organize.

44. Lawrence Mishel and Joydeep Roy, *Rethinking High School Graduation Rates and Trends* (Washington: EPI Press, April 2006), have compiled a list of issues regarding the measurement of high school dropout rates and their use as a measure of student achievement.

45. One study, for example, finds that even within the traditional organization of classroom instruction, the use of hourly tutors for selected students improves student performance, especially among disadvantaged students. G. Farkas, "Structuring Tutoring for At Risk Children in the Early Years," *Applied Behavioral Science Review* 1 (1993): 69–2.

46. Argys and Rees, "Unionization and School Productivity" (see note 40). Studies have found differential effects of union schools on minorities. Both Milkman and Grimes and Register (see note 40) find that African Americans do better in union than nonunion districts. Furthermore, Milkman finds that the union effect on minorities depends on the level of racial diversity in the school.

47. Johnson and Kardos, "Reform Bargaining" (see note 12).

48. Lorraine McDonnell and Anthony Pascal, "Teachers Unions and Educational Reform," Center for Policy Research in Education (Santa Monica, Calif.: RAND, 1988).

49. Johnson and Kardos, "Reform Bargaining" (see note 12).

50. Al Shanker, the long-time president of the AFT, was regarded by many as a champion of educational reform among the union movement. Like his later counterpart in the NEA, Robert Chase, Shanker believed that the future of public education and teacher collective bargaining depended on teachers unions taking more of a leadership role. Shanker died in 1997, the year in which Chase made his National Press Club speech. His successors, however, did not pursue the reform effort with the same fervor, according to Julia Koppich, "The As-Yet-Unfulfilled Promise of Reform Bargaining: Forging a Better Match between the Labor Relations System We Have and the Education System We Want," in *Collective Bargaining in Edu-*

cation: Negotiating Change in Today's Schools, edited by Hannaway and Rotherham (see note 14), pp. 203–27.

51. Charles Kerchner and Julia Koppich, "Organizing around Quality: The Struggle to Organize Mind Workers," in *Teachers Unions and Education Policy: Retrenchment or Reform?* edited by Ronald Henderson, Wayne Urban, and Paul Wolman (London: Elsevier, 2004), pp. 187–221.

52. Koppich, "The As-Yet-Unfulfilled Promise of Reform Bargaining" (see note 50).

53. Kerchner and Koppich, "Organizing around Quality" (see note 51).

54. Christine Murray, "Innovative Local Teachers Unions: What Have They Accomplished?" in *Teachers Unions and Education Policy: Retrenchment or Reform?* edited by Henderson, Urban, and Wolman (see note 51), pp. 149–66.

55. J. Archer, "Districts Targeting Teacher Seniority in Union Contracts," *Education Week,* April 12, 2000.

56. Donald Gratz, "Lessons from Denver: The Pay for Performance Pilot," *Phi Delta Kappan* 86, no. 8 (April 2005).

57. Johnson and Kardos, "Reform Bargaining" (see note 12).

58. Julian Betts and Anne Danenberg, "School Accountability in California: An Early Evaluation," *Brookings Papers on Education Policy* (2002).

59. Gratz, "Lessons from Denver" (see note 56).

60. In this discussion I rely heavily on arguments presented in Richard J. Murnane and David K. Cohen, "Merit Pay and the Evaluation Problem: Why Most Merit Pay Plans Fail and a Few Survive," *Harvard Educational Review* 56, no. 1 (1986): 1–17. The analysis by Avinash Dixit, "Incentives and Organizations in the Public Sector: An Interpretative Review," *Journal of Human Resources* 37, no. 4 (Fall 2002): 696–727, of incentives in education also coincides closely with ours. Dixit suggests four complications that confound the simple "principal-agent" model of implicit contracting in educational settings: multiple goals, multiple principals, lack of competition in the product market, and agents motivated by intrinsic values.

61. Harry P. Hatry, John M. Greiner, and Brenda G. Ashford, *Issues and Case Studies in Teacher Incentive Plans,* 2nd ed. (Washington: Urban Institute Press, 1994). Murnane and Cohen, "Merit Pay and the Evaluation Problem" (see note 60), also emphasize the short-lived nature of merit pay systems.

62. Dennis J. Tulli, "An Assessment of Student Achievement before and during a Merit Pay Program for Teachers of the Penn Manor School District," Ed.D. diss. (Temple University, 1999).

63. Charles Clotfelter and Helen Ladd, "Recognizing and Rewarding Success in Public Schools," in *Holding Schools Accountable, Performance-Based Reform in Education,* edited by Helen F. Ladd (Brookings, 1996), pp. 23–63. Unfortunately, the study did not use a true control group and there was a similar rate of improvement in the year prior to the implementation of the performance-based system. In contrast, Candice Prendergast, "The Provision of Incentives in Firms," *Journal of Economic Literature* 37 (1999): 7–63, documents that private sector businesses reward workers more through promotions and group-based merit systems, such as gain sharing or profit sharing, than through individual merit rewards.

64. Betts and Danenberg, "School Accountability in California" (see note 58).

65. Gratz, "Lessons from Denver" (see note 56).

66. Kathryn Parker Boudett, Elizabeth A. City, and Richard J. Murnane, eds, *Data Wise: A Step-by-Step Guide to Using Assessment Results to Improve Teaching and Learning* (Cambridge, Mass.: Harvard Education Press, 2005).

67. Courts have interpreted the National Labor Relations Act to reserve functions such as peer review, curriculum development, resource allocation, and assessment as the sole prerogative of management, not labor. The Yeshiva University case, which went before the U.S. Supreme Court, denied faculty collective bargaining rights on the grounds that they exercise managerial decisions in their determination of tenure and the promotion of other faculty members. Some states, such as California, have passed legislation to circumvent this law and allow members of a bargaining unit to participate in decisions as listed above.

68. Phi Delta Kappa/Gallup Poll, September 1998.

69. Sandra Black, "Reforming the Unions," *American School Board Journal* (February 2002), offers several of these critical points.

Teacher Labor Markets in Developed Countries

Helen F. Ladd

Summary

Helen Ladd takes a comparative look at policies that the world's industrialized countries are using to assure a supply of high-quality teachers. Her survey puts U.S. educational policies and practices into international perspective.

Ladd begins by examining teacher salaries—an obvious, but costly, policy tool. She finds, perhaps surprisingly, that students in countries with high teacher salaries do not in general perform better on international tests than those in countries with lower salaries. Ladd does find, however, that the share of underqualified teachers in a country is closely related to salary. In high-salary countries like Germany, Japan, and Korea, for example, only 4 percent of teachers are underqualified, as against more than 10 percent in the United States, where teacher salaries, Ladd notes, are low relative to those in other industrialized countries.

Teacher shortages also appear to stem from policies that make salaries uniform across academic subject areas and across geographic regions. Shortages are especially common in math and science, in large cities, and in rural areas. Among the policy strategies proposed to deal with such shortages is to pay teachers different salaries according to their subject area. Many countries are also experimenting with financial incentive packages, including bonuses and loans, for teachers in specific subjects or geographic areas.

Ladd notes that many developed countries are trying to attract teachers by providing alternative routes into teaching, often through special programs in traditional teacher training institutions and through adult education or distance learning programs. To reduce attrition among new teachers, many developed countries have also been using formal induction or mentoring programs as a way to improve new teachers' chances of success.

Ladd highlights the need to look beyond a single policy, such as higher salaries, in favor of broad packages that address teacher preparation and certification, working conditions, the challenges facing new teachers, and the distribution of teachers across geographic areas.

www.futureofchildren.org

Helen F. Ladd is Edgar Thompson Professor of Public Policy Studies and Professor of Economics, Sanford Institute of Public Policy, at Duke University. The author is grateful to Christian Bonilla of Duke University for superb research assistance.

Despite differences in their histories, cultures, and economies, all industrialized countries face the challenge of how to ensure a supply of high-quality teachers sufficient to meet demand. The demand for teachers differs from one country to the next primarily because of differences in the number of school-age children and in politically determined pupil-teacher ratios. Demand also varies with the ambitiousness of a country's educational aspirations. My focus in this article, however, is not on differences in demand but rather on the policies that countries use to affect the supply of teachers—namely, the level and structure of teacher salaries, financial incentives to recruit teachers to areas of shortage, and entry requirements into the teaching profession. For simplicity I define industrialized countries as the thirty member nations of the Organization for Economic Cooperation and Development (OECD) and draw heavily on a recent major OECD study of teacher recruitment and development.[1] Although this analysis generates no simple policy lessons for the United States, it does provide perspective on a variety of matters, including the fact that the United States pays its teachers less generously than many other industrialized countries.

Teacher Salaries and Teacher Shortages

Salaries are one of the most obvious, but costly, policy tools available to governments in their quest to ensure a supply of high-quality teachers. Because teacher salaries are such a large share of the education budget—about 64 percent in the OECD countries—any across-the-board increase in teacher salaries can translate into significant increases in education spending. But when a country does not pay salaries high enough to attract high-qual-

ity teachers, it must either face vacancies or rely on teachers who, based on the stated standards, are underqualified.

Comparing Teacher Salaries across Countries

In many countries, teacher salaries are determined by a national bargaining process between the government and one or more unions. In the United States, in contrast, salary setting is far more decentralized. Therefore any simple comparison of salaries in other countries with those in the United States does not take into account the large variation in U.S. salaries from one school district to another.[2]

By almost any measure, Germany, Japan, and Korea pay generous salaries to their teachers relative to other counties, including the United States. But the relative ranking of U.S. salaries varies with the measure used. For example, a comparison of absolute salaries (adjusted for differences in purchasing power across countries) finds the United States in the top third of OECD countries. In 2003 its average salary for mid-career teachers in lower secondary schools was $43,999— exceeded only by Luxembourg at $80,520, Switzerland at $58,520, Germany at $48,804, Korea at $46,516, and Japan at $45,515. Also in the top ten by this absolute measure are Scotland, the Netherlands, Australia, and England.[3]

But measuring teacher salaries relative to a country's gross domestic product (GDP) per capita puts the United States in the bottom third (see table 1). By that measure, at 117 percent of GDP per capita, the average salary paid to U.S. teachers is on a par with those in Italy and Austria and far below those of Korea (242 percent), Germany (180 percent), and Japan (160 percent). Countries such as

Table 1. OECD Countries Ranked by Ratio of Teacher Salaries to GDP per Capita, 2003

Highest third		Middle third		Lowest third	
Country	Ratio	Country	Ratio	Country	Ratio
Korea	2.42	Netherlands	1.42	Italy	1.18
Mexico	2.23	Australia	1.40	**United States**	**1.17**
Portugal	1.81	England	1.40	Austria	1.13
Germany	1.80	Greece	1.38	Czech Rep.	1.06
Switzerland	1.80	Finland	1.29	Sweden	1.03
Japan	1.60	Belgium (Fl.)	1.28	Hungary	0.98
Spain	1.59	Belgium (Fr.)	1.24	Norway	0.96
New Zealand	1.51	Ireland	1.22	Poland	0.82
Luxembourg	1.50	Denmark	1.21	Iceland	0.73
Scotland	1.45	France	1.21	Slovak Rep.	0.56

Source: OECD, *Education at a Glance* (Paris, 2005), chart D3.1. Based on mid-career salaries of teachers in lower secondary education.

the Netherlands, England, and Finland fall in the middle third.

Though not perfect, this relative measure provides a more accurate picture of whether salaries are generous enough to attract a quality teaching force than does the absolute measure and is thus the measure I use throughout this article. Even better would be a measure of how teacher salaries compare with salaries paid for specific competing occupations, such as computer operators or librarians, but relevant data are not available on a systematic basis across countries.[4] Presumably, though, the richer a country is as measured by its GDP, the higher competing salaries are. Thus, the fact that average U.S. teacher salaries are low relative to GDP per capita indicates both that the United States has the capacity to pay higher salaries and that current salaries may not be high enough to attract a quality teaching force.

Of course, working conditions for teachers may also differ across countries. Hence, a third way of comparing salaries is to express them relative to an important measure of working conditions, such as hours of net teaching time. By this metric, U.S. salaries rank in the lowest third of twenty-seven OECD countries for high school and in the middle third for primary school. Once again, Germany, Japan, and Korea are consistently in the top third.[5]

Maintaining Teacher Supply

Of particular relevance to policymakers is whether salaries are high enough to avoid widespread teacher shortages. Though such shortages are sometimes measured in terms of vacancies, schools typically find some way to fill most positions. A better measure is the share of positions filled by teachers without full qualifications. In high-salary OECD countries such as Germany, Japan, and Korea, the share of such teachers in primary and secondary schools is low: less than 4 percent, as against more than 10 percent in countries such as Sweden and the United States, where salaries (relative to GDP per capita) are low.[6] Though Hungary and Italy are exceptions (both have low salaries and less than 4 percent underqualified teachers), higher salaries are generally linked with a lower share of underqualified teachers.

Several studies in England and Switzerland offer more detailed analysis of how teacher salaries affect teacher supply. A careful empirical study, based on a large sample of U.K. university graduates, of the decision to become a teacher found that expected earnings

---

There is little doubt that uniform salaries across academic subject areas and across geographic regions can lead to shortages in certain subjects and in certain regions.

---

in teaching relative to earnings in other occupations clearly affects the supply of new teachers, and hence that increases in teacher salaries may be a potent tool for increasing the supply of teachers.[7] A subsequent analysis of the U.K. market for teachers between 1960 and 2002 confirmed that conclusion but emphasized that the power of relative wages to affect the supply varies with the state of the labor market.[8] In particular a policy-driven increase in teacher salaries relative to those in competing professions raises the supply of teachers more when teacher salaries are relatively low than when they are high. This insight may explain an empirical finding from Switzerland that the supply of teachers is not very responsive to salaries. The weaker salary effect in Switzerland could simply reflect the fact that teacher salaries are much higher relative to other occupations there than they are in the United Kingdom.[9]

Regardless of the average relationship between teacher salaries and teacher shortages, there is little doubt that uniform salaries across academic subject areas and across geographic regions can lead to shortages in certain subjects and in certain regions. The subjects most susceptible to teacher shortages are math and science, fields in which salaries are relatively higher in occupations outside teaching. The regions most susceptible to shortages are large cities, where the costs of living are higher, where other job opportunities are plentiful for educated workers, and where teaching conditions associated with concentrations of immigrant children from impoverished families can be difficult, and rural areas, where it can be hard to attract teachers. Both types of shortages emerge in most developed countries.

Various policy strategies have been proposed, both in the United States and in other developed countries, to address these shortages. One strategy commonly proposed by economists is to pay teachers different salaries according to their subject area. Analysis for England, however, implies that although higher pay could reduce the shortage of teachers in certain subjects, the salary differences might need to be substantial, because graduates in engineering, science, and social sciences are likely to respond to an increase in wages at only half the rate of graduates of other programs.[10]

Some OECD countries use higher salaries to attract teachers to certain geographic areas. Higher salaries, for example, are offered in London both to offset the high cost of living and to compensate for the challenges of educating disadvantaged urban students. Salaries in London now exceed those in the rest of England by £2,000–£2,500, or about 12 percent. Even this difference, though, has not lowered teacher vacancy rates and the share of teacher slots filled by substitute teachers in London enough to match rates elsewhere in England.[11]

Sweden, a country with a tradition of strong teacher unionism, also uses differential salaries.[12] In 1995, as part of its broader effort to decentralize its schooling system, Sweden modified its centrally bargained fixed-pay scheme and gave municipalities greater flexibility to tailor salaries for individual teachers. As a result, salaries are now negotiated according to teacher characteristics (for example, secondary versus primary), the labor market situation (with teachers in shortage areas able to garner higher salaries), the performance of the teacher, and the range of the teacher's responsibilities. Salaries thus now vary far more than they once did. Although evidence is still limited, the new system appears to have helped some schools overcome some teacher shortages, though the ability of a municipality to make salary adjustments depends on its own economic situation. Notably, poor municipalities can compete effectively for teachers only with the help of grants from the central government.

Teacher Salaries and Teacher Quality

Exactly how teacher salaries affect the quality, in contrast to the quantity, of teachers is not yet clear, though one careful study based on fifteen years of variation in teacher salaries across states in Australia sheds some light on the matter.[13] Using sophisticated statistical techniques, the author concludes that increases in teacher salaries relative to salaries in other occupations raise the quality of potential teachers, as measured by the test scores of students pursuing education courses at Australian universities. (Unlike U.S. university students, those in Australia and in most other OECD countries choose their career paths before they enroll in college.) One of the study's findings is that increasing relative salaries by 10 percent raises the quality of students choosing to pursue an education degree by 8 percentile ranks on their test scores. Much less clear, however, is the potential effect of a differential increase in salaries for new teachers, with higher salaries going to those at the top of the aptitude distribution.

Financial Incentive Packages to Recruit New Teachers

Some countries such as Korea and Japan, both of which feature high teacher salaries, have little difficulty recruiting teachers. In 2001 in Japan, for example, only 6–11 percent of qualified applicants, depending on the grade, were appointed as teachers. In Korea, only about 20 percent of the qualified teachers are appointed.[14] Too great a supply, however, is not necessarily a blessing. Some countries with teacher surpluses find it hard to ensure that talented young people choose to enter teaching. And surveys find that school principals in countries with a teacher surplus worry more about teacher morale and enthusiasm than do those in countries without such a surplus.[15]

Although the number of university students entering as teachers has been growing in several OECD countries, that number fell 10 percent or more between 1997 and 2001 in others, including Belgium (the French community), France, Germany, Mexico, and Scotland.[16] In efforts to attract new teachers, to improve the quality of the teachers who apply, and to recruit teachers for specific subjects or geographic areas, various countries have experimented with financial incentive packages.

The incentives available in England are illustrative. A training bursary offers a tuition waiver and a £6,000 training grant to encourage students to enter a teacher education program. The Golden Hello provides a £4,000 bonus (more than 20 percent of a starting salary) for teachers in shortage subject areas who complete an induction program within a specified period. Student loans are also available for newly qualified teachers who voluntarily take classes in a designated shortage subject area. And Fast Track offers trainees participating in an accelerated program for highly talented graduates a grant of £5,000—£3,000 at the start of the program and £2,000 when they take up their first Fast Track teaching post. The Teach First program, which I discuss below, is specifically designed to induce graduates to enter teaching in London.

Little research is as yet available on the effectiveness of these programs. Although the number of entrants to teacher education programs has risen in England over the past few years, it is difficult to attribute the increase to any specific recruitment initiative. And some surveys have found a downside to such programs: some existing teachers and teacher candidates find it unfair that teachers newly entering the profession should be eligible for benefits that they did not get.[17]

Australia provides incentive packages primarily to attract teachers to rural areas. Because its education system is decentralized, packages vary from one state to another. For example, South Australia provides teaching scholarships of $10,000 to students from rural locations who are offered permanent employment in a rural school for a minimum of two years. In Queensland the rural area incentive scheme offers such benefits as cash, extended leave provisions, and induction programs for new teachers who commit to teach in rural areas. New South Wales has piloted a retention benefit program to attract and retain teachers in difficult-to-staff positions and schools. Starting in 2002, teachers who complete their initial service requirement of two or three years in a hard-to-staff area are paid an annual retention bonus of $5,000. Eligible teachers continue to receive the benefit for a maximum of five years. New South Wales also offers rent subsidies of up to 90 percent in certain rural areas.[18]

The salary adjustments in London and in the Australian provinces suggest the importance of providing financial benefits over an extended period. If certain geographic areas are indeed far less appealing to teachers and if the goal is not only to attract but also to retain quality teachers in those areas, the most logical incentive program is a long-term financial package rather than a one-time bonus.

Salary Structures, Working Conditions, and Teacher Attrition

A teacher's decision to enter or remain in teaching depends not only on his or her initial salary but also on the expected growth in that salary over time. A key question is what a potential teacher could expect to earn over his or her lifetime as a teacher compared with other occupations. To the extent that the potential for salaries to increase with experience in teaching is lower than it is in competing occupations, teachers might be tempted to switch jobs or to retire earlier than their counterparts in other occupations.

Salary structures vary widely across OECD countries. For teachers at the lower secondary level, the top salary exceeds the entering salary by only 10 to 20 percent in Denmark, Finland, and Norway but by more than 130 percent in Japan, Portugal, and Korea. Germany, which along with Japan and Korea has high average salaries, has a relatively narrow salary range of only 38 percent. The high starting salaries thus grow relatively little as teachers gain experience. By comparison, top salaries in the United States exceed entry-level salaries, on average, by about 73 percent.[19] National policies also vary with respect to how long it takes a teacher to reach the top salary. In England and Scotland it takes only six years, compared with more than thirty years in eight countries, including France, Korea, and Spain.[20]

One model of teacher salary progression, as exemplified by Germany, is high starting salaries with relatively rapid growth to a salary plateau. That model is presumably most attractive to those who are willing to make a substantial initial commitment to teaching, as is required by the German system of initial teacher preparation (see below), but may not succeed in keeping teachers in the profession until the normal retirement age. Not surprisingly, the average retirement age for teachers in Germany is only 59, far below 65, the age for retirement with full benefits.[21] In 2001, only 6 percent of German teachers worked until age 65.[22] Korea exemplifies a second model, in which salaries start low but climb steadily over a long period. That model is presumably less attractive to teachers who are unsure about whether they wish to become a lifetime teacher, but it may succeed in retaining teachers as they age. In yet a third model, exemplified by England, salaries start relatively low but then rise quite rapidly to a plateau. That model is associated with the most severe challenges of retaining teachers.

A prospective teacher's decision to enter, or the decision later to stay in, the teaching profession also depends on how a country's salary structure for teachers compares with those in competing occupations—and thus

how lifetime earnings compare across professions. Careful analysis of salaries over time in England, for example, finds that the expected lifetime earnings of both men and women in teaching have been declining relative to lifetime earnings of professionals in other occupations. For women in England, teaching nevertheless remains a relatively attractive career, while for men the lifetime return

> *A prospective teacher's decision to enter, or the decision later to stay in, the teaching profession also depends on how a country's salary structure for teachers compares with those in competing occupations.*

from teaching relative to other occupations is negative.[23] That negative return could well explain why men have increasingly been leaving teaching in England.[24] The departure of male teachers is of particular concern because men are overrepresented both in high schools, which are more subject to teacher shortages than primary schools, and in the shortage areas of science and math.

To counter the effects of having relatively low top salaries (only 46 percent higher than the entry salaries) that are reached at a relatively young age, England has introduced two new salary-related programs within the past ten years to retain effective teachers.

Since 2000, England and Wales have had a program that resembles National Board Certification in the United States. The program gives teachers the option of being assessed against national criteria for teaching effectiveness when they reach the top of the standard pay scale. Those who pass the assessment gain access to significantly higher pay. Unlike the more restrictive U.S. program, more than 230,000 U.K. teachers, or 80 percent of those who were eligible, applied in the first year, and 97 percent of them passed.[25] Critics argue that the process is too time-consuming, both for the applicants and for the head teachers (that is, school principals) who do the evaluation. And no evidence to date shows that the program improves teacher quality and student achievement, though that fact is not surprising because passing the threshold requires evidence of successful past, rather than current, performance. The program does, however, indicate a strong interest among teachers in higher pay and gives successful teachers access to an "upper pay scale" that offers performance pay.

Teachers in England can also increase their pay by becoming an Advanced Skills Teacher (AST). This option, introduced in 1998, keeps teachers in the classroom by allowing them to augment the top salary by up to 40 percent. Teachers can apply at any stage in their career and must pass an AST assessment based on an externally evaluated portfolio. They then typically spend up to 20 percent of their time providing support to other teachers. The hope is that ultimately ASTs will make up about 5 percent of the workforce.[26]

Such programs are not unique to England. Other OECD countries have also searched for ways to diversify a "flat" career structure that offers only limited options outside the classroom as well as limited opportunities for promotion and career diversification. A com-

mon approach is to provide opportunities for established teachers to mentor young teachers. In addition, many countries are shifting more management authority to the school level and creating new roles for teachers, including a variety of "middle management" positions such as departmental heads, team leaders, or management or curriculum development personnel. Typically these positions bring with them higher pay and reduced classroom teaching hours.[27] Nonetheless, opportunities for roles outside the classroom remain quite limited. In 2001, on average, only about 5 percent of staff positions in upper secondary schools across fourteen OECD countries were classified as management and 4 percent as professional development.[28]

Attrition and Nonsalary Considerations

Teachers in England leave the profession at far higher rates than those in many other developed countries, including the United States, where teacher attrition rates increased from 5.1 percent in the early 1990s to 7.4 percent in the late 1990s. In England the rate of attrition rose from 8 percent to 10 percent between 1999–2000 and 2001–02.[29] By contrast, in Italy, Japan, and Korea departure rates are less than 3 percent.[30] Part of the explanation for England's higher attrition rates is undoubtedly the salary structure, but concerns about salary are not the sole explanation.

Indeed, in a 2002 survey of more than 1,000 departing teachers in England, 45 percent of respondents cited the heavy workload, 36 percent cited government initiatives, and 35 percent cited stress as the most important reasons for leaving the profession.[31] Only 11 percent cited low salaries. Concerns about workloads and government initiatives were particularly prevalent among those leaving primary schools, where low ratios of teachers to pupils and the government's drive to promote literacy and numeracy have put a significant burden on teachers. Many teachers, especially older ones, appeared to be increasingly frustrated with the administrative duties associated with new government initiatives, including school testing reports and the stress of meeting performance thresholds. Although some teachers said that higher salaries might have compensated them for these heavier workloads, more than 40 percent said that nothing could induce them to stay.[32]

Concern about work-related stress is also evident in a recent study of teacher supply in Sweden, where the share of teachers suffering mental stress rose from 5.3 percent in 1991 to 21.1 percent in 2002, an increase far exceeding that for all Swedish employees or for white-collar workers. One plausible explanation for the rising stress among teachers is the deterioration in working conditions associated with a continuous fall in the ratio of teachers to pupils during the 1990s.[33]

The lesson for the United States is that government policies that put significant new pressure on teachers could increase departures from the profession. Further, both in the United States and internationally, it is likely to be the more qualified teachers who leave.[34]

Strategies to Retain Teachers

Nonsalary policies used by various OECD countries to try to retain effective teachers include providing additional support staff for teachers, recognizing and celebrating effective teachers, improving school leadership, and reducing teacher burnout through part-time work, sabbaticals, and extended leaves.[35] Some of these efforts appear to be useful, at least for some teachers and in some countries.

Figure 1. Program in International Student Assessment Test Scores versus Teacher Salaries

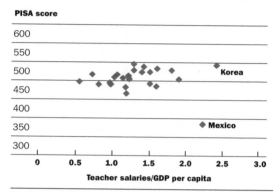

Source: Data on test scores accessed from *International Outcomes of Learning in Mathematics Literacy and Problem Solving: PISA 2003 Results from the U.S. Perspective* (http://nces.ed.gov/surveys/pisa/PISA2003HighlightsFigures.asp?figuure=9&qquest=1). Based on data for combined math literacy scores for fifteen-year-olds in twenty-four countries.

Teacher Salaries and Student Achievement

If high teacher salaries relative to GDP generate a teaching force of high-quality teachers, one might expect students in countries with high teacher salaries to perform better on international tests than those in countries with lower salaries. Although the high test scores of students in Korea and Japan appear to support the link between high salaries and high student performance, a closer look at the data gives a different picture. For example, in the combined mathematics literacy results of fifteen-year-olds from the Program in International Student Assessment (PISA) in 2003, U.S. students scored an average of 483, compared with the OECD average of 500, leaving the United States ranked twenty-fourth among the twenty-nine participating OECD countries.[36] Figure 1 shows no clear relationship between teacher salaries and PISA test scores for the twenty-five OECD countries for which data are available on both measures.[37]

The Trends in International Mathematics and Science Study (TIMSS) data present a similar picture. The average score of U.S eighth graders on that test in 2003 was 504, well above the international average of 466, but far below the scores of Korea (589), Japan (570), Belgium–Flemish community (537), Netherlands (536), and Hungary (529). Among those five countries, the first two have high salaries; the next two, middle-range salaries; and the fifth has low salaries. Again, no clear positive link emerges between teacher salaries and student performance.[38]

The absence of a simple link between teacher salaries (relative to GDP per capita) and student achievement should come as no surprise given the many differences among these countries, including culture, the education level of the adult population, the quality of the teacher training programs, and the presence or absence of national standards. Even if a relationship had emerged from the data, the complexity of the interrelationships between all these variables would make it difficult, if not impossible, to tease out causal linkages between teacher salaries and student achievement.[39]

Teacher Preparation, Including Qualifications and Induction Programs

Though expectations about relative salaries are important to the decision to become or remain a teacher, the expected monetary rewards for teaching must be traded off against other costs or benefits of entering the profession. The main costs are two: training and the possibility of having a poor experience in the early years of teaching.

Teachers are almost always required to have a university degree. Some countries, including the United States, require an additional teaching credential. OECD countries differ not only in how many years of education they

require, but also in whether they require a pre-service exam and practical classroom teaching experience. The wide variation across countries suggests a lack of consensus about how best to prepare teachers.

Length of Education Programs

As in the United States, the typical postsecondary education program for teachers is uniformly four years in Australia, Canada (Quebec), England, and Korea. In many other countries, the length differs for teachers at the primary and secondary levels, but programs tend to be longer than in the United States, particularly for high school teachers. The average across the OECD countries is 3.9 years for primary school teachers, 4.4 years for lower secondary school teachers, and 4.9 years for upper secondary teachers.[40] The general OECD trend has been to lengthen teacher education programs and to raise standards, for example by requiring graduate training for secondary school teachers.[41]

In Europe, Germany has one of the longest, most rigorous, and most inflexible programs of teacher preparation. Initial teacher education takes five years for primary teachers and at least six years for secondary teachers.[42] The first phase of the training, which lasts three to four years, takes place in universities and ends with a thesis and written and oral examinations. Upon successful completion of these examinations, students are eligible to move to the second, or preparatory service, phase, which lasts between one and a half and two years. In this phase, students work at schools at a reduced salary and participate in training seminars run by various ministries of education countrywide. Immediate enrollment in the second phase is not guaranteed, because it is subject to the availability of vacancies at the relevant training institute. At the end of this phase, candidates take another state examination, which consists of another written thesis, an oral examination, and an evaluation of classroom teaching.

Only then are graduates able to enter the profession as probationary teachers. At the end of a two-year probation period, they are appointed for life, provided they are at least twenty-seven years old. Because of the long training program, the average age of teachers entering tenured employment was thirty-two in 1998. And because the training is oriented toward particular levels of schooling (primary, lower secondary, or upper secondary) and types of schools (general or vocational), teachers are not easily able to transfer from one type of teaching position to another.[43] Although reasonable people may disagree about the appropriate length and form of teacher preparation programs, one thing is quite clear. Potential teachers are likely to be willing to make such an investment only if the payoffs in terms of future salary make the effort worthwhile. Thus it is not surprising to find that the long and rigorous teacher preparation program in Germany is associated with high initial salaries.

Practical Field Experience

The general trend across OECD countries is to increase opportunities for practical classroom experience, to start the practical training earlier in the education program, to connect teacher education institutions more closely with the schools where their graduates will teach, and to broaden the scope of the experience beyond classroom teaching.[44] These changes come in response to growing dissatisfaction with having prospective teachers do their practice teaching only at the end of their education.

Teacher education in Sweden, for example, now includes a twenty- to thirty-week program in which a student works with a teacher team within a school on a wide range of professional skills and pursues a research project linked to his or her academic program. Student teachers then stay in touch with "their school" throughout their teacher education.[45] In Ireland, practical experience at the secondary level no longer focuses just on teaching but now extends to planning, supervision,

---

In Ireland, practical experience at the secondary level no longer focuses just on teaching but now extends to planning, supervision, and extracurricular activities.

---

and extracurricular activities. In Israel, practical field experiences now account for 15 percent of the total program time. Also, much of the fourth year of college work is devoted to work in school as regular teachers, combined with reflection with a mentor at the school and with a tutor in the college.

The lessons emerging from the OECD countries are that practicum experience works best when there is close cooperation between the teacher training program and the schools, including some shared training of teacher educators and supervising teachers; when trainees are given opportunities to conduct research in the classroom; and when the course-based and fieldwork components are integrated.[46]

Certification of New Teachers

Some countries, such as Finland, impose no requirements on prospective teachers beyond completion of a teacher education program. Finland can afford such a simple approach because its teacher education programs are standardized, the demand for teaching education opportunities is high, and connections between training institutions and the education profession are close. About half the OECD countries, however, have additional requirements in the form of competitive examinations and mandatory teaching experience or both, as criteria for entrance to the teaching profession.[47]

Competitive examinations are used in France, Germany, Greece, Italy, Japan, Korea, Mexico (in some states), and Spain. In some cases the exam scores determine whether one gets a teaching license; in others, scores determine who gets positions in particular schools. Both Italy and Spain also require one year of teaching. Interestingly, only one in three OECD countries, including the United States, requires teaching experience in order to receive a regular teaching license. Further, the typical U.S. three-year teaching requirement is longer than that in all other countries. Several other countries, though, call for a probationary period before a teacher can get tenure in the form of a permanent teaching post.[48]

Alternative Routes into Teaching

Faced with teacher shortages in some areas, many countries now provide alternative routes into teaching. Of twenty-five OECD countries for which information is available, seventeen make it possible for side entrants—that is, people who have pursued nonteaching careers—to enter the teaching profession. These programs last from one to three years and vary in form. The most common form, used in twelve countries, provides special programs in traditional teacher training institutions, but some offer adult education or distance learning programs. In most

countries, side entrants are permitted to start teaching before they are fully qualified.

An interesting version of this program, which resembles the Teach for America Program in the United States, is England's Teach First program, which specifically addresses teacher shortages in London. A two-year program for graduates who had intended to pursue business careers, it provides intensive employment-based teacher training during the summer after graduation and additional support and training during the first year of teaching, culminating with a teaching qualification.

Among the countries that provide no alternative routes into teaching are Japan, Korea, and Scotland, all of which have relatively high teacher salaries.[49] Germany appears to be a counterexample, in that even though it pays high salaries it does have a side entrant program. But the program is quite limited, with only 3 percent of new appointees entering through that route in 2003. Moreover, though some side entrants in Germany teach in shortage areas in the general education system, such as physics and mathematics, most work in vocational areas.

Not much information is available on the extent to which these programs are used in various countries or on how successful they are at attracting and retaining teachers. In general, the side entrant programs appear to be more a response to the need for teachers than a general movement toward greater flexibility in the teaching profession.

Induction and Mentoring Programs

Beginning teachers in all countries tend to be overwhelmed and to struggle with classroom management and other problems.[50] Increasingly, developed countries have been using formal induction or mentoring programs as a

Table 2. Formal Induction Programs for Beginning Teachers, Selected OECD Countries, 2004

Mandatory (1 year)	Varies (by school)	Not offered
England and Wales	Australia	Austria
France	Canada	Belgium (Fl.)
Greece (8 months)	Denmark	Belgium (Fr.)
Israel	Netherlands	Chile
Italy	Sweden	Finland
Japan	**United States (by district)**	Germany*
Korea (7 months)		Hungary
Northern Ireland		Ireland
Scotland		
Switzerland (2 or 4 weeks over 2 years)		

Source: OECD, *Teachers Matter: Attracting, Developing and Retaining Effective Teachers* (Paris, 2005). *In Germany, the induction program is part of the final year of initial teacher education.

way to improve beginning teachers' chances of success and thereby to reduce the rate of teacher attrition. This trend is consistent with research literature that shows positive benefits not only for the novice teachers but also for the mentors.[51]

Nonetheless not all countries have such programs. Of the OECD countries listed in table 2, ten have national mandatory induction programs, the majority of which last a year. Six countries have such programs in some schools or, in the case of the United States, some districts. In the United States only twenty-three states require some form of mentorship or induction program, and those programs are generally designed and controlled at the local level.[52] Eight countries have no formal induction program. Note, though, that while Germany is included in this group, it does include an induction program in its basic teacher preparation program.

Scotland appears to have one of the more generous induction programs. It guarantees a one-year teaching post to any eligible student who has graduated with a teaching qualification from a Scottish institution of higher education and sets a maximum teaching load of 70 percent, with the rest of the time set aside for personal development. When new teachers apply for a teaching position, they are asked to rank the five local authorities in which they would most like to work. If they are assigned to and accept a position outside their top five authorities, they are eligible for a location bonus of £6,000. Thus, the program is being used not only to make beginning teachers more successful but also to reduce teacher shortages.[53] Beginning in 1999, England introduced a statutory induction period of one year for newly qualified teachers. In contrast to the Scottish program, however, the English program frees up only 10 percent of the teaching time for personal development.

Conclusion

Because of their divergent histories, cultures, values, and economic situations, industrialized countries have developed a wide range of policies related to the supply of teachers. Although it is not possible to derive any simple policy lessons for the United States from this complicated mix, the international experience is useful for providing perspective on the U.S. situation and for generating potential strategies to deal with specific issues. These strategies, however, require more study and formal evaluation.

The clearest finding of this review is that salaries are quite low in the United States relative to those in other developed countries. Although this may well mean that higher salaries would be desirable, the evidence also shows no clear relationship across countries between teacher salaries and student achievement. Moreover, the review highlights the importance of looking beyond single policy levers in favor of broader policy packages. Higher salaries alone, for example, without attention to the nature of teacher preparation and certification, working conditions, the challenges facing new teachers, and the distribution of teachers across geographic areas, are unlikely to elicit the desired widespread improvements in student achievement.

Notes

1. See OECD, *Teachers Matter: Attracting, Developing and Retaining Effective Teachers* (Paris, 2005), and the background reports for individual countries on which the report was based. This OECD project represents the most comprehensive analysis to date of teacher policies at an international level. OECD member countries are listed in table 1.

2. A similar averaging problem arises for other countries, such as Australia, that also have relatively decentralized education systems.

3. OECD, *Education at a Glance: OECD Indicators 2005* (Paris, 2005), table D3.1, p. 370. All figures are converted to U.S. dollars using purchasing power parity.

4. One exception is a comparison of the salaries of secondary school teachers with other public sector employees across a number of OECD countries in 1999. That analysis shows that with a few exceptions, teacher salaries are the same as or higher than those for computer operators, librarians, and social workers. In contrast, secondary school teachers receive lower salaries than university lecturers and civil engineers in most countries, except in Australia, Germany, and Luxembourg, where they are comparable. See OECD, *Teachers Matter* (see note 1), table 3.2., p. 76.

5. OECD, *Education at a Glance* (see note 3), chart D3.1, p. 370. Information is missing for England, Mexico, Sweden, and Switzerland at the high school level; and for England, Sweden, and Switzerland at the primary level.

6. OECD, *Teachers Matter* (see note 1), table 3.1, p. 48.

7. Peter Dolton, "The Economics of UK Teacher Supply: The Graduate's Decision," *Economic Journal* 100 (1990): 91–104.

8. Arnaud Chevalier, Peter Dolton, and Steven McIntosh, "Recruiting and Retaining Teachers in the U.K.: An Analysis of Graduate Occupation Choice from the 1960s to the 1990s," *Economica* (forthcoming).

9. S. Wolter and S. Denzler, "Wage Elasticity of the Teacher Supply in Switzerland," Discussion Paper 733 (Bonn: Institute for the Study of Labor, 2003), as cited in OECD, *Teachers Matter* (see note 1), p. 70.

10. Chevalier, Dolton, and McIntosh, "Recruiting and Retaining Teachers in the U.K." (see note 8), p. 28.

11. For data on vacancy rates in London, see Alistair Ross and Merryn Hutchings, *Attracting, Developing and Retaining Effective Teachers in the United Kingdom of Great Britain and Northern Ireland: OECD Background Report* (Paris, March 2003), para. 157, p. 33.

12. The following discussion is based on OECD, *Teachers Matter* (see note 1), pp. 146 and 147.

13. Andrew Leigh, *Teacher Pay and Teacher Aptitude,* Australian National University, Manuscript, November 2005.

14. OECD, *Teachers Matter* (see note 1), p. 60.

15. Ibid., p. 60.

16. Ibid., p. 52.

17. Ibid., p. 53.

18. Ministerial Council on Education, Employment, Training, and Youth Affairs (MCEETYA), *Demand and Supply of Primary and Secondary Teachers in Australia* (Melbourne, Victoria, 2004).

19. OECD, *Education at a Glance* (see note 3), table D3.1, p. 369.

20. OECD, *Teachers Matter* (see note 1), figure 6.4, p. 181.

21. Ibid., table 6.3, p. 175.

22. Ibid., p. 202.

23. Peter J. Dolton, "Teacher Supply," in *Handbook of the Economics of Education*, edited by E. A. Hanushek and F. Welch (forthcoming).

24. Peter Dolton, A. Tremayne, and T. Chung. "The Economic Cycle and Teacher Supply," paper commissioned for the OECD Activity, "Attracting, Developing and Retaining Effective Teachers" (Paris: OECD Directorate for Education, 2003), available from www.oecd.org/edu.teacherpolicy; cited in OECD, *Teachers Matter* (see note 1), p. 180.

25. Ross and Hutchings, *Attracting, Developing and Retaining Effective Teachers* (see note 11), para. 343, p. 66.

26. OECD, *Teachers Matter* (see note 1), p. 195.

27. Ibid., p. 196.

28. Ibid., p. 194.

29. Ibid., p. 173.

30. OECD, *Teachers Matter* (see note 1), table 6.1A.

31. Alan Smithers and Pamela Robinson, *Teachers Leaving* (Buckingham, U.K.: Centre for Education and Employment Research, 2003), table 7.1, p. 49. Data are based on responses of teachers leaving schools for destinations other than teaching in another publicly supported school. The sample of 1,051 teachers excludes those leaving because they have reached normal retirement age or because of maternity.

32. Ibid., p. 63.

33. Anders Bjorklund and others, *The Market Comes to Sweden* (New York: Russell Sage Foundation, 2006), table 5.1, p. 63, and related discussion.

34. See OECD, *Teachers Matter* (see note 1), p. 176, for references to the relevant studies.

35. Ibid., chap. 6.

36. *International Outcomes of Learning in Mathematics Literacy and Problem Solving: PISA 2003 from the U.S. Perspective* (http://nces.ed.gov/surveys/pisa/PISA2003HighlightsFigures.asp?figure=9&quest=1). In addition, the United States scored below three non-OECD participating countries or areas—Hong Kong-China, Lichtenstein, and Macao-China—but above seven others.

37. A simple linear regression between test scores and salaries generates a slight negative and statistically insignificant coefficient. If the two outliers, Mexico and Korea, are omitted, the relationship is slightly positive but not statistically significant.

38. Trends in International Mathematics and Science Study: TIMMS 2003. Accessed from http://nces. ed.gov.timss/TIMSS)#Tables.asp?figure=6&Quest.

39. For an example of the complexities involved in explaining achievement differences across countries, see Thomas Fuchs and Ludger Woessman, "What Accounts for International Differences in Student Performance? A Re-examination Using PISA Data," Working Paper 1235 (Munich: CESifo, July 2004).

40. OECD, *Teachers Matter* (see note 1), table 4.1, p. 105.

41. Ibid., p. 105.

42. Gabor Halasz and others, *Attracting, Developing and Retaining Effective Teachers. Country Note: Germany* (Paris: OECD, September 2004), para. 47, p. 14.

43. Ibid., para 63, p. 19; and OECD, *Teachers Matter* (see note 1), p. 107.

44. OECD, *Teachers Matter* (see note 1), p. 108.

45. Ibid., p. 110.

46. Ibid., p. 109.

47. Ibid., p. 114.

48. Ibid., table 4.1 and discussion on p. 115.

49. Ibid., p. 84

50. S. Veenmann, "Perceived Problems of Beginning Teachers," *Review of Educational Research* 54 (1984): 143–78; and E. Britton, L. Paine, and S. Raizen, "Middle Grades Mathematics and Science Teacher Induction in Selected Countries: Preliminary Findings, National Center for Improving Science Education" (Washington: WestEd, 1999), cited in OECD, *Teachers Matter* (see note 1), p. 117.

51. OECD, *Teachers Matter* (see note 1), p. 21.

52. National Council on Teacher Quality, *Attracting, Developing and Retaining Effective Teachers: Background Report for the United States* (U.S. Department of Education, International Affairs Office, 2004), p. 37.

53. Scottish Executive Education Department, *Scottish Teacher Induction Scheme* (2005), www.scotland. gov.uk/publications.

Teacher Labor Markets
in Developing Countries

Emiliana Vegas

Summary

Emiliana Vegas surveys strategies used by the world's developing countries to fill their class-rooms with qualified teachers. With their low quality of education and wide gaps in student outcomes, schools in developing countries strongly resemble hard-to-staff urban U.S. schools. Their experience with reform may thus provide insights for U.S. policymakers.

Severe budget constraints and a lack of teacher training capacity have pushed developing nations to try a wide variety of reforms, including using part-time or assistant teachers, experimenting with pay incentives, and using school-based management.

The strategy of hiring teachers with less than full credentials has had mixed results. One successful program in India hired young women who lacked teaching certificates to teach basic literacy and numeracy skills to children whose skills were seriously lagging. After two years, student learning increased, with the highest gains among the least able students.

As in the United States, says Vegas, teaching quality and student achievement in the developing world are sensitive to teacher compensation. As average teacher salaries in Chile more than doubled over the past decade, higher-quality students entered teacher education programs. And when Brazil increased educational funding and distributed resources more equitably, school enrollment increased and the gap in student test scores narrowed. Experiments with performance-based pay have had mixed results. In Bolivia a bonus for teaching in rural areas failed to produce higher-quality teachers. And in Mexico a system to reward teachers for improved student outcomes failed to change teacher performance. But Vegas explains that the design of teacher incentives is critical. Effective incentive schemes must be tightly coupled with desired behaviors and generous enough to give teachers a reason to make the extra effort.

School-based management reforms give decisionmaking authority to the schools. Such reforms in Central America have reduced teacher absenteeism, increased teacher work hours, increased homework assignments, and improved parent-teacher relationships. These changes, says Vegas, are especially promising in schools where educational quality is low.

www.futureofchildren.org

Emiliana Vegas is senior education economist at the World Bank. Rekha Balu provided excellent research assistance.

eveloping countries in Africa, Asia, and Latin America are struggling, just as the world's industrialized countries are, to fill classrooms with qualified teachers.[1] But the challenges they face are even more complicated. Demographers have projected that developing countries have the fastest-growing populations of people aged six to twenty-four in the world.[2] The swelling ranks of school-age populations are driving up demand for teachers. In accordance with the Millennium Development Goals set forth by the United Nations, every country must ensure universal primary education by 2015.[3] Although the majority of children in all regions of the world except sub-Saharan Africa attend primary school, the quality of education is low and disparities in student learning outcomes are large.[4] Children in developing countries have the lowest mean test scores in international assessments of student learning, and they often show the largest variation in test scores as well.[5] The severe challenges facing the developing world are not unique, however. In many ways, in fact, they resemble those facing the U.S. schools with the lowest-income student populations. Could strategies used by developing countries offer lessons to policymakers in the United States seeking to improve their nation's lowest-performing schools?

Budget constraints and a lack of teacher training capacity have led developing nations to try a wide variety of reforms. Some are hiring part-time, contractual, or assistant teachers. Others are using pay incentives to attract and retain qualified teachers. Still others are trying to attract more teachers and raise the quality of teaching by experimenting with school-based management or the devolution of decisionmaking authority, including teacher hiring and firing, directly to schools. The results in terms of student achievement vary widely, depending on the context and the country.

Teacher Labor Markets

The supply of teachers in developing countries, as in developed countries, depends on working conditions and teacher salaries, as well as on how salaries and entry requirements in the teacher labor market compare with other labor markets. Many teachers work in schools that lack adequate teaching materials or basic infrastructure. Pupil-teacher ratios, as shown in table 1, can be large: an average of 43:1, for example, in sub-Saharan Africa, though in some countries the ratio is even larger. Many teachers in developing countries cite lack of resources, such as adequate facilities, textbooks, and teaching materials, as a primary obstacle to effective teaching.[6] Location also affects teacher supply. In most developing countries, unlike in the United States, working conditions tend to be better in urban schools and teachers prefer to work there.

Large cities in the United States have only recently begun using housing subsidies to recruit teachers to difficult-to-staff urban schools, but developing countries have long made use of housing incentives, especially for teachers in rural schools. In many poor countries, however, these subsidies have not been effective, in part because most teachers are women and most single women choose not to live alone or to transfer to rural areas for safety-related reasons.[7]

Recent research in Pakistan, however, suggests that placing secondary schools in rural areas—rather than the urban areas where they are now concentrated—may attract some teachers, as many female secondary graduates

Table 1. Teacher Characteristics, by Region

Region	Pupil-teacher ratio		Trained teachers (percent)		Teacher salary (percent of GDP per capita)
	Primary	Secondary	Primary	Secondary	Secondary
Sub-Saharan Africa	43:1	24:1	69	78[a]	6.7
Middle East/North Africa	23:1	18:1	96	85[b]	
Latin America and the Caribbean	26:1	19:1	87	77	1.4
South Asia	42:1	33:1	62[a]	. . .	. . .
East Asia	22:1	19:1	96	71[a]	. . .
Eastern Europe and Central Asia	17:1	12:1	93[a]	. . .	. . .
OECD	16:1	14:1	. . .	. . .	1.3

Source: UNESCO Institute for Statistics, *Global Education Digest 2003—Comparing Education Statistics across the World* (Montreal, Canada: 2002). Countries with populations of less than 1 million are excluded.

a. Data are based on 10–25 ppercent of the total population of the country group or region.

b. Data are based on 25–50 ercent of the total population of the country group or region.

who aspire to teach higher grades can then teach in their native villages instead of moving to the cities.[8] The strategy of recruiting local teachers and assigning them to schools close to home may also be effective in the United States, where, as researchers have shown, teacher labor markets are mostly local.[9]

Turning to compensation, in Latin America, at least, teachers do not appear to be severely underpaid compared with similar workers in other occupations.[10] Lucrecia Santibáñez examined urban professional salaries in Mexico during the late 1990s.[11] Controlling for education, experience, and hours worked, she estimated that the hourly wage premium in 1998 was 13 percent for male secondary teachers and 30 percent for female teachers. She also analyzed salary differences among states in Mexico and found that, on average, teachers in more developed northern states earned relatively less compared with other professions than did teachers in the rest of the country.

In Chile, teachers' wages were higher, on average, than those of nonagricultural employees, but much of this difference could be attributed to the teachers' higher levels of schooling. One study demonstrated that although entry-level wages for teachers are low, teachers are compensated as well as other professionals who work in similar locations or have similar levels of education and experience.[12] And in Bolivia, a study found that the concentration of teachers in the public sector and the influence of union-negotiated contracts on teacher wages for the entire country reduced geographic variation in teacher salaries, which meant that teachers in rural areas, in particular, were better compensated than other professional workers in similar locations. In addition, union influence set teachers' wages in a way that minimized the salary differences by gender, ethnicity, and marital status that are apparent for some private sector professionals subject to market wages.[13]

In many developing countries, teacher salaries make up a large share of total public education spending—as much as 95 percent of total education costs. Governments in countries such as Uganda, Kenya, and Tanzania, which have recently expanded access to primary schools, cite high spending on teacher salaries as the biggest constraint on improving the supply and quality of teacher recruits. Education advocates have suggested a variety of strategies to minimize this constraint, such as de-linking teacher salaries from civil service salaries or changing the pace at which teachers progress along the salary scale. But research has centered primarily on subsidies and incentives, such as merit-based pay and supplementary allowances (housing, transport), as discussed below.

Alternatives to Hiring Regular Teachers

Many developing countries are upgrading the training credentials required of teachers at the same time as their governments are resorting to hiring part-time, uncredentialed, or contract teachers to meet demand or cut costs. For example, in the Kyrgyz Republic, policymakers emphasized teacher training requirements even as teacher training colleges were being closed for lack of funding. One approach, which Tajikistan has tried, has been to shorten the length of teacher training programs.[14] To limit expenses while responding to increased demand in the 1990s, India hired more than 200,000 "para-teachers," while Pakistan hired contract teachers who were excluded from training and other benefits.

As in the United States, research findings on how teacher training programs affect the quality of education are, at best, inconclusive. A survey of case studies in Latin America found that several different methods of teacher preparation and training—for example, stopgap training that covers only missing skills and competences—achieved consistently poor results, thus sounding a cautionary note for U.S. education programs. The

study also found that professionalizing teacher training by elevating its status to a university degree had the paradoxical effect of causing qualified teachers to move to more remunerative professions.[15]

In addition, a UNICEF strategy paper warns of the cost consequences of expanding alternative teacher hiring. Even if alternative hires start at lower salaries or with fewer benefits, the study finds, they will eventually demand or qualify for higher salaries. Salary increases for a large pool of teachers can financially strain the system over the long term as much as hiring regular teachers would.[16]

Contract Teachers

Many developing countries are addressing shortages by turning to contract teachers— graduates of regular teacher training institutes who receive lower wages than do regular teachers (just 40 percent of civil salaries) and no benefits. Togo recently reported that as much as 55 percent of its teaching force was contractual. The strategy, though, does not appear to have been successful, as the advent of contractual hiring in Togo reduced the supply of high-quality candidates, while also raising absenteeism and creating resentment over unfair pay. A retrospective evaluation found that the performance of students taught by contractual teachers lagged behind that of students taught by regular teachers, even after controlling for prior achievement, household characteristics, and school, classroom, and teacher variables.[17] Not surprisingly, schools whose limited budgets forced them to hire contractual teachers also had less pedagogic supervision and poor facilities.

Assistant Teachers

Some countries are also experimenting with hiring assistant teachers, who often have fewer qualifications than do regular teachers and are paid at substantially lower rates. In rural areas in India, a remedial education program reached more than 15,000 students who had not attained basic literacy and numeracy skills by third grade by hiring as teachers young women from the community who lacked teaching certificates. A randomized evaluation found that after two years, the program had increased student learning by 0.39 standard deviation, with the highest gains among the least able students. This finding suggests that it is possible not only to keep poorly performing students in school but also to ensure that they do not fall behind. It is conceivable that a similar catch-up program could help U.S. cities maintain high net enrollment rates in the grades when students are most likely to drop out. Because the program in India hires local high-school-educated girls to teach classes of approximately twenty students, the average cost is less than $5 a year for each child—far less than the average cost of outfitting classrooms with regular teachers.[18] While these findings are compelling, the validity of the evaluation has been called into question on several points and it was also found that the children's gains began to fade out within one year of leaving the program.

Teacher Pay

Although some disagreement exists about the importance of the absolute level of teacher salaries in attracting qualified people to and retaining them in the profession, there is broad consensus that teacher salaries influence the type of people who enter the field and how long they remain in it. At the same time, research indicates that working conditions and regulations can counteract or amplify the influence of wages on teachers. In this section I describe how salary levels, salary structures, and scholar-

ship programs have influenced teacher recruitment, quality, and retention in developing countries.

Salary Levels

During the 1990s in Chile, teachers' real wages increased and the quality of applicants to the teaching profession improved. Between 1990 and 2002 real salaries grew 156

Even if alternative hires start at lower salaries or with fewer benefits, the study finds, they will eventually demand or qualify for higher salaries.

percent, while the government launched a publicity campaign to encourage college students to become teachers and also created a scholarship program for outstanding students to study pedagogy. Simultaneously, the government allocated substantial additional resources to schools, in the process improving overall working conditions for teachers. Although the individual effect of each of these reforms on student outcomes remains unclear, during the period the number of teacher education applicants increased 39 percent, and the average university entrance exam score of applicants to teacher education programs increased 16 percent. Even though the number of applicants to other degree programs, such as engineering, also increased, the average exam scores of these applicants remained more or less constant. These patterns suggest that changes in salary level can affect an individual's choice to become a teacher.[19]

Some evidence also suggests that salary levels and salary equalization for teachers can improve student outcomes. In Brazil, a finance equalization reform that targeted redistributed funds to teachers resulted in smaller class sizes, fewer overaged children in primary and secondary schools, and a diminishing gap between high- and low-performing students. Brazil, like the United States, is a vast country characterized by large inequalities in educational spending and educational outcomes not only among states but also among different municipalities within each state. The Fundo de Manutenção e Desenvolvimento do Ensino Fundamental e de Valorização do Magistério (Fund for the Maintenance and Development of Basic Education and Teacher Appreciation, or FUNDEF) is a federal fund that addresses spending inequalities within states. State and municipal governments contribute a share of their tax and transfer revenues to the fund, which then redistributes revenues to the state and municipal governments in each state on the basis of the number of students enrolled in their basic education systems. The federal government also promotes funding adequacy across all states by providing supplemental funding in states where FUNDEF revenues per student are below a yearly established spending floor. These "top-ups," which have benefited the poorer states of Brazil, located primarily in the Northeast, point to the importance of additional federal financing when state and local revenues fall short.

Unlike teacher incentive programs in several states in the United States, FUNDEF earmarks 60 percent of funds specifically for teachers, with funds going to hire new teachers, train underqualified teachers, and increase teachers' salaries. A 2005 study found that governments that increased mandated per-pupil spending lowered average teacher-pupil ratios; the study inferred, because there was no decrease in enrollment, that the governments hired new teachers.[20] The share of teachers who had completed only primary education also fell dramatically, most noticeably in Brazil's poorer regions and in the earlier primary school grades, where higher shares of teachers had previously been underqualified. That the reform was introduced at about the same time as legislation requiring teachers to have at least a secondary education degree complicates any assessment of the results. But the 2005 study found that funds received from FUNDEF were not significantly linked with the steep decline in underqualified teachers, though FUNDEF revenue was used to train and educate teachers.[21]

The FUNDEF-related changes in educational inputs have, in turn, generated changes in student outcomes. More students are now attending school in the poorer states of Brazil, particularly in the higher grades of basic education. The reform is also linked with lower levels of overaged students in the classroom. Having qualified teachers thus appears to help students stay on track in school, repeat grades less often, drop out and reenter less often, and perhaps also enter first grade on time. Because low-performing students suffer most from inequalities in per-pupil spending, finance equalization reforms that decrease these spending inequalities may also narrow the performance gap between high-performing and low-performing students and between white and nonwhite students. Studies of school finance reform in the United States, however, have not shown consistent effects on student outcomes.[22]

Salary Structure

Although teacher pay in developing countries is seldom linked to teacher performance, a few countries have recently experimented with performance-based pay to raise teaching quality and student outcomes (see the article in this volume on performance-based pay by Victor Lavy). Because few large-scale pay-for-performance programs have been implemented in the United States, programs in developing countries provide particularly valuable evidence of the extent to which incentives affect performance.

The effect of performance-based pay depends critically on how it is designed and linked to teacher performance. Chile and Mexico, for example, have instituted different types of performance-based incentives for teachers. In Chile's Sistema Nacional de Evaluación de Desempeño de los Establecimientos Educacionales (National System of School Performance Assessment, or SNED), top-performing schools within predetermined groups earn a financial bonus for student performance; the bonus is distributed among the teachers in the winning schools. Initially Chile's school-based bonus had no effect on student performance, but a recent study found that in schools that have some likelihood of receiving the prize in each of the three years they apply, average student test scores increase slightly.[23]

Mexico's Carrera Magisterial (Master Training, or CM) program, instituted in 1993, allows teachers to move up consecutive pay levels based on year-long assessments of their professional development and education, years of experience, a peer review, and, importantly, their students' performance. The awards are substantial—they can represent between 25 and 200 percent of the teacher's annual wage—and last throughout a teacher's career, just as a salary increase does. Since 1993, more than 600,000 teachers have received the lowest level of award. The Carrera Magisterial reform resembles an across-the-

board wage increase for "good" teachers and may thus be expected to have led to an increase in the quality of entering cohorts of teachers in the past decade.

A study by Patrick McEwan and Lucrecia Santibáñez examined how effective the Carrera Magisterial incentives were in improving students' test scores.[24] The study compared a

---

Although teacher pay in developing countries is seldom linked to teacher performance, a few countries have recently experimented with performance-based pay to raise teaching quality and student outcomes.

---

group of teachers who had participated in the program but whose characteristics put them far below or above the threshold for a bonus payment with a small group of teachers who were close to, but not assured of, receiving the bonus. The study found that the mean test scores of students of teachers in the latter "incentivized" group rose by a small to moderate amount, roughly 0.15–0.20 points (less than 10 percent of a standard deviation), relative to teachers without the incentive. The effect was robust to a variety of alternative specifications and subsamples.

Although Mexico's Carrera Magisterial and Chile's SNED are both nationwide programs involving most of the country's teachers, only a minority of teachers has any real likelihood of receiving a promotion (in the case of Carrera Magisterial) or a bonus (in the case of SNED) each time they apply.[25] Thus, most teachers who apply have no real incentive to improve performance. To be effective, as Victor Lavy explains in his article in this volume, an incentive scheme must give all or most teachers a reason to exert extra effort.

The size of the reward relative to a teacher's base pay also matters. When a teacher's base salary accounts for a large share of total compensation, incentives for specific behaviors, such as working in rural schools or serving children with special needs, will be relatively less powerful. Figure 1 portrays the share of teacher pay that comes from education and training, years of service, and performance in two Latin American countries, Chile and Bolivia. In Bolivia's pay structure—one common in both developing and developed countries—by far the largest part of a teacher's salary depends on experience and education. Chile has tried to increase the share of teacher pay that is related to performance, but even there more than 60 percent of pay continues to depend on characteristics, such as years of service and education, that are unrelated to performance. The mixed findings on the effectiveness of performance-based pay in Mexico and Chile echo findings from the United States (again, see the article by Victor Lavy in this volume) that make clear the difficulty of designing an effective performance-based pay policy.

Some incentive programs, however, have shown some success. A nongovernmental organization (NGO) project in India used a simple financial incentive program to reduce teacher absenteeism and to stimulate teaching and better learning. The NGO initiated the program in 60 informal one-teacher schools in rural India, randomly chosen out of a sample of 120 schools; the remaining 60

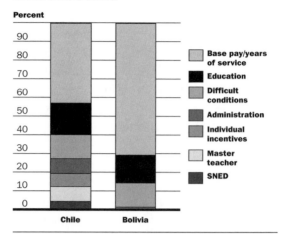

Figure 1. Decomposition of Teacher Pay in Chile and Bolivia

Percent

Legend:
- Base pay/years of service
- Education
- Difficult conditions
- Administration
- Individual incentives
- Master teacher
- SNED

(X-axis: Chile, Bolivia)

Sources: Cristián Cox, "Las políticas educacionales de Chile en las últimas dos décadas del siglo XX," in *Políticas educacionales en el cambio de siglo: la reforma del sistema escolar en Chile*, edited by Cristián Cox (Santiago, Chile: Editorial Universitaria, 2003); and Miguel Urquiola and Emiliana Vegas, "Arbitrary Variation in Teacher Salaries," in *Incentives to Improve Teaching: Lessons from Latin America*, edited by Emiliana Vegas (Washington: World Bank Press, 2005).

schools served as comparison schools. Teachers were given a camera with a tamper-proof date and time function, along with instructions to have one of the children photograph the teacher and other students at the beginning and end of the school day. The time and date stamps on the photographs were used to track teacher attendance. Salary was a direct function of attendance.

An evaluation of the program by Esther Duflo and Rema Hanna reported that it immediately reduced teacher absenteeism.[26] The absenteeism rate, measured using unannounced visits in all 120 schools, averaged 42 percent in the comparison schools and 22 percent in the schools under study. When the schools were in session, teachers were as likely to be teaching in both types of schools; the number of children present was roughly the same. The program also improved student achievement. A year after its start, test scores in the schools participating in the incentive program were 0.17 standard deviation higher than those in the comparison schools, and children were 40 percent more likely to be admitted into regular schools.

The study by Duflo and Hanna demonstrates how random assignment studies can be used to learn about program effects, though the results may be specific to the context in which they are implemented. The scheme in India was tested in a small group of one-teacher schools; the question is whether the results would be similar in different contexts. For example, would the teacher attendance effect be smaller in regular public schools or in larger schools with many other teachers who can substitute for an absent teacher? Another issue of practical importance for public policy is whether the camera mechanism would share the fate of other already existing formal mechanisms for punishing absentees: weak enforcement.

Scholarship Programs

To attract talented students to teaching, several countries in South America's Southern Cone have introduced scholarship programs. In Chile, a scholarship program for talented students covers 100 percent of tuition up to 1 million pesos in exchange for a commitment to teach for three years. Priority goes to candidates in natural sciences, mathematics, English, language arts, and basic education.[27] In Uruguay, where teacher education is free, scholarships are provided to talented candidates from disadvantaged backgrounds to cover their living expenses during the three years of intensive training at regional teacher training centers.[28] In Asia, during the 1990s Taiwan offered free pre-service education to those who had taught for five years. Researchers cite the combination of the scholarship and generous salaries and benefits for teachers relative to other professions in Tai-

wan to explain why the country's teacher retention rate remains high beyond the five-year threshold.[29] Such programs imply that strong relative wages and subsidized costs can have an important effect on the quality of teacher supply.

School-Based Management

Some developing countries have tried devolving directly to schools the authority to make decisions regarding teacher hiring and other administrative matters that are usually made by local, regional, or central governments. The idea behind such decentralization is to bring these decisions closer to the school, and thus to parents and students, to generate incentives and conditions to improve teaching quality and student outcomes and make teachers and schools more accountable to the community.

Several countries in Central America have introduced such school-based management reforms. In El Salvador, a retrospective evaluation found that the Programa de Educación con Participación de la Comunidad (Education with Community Participation Program, or EDUCO) has affected management practices, teacher behavior, and student outcomes.[30] A few important powers, most notably the ability to hire and fire teachers, have been transferred to the school, but many other decisions continue to be made primarily by central authorities. Most of the local decisionmaking power has been given to parents rather than principals. The study also finds important behavioral differences: EDUCO schools have fewer school closings, less teacher absenteeism, more meetings between teachers and parents, and longer teacher work hours than control schools. These changes in teacher behavior, in turn, are related to higher achievement in Spanish in EDUCO schools.

Another retrospective evaluation finds similar effects in Honduras's Proyecto Hondureño de Educación Comunitaria (Honduran Community Education Project, or PROHECO).[31] Like EDUCO, PROHECO is a school-based management reform for rural primary schools. Comparing PROHECO schools to similar schools in rural areas (using propensity score matching methods to construct a credible comparison group), the study finds that PROHECO teachers are less frequently absent because of union participation, although they are more frequently absent because of teacher professional development. Teachers in PROHECO are paid less and have fewer years of experience than comparison teachers. And, as in El Salvador's EDUCO program, teachers in PROHECO teach more hours in an average week than comparison teachers; they also have smaller classes and assign more homework. In these examples, at least, decentralized schools appear to encourage greater efficiency and teacher effort.

Although the studies found little evidence that teachers in community-managed schools differ from their colleagues in conventional schools in terms of their classroom processes, planning, or motivation, PROHECO students score higher on math, science, and Spanish exams than students in similar non-PROHECO schools. This higher student achievement is, in part, explained by unique qualities and characteristics of PROHECO schools. Specifically, the more hours a week a teacher works, the higher is the mean student achievement in all three subjects. The frequency of homework is associated with higher achievement in Spanish and math. Finally, smaller classes and fewer school closings are related to higher student achievement in science.

In contrast to PROHECO and EDUCO, Nicaragua's School Autonomy program (Autonomía Escolar) was aimed initially at urban secondary schools, in particular those with higher-than-average resources. Unlike their peers in neighboring El Salvador and Honduras, parent associations and teachers in Nicaragua's autonomous schools report little decisionmaking power. A decade after the reform began, autonomous and nonautonomous schools continue to differ in much the same ways as before reform. Differences in student socioeconomic background continue to explain most differences in student achievement. The reform appears to have had no systematic effect on student learning. Although on average students in autonomous schools outscore students in traditional schools in mathematics in third grade, by sixth grade they score lower on both Spanish and mathematics tests. There is little evidence that differences between autonomous and traditional schools are responsible for these differences in test scores.[32]

Some Lessons for the United States

Although developing countries differ in many ways from the United States, the inequality and poverty in some of their schools closely resembles conditions in some hard-to-staff U.S. schools. Because of their widely varying circumstances, these countries have tried many and varied reforms, often on a large scale. Their experiences with reform may provide insights for U.S. policymakers.

Clearly, educational reforms of many kinds can affect teaching quality and student learning. Research evidence supports the intuitive notion that teaching quality and student achievement are sensitive to the level and structure of teacher compensation. For example, as average teacher salaries in Chile more than doubled over the past decade, higher-quality students entered teacher education programs.[33] Similarly, when FUNDEF increased educational resources in Brazil and distributed them more fairly, school enrollment increased and the gap in student test scores narrowed.[34]

Once a country makes teacher salaries competitive, it can link teacher performance to pay increases to improve teaching quality. Although Chile's school-based teacher bonus for student performance did not initially affect average test scores, it has now begun to increase them modestly, under some circumstances.[35]

The specific design of teacher incentives can have important consequences for teaching quality and student outcomes. Even in the case of nationwide performance-based-pay programs, such as those in Mexico and Chile, few teachers are likely to receive awards and thus few have any real incentive to improve student performance.[36] Effective incentive schemes must be tightly coupled with the desired teacher behaviors and generous enough to give teachers a reason to make the extra effort.

A key lesson from research both in the United States and in developing countries is that teachers do not always respond to incentives in predictable ways. Sometimes, programs designed to reward teachers who adopt specific behaviors or achieve higher student achievement fail to generate the desired behavioral response.[37] Bolivia's bonus for teaching in rural areas, for example, failed to produce higher-quality rural teachers.[38] And Mexico's new

teacher career system, designed to reward teachers for improved student outcomes, failed to change teacher performance—and thus to change student outcomes.[39] These cases highlight the importance of design and implementation issues in teacher incentive reforms.

Finally, reforms that are not specifically designed to affect teachers can nevertheless in-

---

A key lesson from research both in the United States and in developing countries is that teachers do not always respond to incentives in predictable ways.

---

fluence—sometimes even more than changes in compensation can—the characteristics of those who choose to enter and remain in teaching, as well as their work in classrooms. School-based management reforms that devolve decisionmaking authority to the schools, for example, have had important effects on teacher performance and student learning by making teachers (and schools) more accountable to their communities. Devolution of decisionmaking authority to schools in Central America has, in many cases, led to lower teacher absenteeism, more teacher work hours, more homework assignments, and better parent-teacher relationships. These are promising changes, especially in schools where educational quality is low.

Notes

1. In this article, "developing countries" are low- and middle-income countries with high inequality or high poverty, or both.

2. United Nations Population Fund, *State of the World's Population 2005* (New York, 2005).

3. The Millennium Development Goals grew out of the agreements and resolutions of world conferences organized by the United Nations during the 1990s. The goals were accepted as a framework for measuring development progress. The eight goals are to eradicate extreme poverty and hunger; to achieve universal primary education; to promote gender equality and empower women; to reduce child mortality; to improve maternal health; to combat AIDS, malaria, and other diseases; to ensure environmental sustainability; and to build a global partnership for development. For most countries, the self-imposed deadline for achieving these goals is 2015. World Bank, "Achieving the Millennium Development Goals," available at www.web.worldbank.org.

4. For example, though 93 percent of children in East Asia are enrolled in school, only 56 percent have progressed through grades at the expected pace.

5. As an example, while the share of students deemed to have low skills in the Program for International Student Assessment (PISA) is only 0.9 percent in Korea, 4.2 percent in France, and 6.8 percent in the United States, it is 23 percent in Brazil and 54 percent in Peru. Some countries do not participate in such assessments, however, and these findings do not reflect their outcomes. India, for instance, has not participated in the Trends in International Mathematics and Science Study or PISA.

6. Mary H. Futrell, presidential speech delivered to Fourth World Congress of Education International, Porto Alegre, Brazil, July 22, 2004.

7. Donald Warwick and Fernando Reimers, *Hope or Despair? Learning in Pakistan's Primary Schools* (Westport, Conn.: Praeger, 1995); Ya Ping Wang and Alan Murie, "Social and Spatial Implications of Housing Reform in China," *International Journal of Urban and Regional Research* 24, no. 2 (2000): 397–417; P. J. McEwan, "Recruitment of Rural Teachers in Developing Countries: An Economic Analysis," *Teaching and Teacher Education* 15 (1999): 849–59.

8. Tahir Andrabi, Jishnu Das, and Asim Ijaz Khwaja, "Students Today, Teachers Tomorrow? The Rise of Affordable Private Schools in Pakistan," mimeo (World Bank, 2005).

9. D. Boyd and others, "Explaining the Short Careers of High-Achieving Teachers in Schools with Low-Performing Students," *American Economic Review* 95, no. 2 (2005): 166–71.

10. Werner Hernani-Limarino, "Are Teachers Well Paid in Latin America and the Caribbean? Relative Wage and Structure of Returns of Teachers," in *Incentives to Improve Teaching: Lessons from Latin America*, edited by E. Vegas (Washington: World Bank Press, 2005).

11. Lucrecia Santibáñez, "¿Están mal pagados los maestros en México? Estimando de los salarios relativos del magisterio," *Revista latinoamericana de estudios educativos* 32, no. 2 (2002): 9–41.

12. A. Mulcahi-Dunn and G. Arcia, "An Overview of Teacher's Salaries and Living Standards in Ecuador. Center for International Development," mimeo (North Carolina: Research Triangle Institute, 1996).

13. C. Piras and W. D. Savedoff, "How Much Do Teachers Earn?" Working Paper 375 (Washington: Inter-American Development Bank, 1998).

14. D. W. Chapman and others, "The Search for Quality: A Five-Country Study of National Strategies to Improve Educational Quality in Central Asia," *International Journal of Educational Development* 25, no. 5 (2005): 514–30.

15. Juan Carlos Navarro and Aimee Verdisco, "Teacher Training in Latin America: Innovations and Trends," Sustainable Development Department Technical Paper Series (Washington: Inter-American Development Bank, 2000).

16. Santosh Mehrotra and Peter Buckland, "Managing Teacher Costs for Access and Quality," Staff Working Paper EPP-EVL-98-004 (UNICEF, 1998).

17. Joost De Laat and Emiliana Vegas, "Do Differences in Teacher Contracts Affect Student Performance? Evidence from Togo," mimeo, 2005, Harvard University and The World Bank.

18. Abhijit Banerjee and others, "Remedying Education: Evidence from Two Randomized Experiments in India," Working Paper 11904 (Cambridge, Mass.: National Bureau of Economic Research, 2005).

19. Cristián Cox, "Las políticas educacionales de Chile en las últimas dos décadas del siglo XX," in *Políticas educacionales en el cambio de siglo: la reforma del sistema escolar en Chile*, edited by Cristián Cox (Santiago, Chile: Editorial Universitaria, 2003).

20. Nora Gordon and Emiliana Vegas, "Educational Finance Equalization, Spending, Teacher Quality, and Student Outcomes: The Case of Brazil's FUNDEF," in *Incentives to Improve Teaching: Lessons from Latin America*, edited by Vegas (see note 10).

21. The study used an instrumental variables approach to estimate the causal effect of FUNDEF.

22. For example, David Card and A. Abigail Payne, "School Finance Reform, the Distribution of School Spending, and the Distribution of Student Test Scores," *Journal of Public Economics* 83 (2002): 49–82, find evidence that equalization of educational expenditures across U.S. school districts led to less dispersion in SAT test scores among children of diverse socioeconomic backgrounds. But Melissa A. Clark, "Education Reform, Redistribution, and Student Achievement: Evidence from the Kentucky Education Reform Act" (Princeton, N.J.: Mathematica Policy Research, 2003), finds no evidence that the education expenditure equalization resulting from the Kentucky Education Reform Act narrowed the gap in test scores between rich and poor districts.

23. Alejandra Mizala and Pilar Romaguera, "Teachers' Salary Structure and Incentives in Chile," in *Incentives to Improve Teaching: Lessons from Latin America*, edited by Vegas (see note 10).

24. Patrick McEwan and Lucrecia Santibáñez, "Teacher and Principal Incentives in Mexico," in *Incentives to Improve Teaching: Lessons from Latin America,* edited by Vegas (see note 10).

25. Ibid. and Mizala and Romaguera, "Teachers' Salary Structure and Incentives in Chile" (see note 23).

26. Esther C. Duflo and Rema Hanna, "Monitoring Works: Getting Teachers to Come to School," Working Paper 11880 (Cambridge, Mass.: National Bureau of Economic Research, 2005).

27. Paula Pogre and Graciela Lombardi, *Schools That Show How to Think: Teaching to Understand, A Theoretical Mark for Action* (Argentina: Consorcio de Editores, 2004).

28. Denise Vaillant, "Reforma Del Sistema Formación Inicial De Docentes En Uruguay," paper presented at Los Maestros en América Latina: Nueva Perspectivas Sobre su Desarrollo y Desempeño, San Jose, Costa Rica, 1999.

29. Bih-Jen Fwu and Hsiou-Huai Wang, "The Social Status of Teachers in Taiwan," *Comparative Education* 38, no. 2 (2002): 211–24.

30. Yasuyuki Sawada and Andrew Ragatz, "Decentralization of Education, Teacher Behavior, and Outcomes: The Case of El Salvador's EDUCO," in *Incentives to Improve Teaching: Lessons from Latin America*, edited by Vegas (see note 10).

31. Jeffrey Marshall and Emanuela Di Gropello, "Teacher Effort and Schooling Outcomes in Rural Honduras," in *Incentives to Improve Teaching: Lessons from Latin America*, edited by Vegas (see note 10).

32. Caroline E. Parker, "Teacher Incentives and Student Achievement in Nicaraguan Autonomous Schools," in *Incentives to Improve Teaching: Lessons from Latin America*, edited by Vegas (see note 10).

33. Mizala and Romaguera, "Teachers' Salary Structure and Incentives in Chile" (see note 23).

34. Gordon and Vegas, "Educational Finance Equalization, Spending, Teacher Quality, and Student Outcomes" (see note 20).

35. Mizala and Romaguera, "Teachers' Salary Structure and Incentives in Chile" (see note 23).

36. Ibid.; McEwan and Santibáñez, "Teacher and Principal Incentives in Mexico" (see note 24).

37. See, for example Paul Glewwe, Nauman Ilias, and Michael Kremer, "Teacher Incentives," Working Paper 9671 (Cambridge, Mass.: National Bureau of Economic Research, 2003); Charles T. Clotfelter and others, "Do School Accountability Systems Make It More Difficult for Low Performing Schools to Attract and Retain High Quality Teachers?" *Journal of Policy Analysis and Management* 23 (2004): 251–71. Brian A. Jacob and Steven D. Levitt, "Rotten Apples: An Investigation of the Prevalence and Predictors of Teacher Cheating," *Quarterly Journal of Economics* 118, no. 3 (2003): 843–78, present some evidence of the behavioral reactions to teacher incentive mechanisms in the United States.

38. Miguel Urquiola and Emiliana Vegas, "Arbitrary Variation in Teacher Salaries," in *Incentives to Improve Teaching: Lessons from Latin America*, edited by Vegas (see note 10).

39. McEwan and Santibáñez, "Teacher and Principal Incentives in Mexico" (see note 24).